# The Trials of Counsel—Francis Bacon in 1621

*Sir Francis Bacon, a woodcut made in 1641*

Certainly men in great
fortunes are strangers to themselves, . . .
–*Of Great Place*
Sir Francis Bacon

# THE TRIALS OF COUNSEL

# FRANCIS BACON

# IN 1621

*By Jonathan Marwil*

*Wayne State University Press*

*Detroit 1976*

Marwil, Jonathan, 1940-
    The trials of counsel—Francis Bacon in 1621.

    Includes bibliographical references and index.
    1.   Bacon, Francis, Viscount St. Albans, 1561-1626.
I.   Title.
B1197.M46        192   [B]   75-33650
ISBN 0-8143-1549-6   .

*To my father and in memory of my mother*

# Contents

# Acknowledgments

Several friends assisted in making this book; they offered advice, encouragement, and love. What I have written is the better for their help. But a man altogether unaware of these pages contributed most. In my university days John Van Doren taught me more about reading and writing than words can properly honor.

*December, 1974*

### Textual Note

Days and months are given in old style, but the year is dated from January 1.

Parenthetical references in the text are to *The Works of Francis Bacon*, edited by James Spedding, R.L. Ellis, and D.D. Heath, 14 volumes, London, 1857–74. In the Notes section, citations identified only by volume and page are to this source.

# *Introduction*

nce upon a time there lived a king by the name of Henry. He lived (like most kings) in a time when swords rather than words counted in the winning of kingdoms, and when marriages rather than purges kept new rulers awake at night. Having won his kingdom by ousting a tyrant whose cruelties were of such magnitude that even his few virtues were thought to be feigned, Henry ruled for twenty-four years, bringing peace and a small measure of the good things to his people. During his reign many ambitious men coveted his throne, but the King always proved himself too clever for them. A silent and self-concealing man, he won the respect, if not the love, of his subjects. When he died in his bed he was rich, powerful, lonely, and famous: the very model of a successful king.'

So might have Francis Bacon described Henry VII had he penned only a conceit. Instead he wrote a history. Composed in the summer of 1621 while he recovered from the shock of his impeachment, the *History of the Reign of King Henry VII* was intended to revive its author's fortunes. The intent failed: Bacon never regained favor or influence, although the book was not to blame. Both King James, who read it prior to publication, and Prince Charles, to whom it was dedicated, thought well of it. Bacon stayed in retirement because he was not needed. Besides failing to restore its author to his former eminence, the book, more recently, has damaged Bacon's reputation as a man of learning. For after enjoying the praise of several generations, the *History* has been found to be based on the dubious use of available resources and, accordingly, banished from the shelves of serious historical scholarship.

Is the *History*, then, merely a footnote to the achievement of its author, a *pièce d'occasion* that missed fulfilling its purposes? Certainly not. Indeed, it is absurd to appraise the book solely by modern standards of what a history ought to be. Bacon was not even pretending to write the kind of book he has been condemned for not writing. The work is manifestly an invention: a history composed in the classical style, where the object is to persuade the reader of known truths. Acceptance, not accuracy, is the goal of the writer. With this in mind we might pause to reflect on just how superior a performance the *History* is. For the vision we have of the first Tudor king is still the one Bacon gave us.

But why did Bacon choose to write a history at the nadir of his public fortunes? He never wrote another, though there are some fragments. Why did he choose to write about Henry VII? Except for a two-page portrait of the first Tudor composed during Elizabeth's reign, Bacon's writings up to 1621 scarcely show a fascination with Henry. What, moreover, is the *History* actually about, what are the truths it sought to teach? And, lastly, why is the character of Henry VII so strikingly similar to the received image of his creator?

Answers to these questions will not be found in the *History* itself. The commonplace, 'To understand a history one ought first to study the historian,' applies particularly to any man writing in the classical mode, but it is even more dramatically the case with Bacon. He was not a retiring intellectual, and to appreciate the *History* one must see it in the context of his life. Thus, this study examines the circumstances of the crisis that led to his writing a history, the progress of his mind and career up until his downfall, and, finally, the *History* itself. This unorthodox structure seems best suited to gain perspective on both the man and his book.

In examining the impeachment much more is at stake than determining the truth of the charges against Bacon; his overthrow, in fact, is inexplicable when seen solely in terms of his guilt. What must be explained is how parliament—an institution Bacon prided himself on having mastered—could so briskly defeat him, and how James—a king he had served with exemplary loyalty and skill—could so casually let him fall. It is, then, Bacon's true position in affairs of state that this chapter tries to locate. To do this it will be necessary to look at the parliament of 1621 more closely than might seem warranted. Furthermore, since these months provide us with the most detailed record we have of any portion of Bacon's life, a somewhat rounder view of the man should emerge. This view will suggest that temperament and a shaky status, perhaps even more than misdeeds, caused the Lord Chancellor's ruin.

The discussion of Bacon's development up until 1621 is purposely less exhaustive, and slights the standard categories of inquiry: biography, ideas, and influences. Instead, following the path of his public career, particularly through his writings, it observes the distinctive contours of Bacon's intellect (the way he consciously addressed himself to examining and discussing subjects) and sensibility (the spontaneous responses he was apt to make to situations and people). It also explores how his formidable talents as lawyer and publicist advanced, yet limited, his fortunes, and how they colored virtually all of his writings. Finally, the reliability of Bacon as an observer of his day, as well as of himself, will be questioned; for too long have his words about men and events seemed truth. The decision to compose these middle chapters in the form of a selective commentary on his life was taken so as to impress the reader with a feeling for a man and his predicament. The search here is for pattern and style, while avoiding the reductive error; there is no offer of a complete, or new, biography.

In the last chapter the *History* is studied for its connections with Bacon's career and mind. Analysis replaces narrative; a text serves both as a witness and justification to a career. Necessarily, the book resembles other histories of the period. But like so many of its author's creations, it will not be contained within a type. Its special vitality and persuasiveness can only be explained by knowing the experiences, hopes, and habits of mind that Bacon brought to it. Thus, the analysis urges the reader to grasp how profoundly the life of Francis Bacon establishes meanings and motives for his writings, and how the writings, in turn, provide an interpretation of his life.

# Chapter 1

# King's Pawn,
# October 1620–May 1621

he parliament of 1621 convened during one of the worst winters on record. High winds and freezing temperatures caused great floes of ice shaped "like rockes and mountaines," and having "a straunge and hideous aspect," to clog the Thames. For three weeks in January the river was impassable, and filth submerged the streets and lanes of the capital. Food prices, already high, soared. Men could not remember when conditions had been so bad. Originally scheduled to meet on January 16, but prorogued twice, the Lords and Commons finally gathered at Westminster on January 30.

Seven years had passed since the barren session of 1614. Once again the need for money had prompted writs to be sent out. This time, however, the King commanded a strong position. It was generally assumed that he would seek aid to protect the interests of his son-in-law, Frederick, Elector of the Palatinate, who, having rashly accepted the Crown of Bohemia two years before, was now struggling to defend his own lands against a Spanish army. Pledges of war had been heard in Whitehall, and a benevolence to give substance to the threat was being raised among privy councilors and the nobility; at long last it seemed the King might reap some advantage from the popular contempt for Spain and Catholicism. Despite hard times there was a slight puffing of chests as men realized that the courts of Europe were nervously looking to see if King and parliament would decide to intervene. To unite himself with his people, solve his chronic financial difficulties, and preserve his daughter's inheritance all appeared within the King's grasp. But the neat coincidence of interest between James's dynastic and financial concerns and his subjects' emotions could not alone ensure a bountiful session. High prices and a scarcity of coin persuaded many that the commonwealth was in great trouble, and, together with notorious grievances, threatened to corrode the enthusiasm for a holy war and retard supply. A skillful strategy was required if this parliament was not to repeat the failure of its predecessor.

On January 22, Francis Bacon, 1st Lord Verulam, had celebrated his sixtieth birthday at York House, the mansion where he had been born. Ben Jonson was in attendance and read lines composed for the occasion. Five days later Bacon advanced to the title of Viscount St. Albans. In the midst of all the flattery and panoply of power, the Lord Chancellor of England was probably worrying about the upcoming parliament. He had given much time and thought to the pre-liminaries, but his advice had been rarely followed. A letter he wrote to the King on October 2, 1620, and which, like virtually all his correspondence with James, was sent through the Marquis of Buck-ingham, contains the first notice of his involvement.

> Secretary Naunton this day brought me your pleasure in certain notes; That I should advise with the two Chief Justices (old Parliament-men) and Sir Edward Cook (who is also their senior in that school) and Sir Randall Crewe the last Speaker, and such other Judges as we should think fit, touching that which mought in true policy, without packing or degenerate arts, prepare to a Parliament, in case your Majesty should resolve of one to be held.[14.114]

Promising to "carry the business with that secrecy which apper-taineth," he also added that he would be discreet about informing the privy council of his efforts. Still undecided whether to summon a parliament, James wished to avoid a decisive split in the council, where there was a faction strongly opposed to such a move. A less formal survey of the problems would leave the King uncommitted publicly to a course of action.[1] Bacon was a natural choice to conduct such a survey. He had been offering advice to James on parliamentary business since the beginning of the reign, and had himself sat in every parliament since 1581. Few men could rival his knowledge of its customs and prejudices, fewer still his faith that he could predict and manage its proceedings.

The committee (without Coke) first met on October 6, and divided the business into four categories, the substance of which Bacon reported to Buckingham in a letter the following day. Griev-ances, old and new, headed the list. The committee next considered what sort of proclamation should be issued announcing the parliament. What persons "were fit to be of the House" and how they were to be placed was the third consideration, which meant that lists indicating the expected reliability of possible members had to be made. Lastly, "some commonwealth bills" that might be put before the parliament to demonstrate the King's concern for his subjects' welfare were drawn up, "not wooing bills to make the King and his graces cheap; but good matter to set the Parliament on work, that an empty stomach do not feed upon humour" (14.115-17). This report satisfied the King, Buckingham assured Bacon in a letter of October 9. In the weeks to come, however, James declined to follow through on his Lord Chancellor's suggestions.

The matter of a suitable proclamation was taken up first. On October 18 a draft, "which I thought fit to offer first to his Majesty's perusal, before I acquainted the Council," was passed through Buckingham to the King. The task of composing public declarations was a familiar one to Bacon; hardly another government figure had his facility, or his faith in the potency of words. The proclamation discussed the reasons for summoning a parliament and the kind of member desired. Peace, it stressed, was the "constant purpose and provident care" of the King; he had persisted "in the same resolution" even after his son-in-law's election to the Bohemian Crown. But the late invasion of the Palatinate had forced a reappraisal of policy. Dynastic responsibilities and the "balance of Christendom" demanded "the uttermost of our forces and means, to recover and resettle the said Palatinate to our son and our descendents." War, then, might be necessary. If so, there would be many concerns, "amongst which we hold nothing more necessary than to confer and advise with the common council of our kingdom, upon this so important a subject. For although the making of war or peace be a secret of empire, and a thing properly belonging to our high prerogative royal, and imperial power: yet nevertheless, in causes of that nature which we shall think fit not to reserve but to communicate, we shall ever think ourselves much assisted and strengthened by the faithful advice and general assent of our loving subjects." Money, as well as advice, would be needed, and Bacon contended that although James had subsisted on his own for the last ten years "(a thing unheard of in late times)," supply was necessary. Recalling one of the committee's suggestions, Bacon completed the rationale for summoning a parliament by noting that "in respect of so long intermission of a Parliament the times may have introduced some things fit to be reformed, either by new laws or by the moderate desires of our loving subjects dutifully intimated unto us (wherein we shall ever be no less ready to give them all gracious satisfaction than their own hearts can desire)." The draft concluded with a brief discussion of what constituted a desirable member. Experience, wisdom, and discretion should be the qualities looked for, "and generally such as are interested and have portion in the state." Papists and schismatics were to be kept out, as well as "bankrupts and necessitous persons," "lawyers of mean account and estimation," "young men that are not ripe for grave consultations," and "mean dependents upon great persons." If these were excluded, "a loving and comfortable meeting between us and our people" was assured (14.124-28).

This draft, so typical of Bacon's thought and style, was designed to bind King and nation together, to establish confidence by showing respect. The interests of both are assumed to be intimately involved in the Palatinate question. Consultation on the matter is desirable and altogether feasible. Money will be needed yet grievances will not be neglected. Considerable emphasis is placed on the decisive but not inflexible nature of the King's policy. The part dealing with elections was intentionally brief and restrained so as not to clash with the soothing tone of the whole: "we [Coke, Chief Justices, Crewe] are all of the opinion, that it is not good to have it more peremptory, more particular, nor more sharp" (14.123).

The King was not pleased. Replying through Buckingham the next day, he rejected any discussion "containing matters of state and the reasons of calling the parliament: whereof neither the people are capable, nor is it fit for his Majesty to open now unto them, but to reserve to the time of their assembling, according to the course of his predecessors, which his Majesty intendeth to follow: the declaring whereof in the proclamation would cut off the ground of his Majesty's and your Lordship's speech, at the proper time." The King would draft his own proclamation, one which would discuss only the "well ordering of the election of the burgesses," and which would use "somewhat of the latter part of the draught you have sent" (14.128).

Bacon's attempt to introduce a spirit of accommodation failed.

His quick response to Buckingham's letter contained a sardonic, yet shrewd, observation:

> I did even now receive your Lordship's letter touching the proclamation, and do approve his Majesty's judgment and foresight above mine own. Neither would I have thought of inserting matter of state for the vulgar, but that now-a-days there is no vulgar, but all statesmen. But, as his Majesty doth excellently consider, the time of it is not yet proper. [14.129]

Instead of outright genuflection, his usual gesture when he had misread the King's mind, Bacon offers his wit. He does not actually deny that something more than an admonishment to select responsible members is called for. The King's quibble, that the people were not fit, and that custom argued against such a format, is questioned for its relevancy, not its accuracy. Bacon was, of course, no more eager than James to have all the questions of war and peace discussed openly. But he was anxious to have the King's subjects *believe* that their advice was desired. After all, since a public declaration to intervene in the Palatinate if diplomacy failed had already been made, doubtless with the hope of activating public sympathy, why not go a step further in gathering support? James obviously did not value such a tactic.

The King, as promised, wrote his own proclamation. It casually alluded to "the present Face of Christendom so miserably and dangerously distracted at this tyme," and then exhorted the people to choose sober members. Its tactlessness on the latter issue saved it from being dull. After closely following his Lord Chancellor's lead in enumerating various undesirable members, the King, when he came to mention lawyers, lost his temper. Bacon had cautioned against electing "lawyers of mean account and estimation," a bland scruple; James trumpeted against "curious and wrangling Lawyers, who may seeke reputation by stirring needlesse questions," a remark that could easily be interpreted as a denunciation of all lawyers.[2] Despite efforts by Bacon and Lord Chamberlain Pembroke to persuade James to tone down this description of perhaps the most irritable and influential profession, the proclamation was published on November 6, 1620.[3]

Grievances had been the first item of business in Bacon's survey of October 7. It was inevitable, no matter how "loving and comfortable" the meeting between King and people might be, that there should be complaints and sharp questions. The committee, accordingly, had worked hard to define the probable points of dissatisfaction and to devise methods of contending with them so as to avoid rancorous deadlocks. Sometime after October 7 it met with the King to examine the grievances of the last parliament, and expressed its opinion, "by way of probable conjecture, which of them are like to fall off, and which may perchance stick and be renewed." The committee also informed James that "fresh" grievances, some "Proclamations and Commissions, and many Patents," were likely to be raised. These were not discussed in detail at the time, but as the opening session grew near they drew increasing attention.

On November 29 the committee sent to Buckingham a proposal on how to handle the new grievances. Drafted once again by Bacon, it outlined a strategy calculated to defuse a potentially explosive situation.[4] The Lord Chancellor hoped the King would do something about the anticipated grievances, particularly patents of monopoly, before parliament gathered. Patents were grants of specific privileges or powers to individuals—often courtiers—and were usually very lucrative. In their most common form, as monopolies, they gave to their beneficiaries control over a particular trade or industrial process. Bacon did not disapprove of monopolies in themselves; he simply did not think they were worth the loss of good opinion.

The course to be taken with the unpopular patents was shrewdly conceived. The patents of old debts and concealments—grants permitting private individuals to search out forgotten debts to the Crown and defective land titles—might be abolished by an act of parliament. Surgery of this sort was quick, inexpensive, and left no scars. The law courts were too slow, and to leave the task to the council would result in a swarm of the dispossessed seeking compensation.

> Wherefore we conceive the most convenient way will be, if some grave and discreet gentlemen of the country, such as have least relation to the court, make at fit times some modest motion touching the same; That his Majesty would be graciously pleased to permit some law to pass (for the time past only) no ways touching his Majesty's regal power, to free his subjects from the same; and so his Majesty, after due consultation, to give way unto them. [14.146]

Patents of monopoly were to be dispatched more directly. Those the

King was willing to abolish were to be examined and revoked by the council, "either as granted contrary to his Majesty's book of bounty, or found since to have been abused in the execution, or otherwise by experience discovered to be burdensome to the country." The essential point was to give the impression that such revocations were the ordinary business of the council, and were "not done as matter of preparation to a Parliament." This way the King might "keep his greatness, and somewhat shall be done in Parliament, and somewhat out of Parliament, as the nature of the subject and business requires."

A list of patents to be abolished accompanied the advice. With respect to monopolies Bacon was selective, noting only those most ill-famed. "There be many more, of like nature but not of like weight, nor so much rumoured, which to take away now in a blaze will give more scandal that such things were granted, than cause thanks that they be now revoked." The committee also promised to advise the King about what sort of "Commonwealth Bills" would be appropriate, and the "extent of his Majesty's pardon, which if his subjects do their part, as we hope they will, we do wish may be more liberal than of later times, pardons being the ancient remuneration in Parliament" (14.148).

The prime concern of this report is the King's image: monopolies must be done away with because the King cannot afford their unpopularity. Any method of withdrawal, however, might not be satisfactory; if it was ill-conceived the King stood to lose more than if he neglected the grievances altogether. To begin the process now was to increase the probability of a happy session. This would not diminish the prerogative; rather, it would enlarge the King's reputation. The stress on reputation, on handling the problem so as to win the King some credit, was habitual with Bacon. What James can persuade his subjects to believe he is doing is more important than what is actually done. In politics, as Bacon was wont to say, *opinio est veritate major*.

Similar advice was given to Buckingham. In a letter to the Marquis accompanying the report to the King, Bacon notes the bad odor rising from the patents of Sir Giles Mompesson and Christopher Villiers (the favorite's brother), "your Lordship's special friends, which I account as mine own friends; and so showed myself when they were in suit." He urged Buckingham to heed the advice given the King, and to "put off the envy of these things (which I think in themselves bear no great fruit), and rather take the thanks for ceasing them, than the note for maintaining them." Bacon was careful not to seem too bold; Buckingham, vain and prickly especially in regard to his family, could not be pushed. Thus, having set forth his opinion, Bacon closed his remarks on patents with a proper submission. "But howsoever, let me know your mind, and your Lordship shall find I will go your way" (14.148-49).

The willingness to serve, no matter what policy is adopted, is hardly unique with Bacon. But simple allegiance (and self-interest) graciously expressed is mixed with hints of disappointment. In the same letter Bacon applauds the recent choice of Chief Justice Montagu as Lord Treasurer. Perhaps "now a number of counsels which I have given for the establishment of his Majesty's estate, and have lyen dead and buried deeper than this snow, may now spring up and bear fruit" (14.149). With regard to office and wealth, things that meant much to him, Bacon could not reasonably complain about his years of serving the King: he had prospered. But there was often an oblique sense of frustration over his failure to influence policy. He performed many duties, but recurrently felt he deserved, by virtue of his position and talents, to do more. He was neither as close to the King nor as powerful as he imagined he ought to be, and thus was always signaling his loyalty and readiness. "All your Majesty's business is *super cor meum*."[5]

On December 14 the committee, at the King's request, took the matter of the patents before the council. Arguing vigorously that to revoke at least the most notorious would eliminate a source of bitter debate and move parliament "better and faster to the main errand," Bacon pleaded with the council to take up the project and improve its image as "centinel" of the public interest. The council disagreed, echoing the excuses offered earlier by the King. To revoke patents so near to a parliament would be construed as "an humouring of the Parliament . . . and that after Parliament they would come up again." Besides, custom argued that patents were to be revoked "upon the complaints of particular persons"; as an "offered" grace, they would "leese their thanks." The council also suggested that the Commons should have its choice of grievances to voice, particularly "since they can do nothing of themselves." Bacon, although hardly convinced of their merit, yielded to these arguments. Later, in the letter to Buckingham where he related the events of this council meeting, he reiterated his belief that if the favorite would disengage himself from the patents, "it will sort to your honour." He also expressed concern for how the elections were progressing; this concern doubtless was reinforcing his desire to see the King do *something* before January. "For if his Majesty said well, that when he knew the men and the elections he would guess at the success; the prognosticks are not so good as I expected, occasioned by late occurrences abroad, and the general licentious speaking of state matters" (14.152).

No more is heard of patents until the session itself. Neither the King, Buckingham, nor the council favored discarding a cheap means of rewarding servants and sycophants. Besides, such a move might break with custom or be interpreted as a sign of weakness. Bacon had failed to make James see how severe a tactical disadvantage patents were. As with the proclamation, he had appealed to the King to make a gesture that would have secured, rather than undermined, his authority. James was not a stupid man, and dissimulation was not distasteful to him, but a predisposition to define political problems in personal terms made compromise and flexibility unlikely. He was not about to give away tokens of power, the less so where Buckingham was intimately involved.

The one item on which the King and Bacon found themselves in full accord was a proclamation against licentious speaking and writing in state matters. Feeling against Spain, always strong, had intensified since the news of Frederick's defeat at the White Mountain had reached England on November 24. Writing to Carleton on December 22, Chamberlain suggested how far indiscretion had gone. "The last weeke the bishop of London was willed to call all his Clergie before him, and to charge them from the King not to meddle in their sermons with the Spanish match nor any other matter of State."[6] Disturbed by the extent of political discussion, the King asked Bacon to draft a proclamation of warning. The result was a model of the ambiguous threat. So vague was the definition of "lavish discourse" and so abstract the quality of menace, that it is difficult to envision its having any effect. Bacon was told by Buckingham, in a letter dated December 21, that "his Majesty liketh [it] in every point so well, both in matter and form, that he findeth no cause to alter a word in it, and would have your Lordship acquaint the Lords of the Council with it (though he assureth himself no man can find anything in it to be changed), and to take order for the speedy setting of it forth" (14.154-55). The council was less impressed, as Bacon wrote two days later to Buckingham. "There was a motion to have sharpened it; but better none, than over sharp at first" (14.155). It was published without changes on December 24.

Along with the letter to Buckingham reporting the council's reaction, Bacon sent an analysis of the business expected in the upcoming parliament. Unfortunately, this document has not survived; it might have explained in more detail the fears he had for the session. But the letter speaks of the paper, and of the need for planning.

> Meanwhile as I propounded to the King (which he allowed well), I have broken the main of the Parliament business into questions and parts which I send. It may be, it is an overdiligence; but still methinks there is a middle thing between art and chance: I think they call it providence, or some such thing; which good servants owe to their sovereign, specially in cases of importance and straits of occasions. And these huffing elections, and general license of speech, *ought to make us the better provided*. The way will be, if his Majesty will be pleased to peruse these questions advisedly, and give me leave to wait on him; and then refer it to some few of the Council, a little to advise upon it. [14.155, Emphasis added]

There is no record to show that any use was made of this analysis, and the sentences imply what the sessions were to reveal: the King had thought little about *how* he was going to get what he wanted. Moreover, he appeared less than interested in the urgent proposals offered by his Lord Chancellor.

The King undoubtedly respected his Lord Chancellor's capacities. What is less clear is to what uses he considered them appropriate. As lawyer and writer Bacon was a valuable servant; whether he was trusted as a counselor or liked as a person is, at least, questionable. The often-quoted reaction of James to the *Novum Organum* suggests, albeit humorously, a quality of Bacon's mind that James perhaps found uncongenial. "The King cannot forbeare sometimes in reading his last booke to say that yt is like the peace of

God, that passeth all understanding."[7] Even more revealing, though, is a sentence to be found in the King's letter of October 16, 1620, when he acknowledged receiving his presentation copy of the book.

> I can with comfort assure you, that you could not have made choice of a subject more befitting your place, and your universal and methodick knowledge; and in the general, I have already observed, that you jump with me, in keeping the mid way between the two extremes; as also in some particulars I have found that you agree fully with my opinion. [14.122]

The straggling prose and egregious vanity camouflage poorly a need to protect oneself against a competitor. James demanded that other men regularly accommodate themselves to his fears and passions. Despite his constant flattery, Bacon was a competitor; his intellectual attainments did not bring him the King's affection. He could never win the King's confidence because he could not cope with the King's personality, which intruded itself into all business. This undoubtedly vexed Bacon. Eager as he was to perform any service, he was not satisfied being a secretary. As Lord Chancellor he had position, but his ambition sought the higher reaches: he yearned to make policy. The preliminaries to the parliament of 1621 disclose how far he was from realizing his desire. Those who like their history with a lesson often choose to view Bacon's fall as conforming to the pattern of classical tragedy. Such comparisons distort tragedy as well as misrepresent Bacon's real situation. In truth, he did not fall from a very great height, however guilty of the crimes imputed to him.

The omens were not favorable at the opening of parliament. Dozens of spectators were injured when two of the scaffolds erected to give the thronging crowds around Westminster a better view collapsed. On the royal progress from Whitehall observers marked the private words the King spoke to the mother and wife of Buckingham, as well as to the Spanish ambassador, Count Gondomar. When he arrived at Westminster James had to be carried into the House of Lords in a chair because of his arthritis. Rumors spread that the King, never regal in his bearing, was now virtually a cripple, "beeing so weake in his leggs and feet that yt is doubted he will find litle use in them hereafter."[8] His speech was equally unimpressive; once more grown men heard themselves addressed as errant school boys. "I may truly say with our Saviour, I have often piped unto you and you have not danced. I have mourned and you have not lamented." Instructions as to "what a parliament is" and how the members were to "behave" sounded in the chamber. Substantive issues were ill-defined. Empty coffers were treated as an unfortunate anomaly in a time of peace and plenty. "No man within my dominions can complain of poverty which is not through his own default; that either he doth not work or lives unthrifty." Buckingham's appointment as Lord Admiral was defended on the grounds that faith and loyalty in such a position meant more than expertise. Turning to the Palatinate, James pledged "my crown and my blood and the blood of my son" in its defense; parliament need offer only its purse. The lecture dragged on with promises of reform and effusions of love.[9]

It was a feeble performance. For more than an hour the King had avoided analyzing the issues as problems to be reckoned with on their own terms. Instead, he had defended his relation to them. Alternately apologizing and chastising, he seemed interested only in obtaining subsidies. Parliament was free to discover its own intentions.[10]

Bacon's message afterwards was brief but purposeful. He offered the members a carrot.

> I would have the Parliament know itself, first in a modest carriage to so gracious a Sovereign, and secondly in valuing themselves thus far, as to know now it is in them by their cheerful dealing to procure infinite good to themselves in substance and reputation at home and abroad. As there is great expectation in the beginning of this Parliament, so I pray God it may be as good in the conclusion: that it may be generative, begetting others hereafter.[11]

Struggle between King and parliament was useless, only compromise could be productive. Having tried to caution the King, Bacon was now making the same appeal to parliament. On February 3, after the Commons had presented their speaker, Bacon returned to the same theme with more energy and detail. If the members carried themselves with "moderation" and "affection" in their actions and their speeches, they would find a loving and generous King. Ironically, the detente eventually fashioned rendered the Lord Chancellor's fall possible.

The first days of the session were taken up with cries for privileges and outbursts against papists, both familiar chords. The Commons then turned its attention to what the King had described as the "main errand," money. Astonishingly little trouble was met. On February 15 two subsidies were agreed upon as "a present of love" to the King; more, it was hinted, would later be voted specifically for the Palatinate. James was surprised, and pleased.[12] Such largesse so early in a session was a new experience. The generosity of the Commons, however, was not entirely spontaneous. Hard coin was advanced to propitiate the King and enable a discussion of grievances to go forward.[13] Coke, when reporting to the lower house the King's pleasure at receiving the windfall, underlined the advantage of being generous. "I will now make an observation and a motion. My observation is that God gave us the better success because we began with his cause first. My motion is to strike while the iron is hot and to appoint two days every week to hear grievances."[14] The King's promise to meet their grievances "above half the way" confirmed the wisdom of timely gestures. Bacon's anxious speeches had fallen on willing minds, yet minds with too much determination, if not altogether clear purposes, for a serene meeting. The initiative had been seized.

Bacon had made a shrewd estimate when he warned James and Buckingham how dangerous the issue of monopolies could be. Two decades of complaints had brought no redress; indeed, the number of patents only grew larger. Thus it was to be expected in a time of serious economic worry that men should fix their energies on abuses of their getting and spending. And the members of the Commons, increasingly conscious of their role as physicians of the commonwealth, were eager to operate themselves on this cancerous growth.[15] The attack on monopolies that quickly followed the vote on supply was not, therefore, merely a screen for embarrassing Buckingham and destroying Bacon. Some, like Sir Edward Coke, doubtless appreciated the larger strategic (and personal) value of the attack, but it requires a skillful, not to mention anachronistic, imagination to see a conspiracy in the ragged debates. Each of the monopolies scrutinized was felt as a serious fault in the fabric of daily life. The licensing of inns and alehouses throughout the realm by Londoners was condemned for subverting the local jurisdiction of the Justices of the Peace, while the gold and silver thread monopoly was widely criticized for contributing to the current scarcity of money. The angriest censure was reserved for the projectors, those who actually worked the patents. As the days went by, and more evils were uncovered, the Commons became mesmerized by its rhetoric. The fever soon spread to the Lords. It seemed that the whole structure of things needed looking to. Reformation, not simply the remedying of specific grievances, was called for.

The questioning of the referees was an inevitable step in the logic of reform. Who, after all, had sanctioned such a grievance? On February 6, when the first rumble of monopolies had been heard, Sir Edward Sackville declared that the referees "who misled his Majestie and are worthie to beare the shame of their owne worke" also ought to be investigated.[16] The examination two weeks later of Sir Giles Mompesson, who held the patent for inns and sat for Great Bedwin in the lower house, focused the problem. Before a monopoly was granted the practice had been to refer it to several officials who advised the King of its legality and "conveniency." Based on their recommendation, the monopoly was granted or refused by the King. Thus, with hardly a trace of casuistry, the referees could be considered the persons responsible for monopolies; the King need not come under attack. "If these did certify it," pronounced Coke, "no king in Christendom but would have granted it. Therefore his Majesty is free from all blame in it."[17] Absolved, James could afford to gaze with equanimity on the progress of debate.

Those about him were not so lucky. Buckingham, opposed originally to even summoning parliament, was understandably less sanguine than the King about its progress. His creatures and kinsmen were now into almost every pot of jam, hence cries of reform threatened him even when he was not personally culpable. Mompesson, a relation by marriage, was fast becoming notorious, so widespread had been his activities. The Marquis's brothers, Sir Edward and Christopher Villiers, were both reputed to have reaped large benefits from patents. Consequently, as the debate warmed, Buckingham, imagining himself the real target, grew frightened and begged the King to dissolve parliament. James refused. A paying parliament was not tossed out so quickly. Buckingham desperately turned for advice to John Williams, Dean of Westminster, only to hear what had been told him months before by Bacon: "Follow this Parliament in their undertakings . . . Swim with the Tide, and you cannot be Drown'd."[18] Implicit in Williams's advice was the belief that the lower house was not conspiring to bring down the favorite.

Those who had served as referees had still less relish for the gathering crusade. Two names stood out: Bacon and Lord Treasurer Montagu. Over the years both men had frequently advised the King on monopolies, and both had approved Mompesson's patent for inns. If these persons of eminence had failed as guardians of the commonwealth, whatever the reason, then the House of Commons, proclaimed Sir Francis Seymour on February 27, had the obligation to censure them. "And this will be for the honor of the King, the good of the subject and terror of others in time to come."[19]

It was easier to talk terror, however, than to implement it, for the House of Commons had no punitive jurisdiction except in cases involving its privileges. Over several decades it had increasingly thought of itself and acted as a court in extending its own privileges, but it had not developed any procedures for judging, as distinguished from investigating and condemning, grievances against the commonwealth.[20] Having now worked themselves into a temper where political interest and self-righteousness transformed them into sinless judges, the members rediscovered their impotence. Temporarily they overlooked the difficulty; their illegal and brutal condemnation of Sir Francis Mitchell, a Justice of the Peace accused of misusing his powers in support of the alehouse patent, reveals just how uncalculated the actions of the house could be.[21] In the course of Mompesson's examination, however, two lawyers, William Noy and William Hakewill, were dispatched to the Tower to comb the records and find answers to the jurisdictional problem. They returned with a solution prepared earlier by Sackville: alignment with the Lords. Precedents had been discovered in the reign of Henry VI to justify such a move.[22] Coke was quick to buttress this legal construction with an emotional appeal. "I thank God for three unities of this parliament: 1, betwixt our Sovereign and us; 2, betwixt the Lords and us; 3, betwixt ourselves. This is as weighty a cause as any in my time because it concerns not us only but the Lords also. Therefore we are resolved according to former precedents to address ourselves to the Lords."[23] Many members could not have felt exceptional confidence in these words. The unity "betwixt the Lords and us" would have struck them as a figment of the great man's imagination. Indeed, Nathaniel Rich almost immediately discarded the rhetoric of unity for the more familiar "Libertye of the Howse," and threatened "That if the Lords will not ioyne with us we will punish him ourselves."[24]

A decisive moment had arrived, one that the logic of circumstances and emotion, rather than the schemes of men, had created. Reform demanded punishment. In his motion to inquire what laws were available to punish patentees, Sir Thomas Wentworth had put the matter persuasively on February 21. "If we let them go with laying down their patents, what do we reform. Will not others do the like."[25] To join with the Lords, however, would require ignoring bitter memories, for the unproductiveness of James's first two parliaments had stemmed largely from the discord between the two houses. Rare had been the occasions when they had worked together comfortably. In the parliament of 1604-11 the concerns of the lower house, purveyance, ecclesiastical reform, and trade, were either ignored or roughly handled by the Lords, while the major proposals of the Lords, the union with Scotland and the Great Contract, had come by similar treatment in the Commons. Moreover, considerable ill feeling had been generated in the Commons by the Lords' high-handed practices in conferences.[26] The parliament of 1614 saw the situation worsen, and, significantly, the immediate cause of dissolution had been the King's lack of confidence that the two houses could stop quibbling long enough to accomplish any business. The Lords had refused (though by a close vote) to confer with the Commons on what the latter regarded as the crucial issue of the moment, impositions. Bishop Neile's intemperate remarks on this occasion, which the Commons interpreted as a smear on their reputation as well as their privileges, effectively ended serious debate. The counterblast of Sir Roger Owen, "that he never sawe anye goodnes Come from the Lordes and if the kinge doe not repayre their wronges, it will hinder him more then the bushopp is worthe,"[27] was prophetic; it also accurately caught the mood of disgust felt by the Commons.

In seven years the anger had subsided, but the remaining suspicion offered little hope for a joining of hands.[28] When Sir Robert Phelips, on the morning of February 5, urged the Commons to confer with the Lords on freedom of speech, he found no support. The Lords, he was told, had formerly rejected such advances; to try again was pointless. Undaunted, Phelips that afternoon pushed the argument once more, and with the same result. The Commons did agree, however, to confer on recusants. Two days later, during the debate on whether Sir Henry Cary, the Comptroller of the Household who had been raised to the Scottish peerage as Viscount Falkland after his election, should be admitted to the house, Thomas Mallet voiced a common feeling. "The Higher and Lower House were divided because the Lower House could not have that liberty of speech, there being such a world of Lords their superiors, being such a distance between them and some of the Lords."[29] Such words did not portend well for an alliance. Coke too was not immune from the prevailing suspicion, arguing that the Commons be represented by twice as many members as the Lords when the conference on recusants was held. This was the familiar expedient of using numbers to establish parity between the houses. On February 15 there was a sharp debate when Edward Alford criticized Speaker Richardson for showing too much deference to the Lords.[30] That afternoon Phelips again urged a consultation with the Lords, this time about the disposition of the subsidies to be granted to the King. Sir Thomas Roe, somewhat misconstruing the purpose of the suggestion, objected: "For if we give I would not have them [Lords] to share the thanks." Phelips's reply struck the larger issue and offered a tempting precedent.

> I meant not to go to the Lords about giving but about the way of doing and undertaking. For the 3 of Rich. 2, when the affairs of France were in hand a supply was demanded, and then this House conferred with the Lords about the end of it. It's the Catholic King that means to make himself monarch of the west. And is it not fit to have a consultation.[31]

Mr. Secretary Calvert immediately questioned the wisdom of using a public forum to discuss the King's strategy. Phelips answered with a deceptive distinction: "I meant not what to do but how to maintain that which he intends to do." (Could the latter have been discussed without publicly revealing the former?) At this tense point Coke stepped in to rejoice over the unanimity on the subsidy, thereby closing the argument. But perhaps Phelips's insistence had awakened the great lawyer's mind to a possible strategy.

Distrust, then, was the prevailing mood in the Commons whenever the subject of working with the Lords was brought up. Phelips stands alone in his efforts to persuade the lower house to a rapprochement. He had sat in the two previous parliaments and perhaps had decided that failure would also mark this gathering unless the two houses realized a tactical compromise. It is also possible that he had perceived divisions existing in the Lords that made an alliance of self-interest feasible.

No longer was the upper house comprised of complacent peers, fawning bishops, and a smattering of dissidents.[32] Villiers's rise and the King's empty coffers had instituted a hazardous practice: the direct cash sale of titles. It is very doubtful that the cash obtained balanced the political capital lost, since an essentially obedient body became factious. The contempt of the old peers, who regarded their place as a birthright, for the new, who conceived of theirs as an extension of their property or favor, was easily translated into political issues. How touchy the Lords were becoming can be seen in their reaction in February 1621 to the raising of Sir Henry Cary to the peerage. Thirty-three lords petitioned the King, requesting that no Scottish lord take precedence in England over the lowest member of the English baronage. The King might turn as many Englishmen into Scots and Irish lords as he chose, but their titles were to have no significance in England. Chamberlain's estimate of how this unprecedented petition affected the King is illuminating. "This accident moved him the more, because a misunderstanding having so long continued twixt him and the nether house, (and they now agreeing so well,) the wind shold thus come about into a corner of the upper house."[33] The ascendancy of Buckingham aggravated the resentment of many. The Marquis was treated coldly in this, his first, parliament. Unhappy peers might daily see the embodiment of what was wrong at court. Of course there had always been lords whose sympathies and interests tied them to the more independent-minded in the lower house. The novelty of 1621 is the strong sense of grievance existing within the upper house. Its prestige and honor were felt by many to have been debased. Little wonder, then, that on the first day of the session a committee was appointed to investigate what the Earl of Arundel termed the "many priviliges belonging to us and divers orders which weare anciently observed in this house that by disuse and want of puttinge in practise are now almost lost."[34] Given the opportunity, the House of Lords might discover new (or old) practices that would refurbish its reputation.

Tactical necessity, therefore, prompted and shaped the alliance. The Commons needed a tribunal to press reform; angry debate and royal promises would not suffice. The Lords sought a lever to raise their self-esteem; popular grievances and a suing Commons could supply it. In the following weeks pride of place and remembrance of past insults never quite disappear, but skillful leadership and a measure of luck combine to give substance to Coke's apparition of unity.

Coke's motion on February 28 to take Mompesson's case to the Lords was supported by the house. The splendid qualifications of Sir Giles for the part of Example probably helped some members to swallow their pride.[35] This new strategy did not, however, go un-noticed by the court. That evening the King informed his Lord Chancellor of what was coming and told him to consult with the Prince and the Lord Treasurer on how to handle the proposal in the Lords. Not unexpectedly, the three decided to work for a delay. Their task was simplified by the Archbishop of Canterbury, who, unin-formed of "any part of the business," recommended the next day (Thursday) that the Lords, in conformity with the ancient practice, not sit on Wednesdays and Fridays because of Convocation. There being "no other business at all," Bacon, who had encouraged the Archbishop to make his recommendation, immediately adjourned the house till Saturday.[36] Thus, when a committee of the Commons, at the inspiration of Phelips and with Coke as their speaker, arrived to confer, they found the Lords already risen. Despite the eagerness of some peers to reconvene, the conference was rescheduled for Satur-day, March 3.

The situation had radically altered, however, when the Commons met on Saturday. Mompesson had fled. Angrily the house discussed measures to secure the other patentees under investigation. Coke was dispatched to the Lords to request a conference on grievances and to seek help in capturing the fugitive. His words were carefully chosen. He declared that the grievances of the land were "so unsufferable as that it is for the honor of the king to have a fit reformation," and that "ancient precedents," "your Lordships . . . great power and interest in the redress," and recognition of the Lords' own concern for these matters, induced the Commons to ask their support.[37] After deliberating, the Lords agreed to confer with the Commons on Monday, and to help in the search for Mompesson. When Coke replied that the lower house might not be fully prepared by Monday, but was nevertheless anxious to oblige the Lords in respect to time and place, Bacon answered that the Lords were flexible and would, if necessary, accept a conference at another time. With a promise from the Lords that they would shortly send a further message on Mompesson, Coke returned to the lower house.

The discussion following Coke's departure revealed the growing interest of the upper house in the case. There were now no ambiguities; a man publicly accused had run away. Not to do everything possible to ensure his capture would be interpreted as a dereliction of duty. The Earl of Southampton, who in 1614 had argued for a conference with the Commons on impositions, now strongly urged the Lords to join in the manhunt.

> Whether both howses do not make one howse. Yf so, then to ioine. Both howses to concurre in consideracion of the course to be taken for stopp and taking the offender.[38]

Haughton and Say came to his support, and it was decided to hold a conference with the Commons that very afternoon to discuss the problem of Mompesson. Meanwhile, letters were to be sent out stopping the ports and setting a search in hand. The lower house, perhaps surprised at the Lords' enthusiasm, was slow to respond when the messenger brought word of the above. Only when the Lords sent him a second time did the Commons signify their approval of a meeting, with Edward Alford adding, "to have the Messenger now to acknowledge our well Acceptance of their good Correspondence with the House."[39] So eager, apparently, were some of the Lords appointed to this conference committee to get on with the matter that they withdrew to the conference chamber before the time designated and were, at the motion of Lord Hunsdon, rebuked by the other peers.[40]

Good feeling and tender regard marked the conference that afternoon, as Coke noted when he glowingly reported its substance to the lower house. "A desire accomplished is the tree of life. It is not possible to desire more than they have granted . . . . And they would do else whatsoever we thought fit." Besides dispatching their own letters, the Lords agreed to recommend to the King that a proclamation be issued to quicken the search. The Lord Admiral and the Prince gave their word to speak to his Majesty in this matter.[41] The Lords also promised to draw up a warrant for the seizing of Mompesson's papers; significantly, it was to express that it was made upon the "Conference and Agreement of both Houses." But it was a speech by Buckingham that most of all satisfied Coke. In a palpable gesture of expediency the favorite confessed his original support of Mompesson's patent—though mentioning that he, like the King, had depended on the referees' judgment—but insisted that having discovered "how much the people cryed oute against it" he had subsequently cautioned Sir Giles about his activities. To prove his good will Buckingham, in a dramatic flourish, took from his pocket a letter written by the arch-monopolist two days before and had Coke read it to the conference. In it the fugitive protested "that everyone was heard against him but he could not be heard for himself." Buckingham concluded his singular mea culpa with a promise to be "the cheifest and the forwardest against him."[42] The Marquis had caught the tide. More noteworthy was the implication that James refused still to interfere in the cause of reform.

Hardly a better piece of luck than Mompesson's flight could have been asked for by those seeking an alliance between the two houses. By turning fugitive, Sir Giles had declared his guilt. Instead of the two houses having possibly to irritate each other in working out the judicial forms to be taken, they were thrown together into a chase. Details of form and precedent were submerged in a common enthusiasm. Mompesson also gave Buckingham a chance to get off the hook, which in turn served to renew the appetite of the reformers. No single act did as much to confirm the need for reformation, or, paradoxically, reclaim the prestige of the King and his favorite.

The next few days were spent preparing for the conference on monopolies, now finally scheduled for Thursday, March 8. Great care was taken to keep the King in good humor and free from blame for the actions of both the patentees and referees. Coke, for example, swiftly quashed a motion begging a general pardon in return for the subsidy lest it "derogate from our free gift." Phelips, speaking at length on the gold and silver thread monopoly, insisted that James was not to be blamed. Both in its inception and execution, "His Majesty" had shown a sincere concern for the "common good." Cover was also provided for Buckingham: Sir Lionel Cranfield, Master of the Wards, carefully noted that "Sir Edward Villiers had no countenance from the Marquis" in these matters. Bacon did not fare so well. On March 5 the evils of the gold and silver thread monopoly were aired in the Commons, and his actions as Attorney-General, when he had been one of the referees in the monopoly, and as Lord Chancellor, when he had illegally imprisoned some of its opponents, were heavily condemned by Phelips. Nevertheless, a letter that Bacon wrote to Buckingham on March 7 suggests that he was not greatly concerned.

> I do hear from divers of judgment, that to-morrow's conference is like to pass in a calm, as to the referees. Sir Lionel Cranfield, who hath been formerly the trumpet, said yesterday, that he did now incline to Sir John Walter's opinion and motion not to have the referees meddled with, otherwise than to discount it from the King; and so not to look back, but to the future. And I do hear almost all men of judgment in the House wish now that way. I woo no body: I do but listen, and I have doubt only of Sir Edward Coke, who I wish had some round *caveat* given him from the King; for your Lordship hath no great power with him: but I think a word from the King mates him. [14.192]

The prophecy proved correct—momentarily. Although the Commons had voted to include the referees in its report to the Lords, they were not even named by those assigned to deal with the specific patents, Sir Thomas Crew, Heneage Finch, and William Hakewill. Coke, however, did mention them briefly, even though his part as "a father of the law," was to explain the proceedings of the Commons and supply precedents justifying the appeal to the Lords. This he performed brilliantly. With Latin quotations and medieval precedents tumbling from his mouth, Coke besought the Lords to assume the responsibility for purging the commonwealth of corruption, even if it meant calling parliament every year. He urged the Lords to realize that they might sit as a court to decide cases and dispense penalties. "I find then that in parliaments (besides the way of acts and petitions) there is a power of judicature or judicial proceedings." He was careful, however, to praise the King and to emphasize the modest nature of his request. "I remember Phaeton's counsel to Icarus, *altius egressus etc.,* and concludes *medio tutissimus ibis.* So if we go too high we may wrong the king's prerogative; if too low, we betray our country."[43] But Coke's efforts could not make up for those (Crew, Finch, Hakewill) who had muffed their parts. They were chastised, and it was resolved to request a conference for the afternoon of March 10 so that they might be given another chance. The Lords must be told the whole story, the honor of the King and the good of the commonwealth demanded it.

Bacon's optimism, then, was somewhat misplaced. The outrage directed against monopolies and those responsible for them hardly depended for its vigor on Sir Edward Coke. Even if James had checked him, which was not likely since nothing was to be gained by it, it is not clear that the lower house would have obediently halted its investigation. Bacon, always suspicious and resentful of Coke, naturally selected him as the 'real' adversary; he seems at this point not to have realized that something more than self-interest motivated the attack. As long as the Commons showed great deference to the King and the Lords, and left Buckingham to stew in his fears, there was no predicting the outcome of their campaign. Their tact was amply shown on the morning of March 10 when the Attorney-General, Sir Thomas Coventry, suddenly appeared in the house to ask them to put off their afternoon conference with the Lords so that the subsidy bill might be pushed forward. Since royal messages were normally delivered by privy councilors who served in the house, a tempest over custom might easily have ensued. Instead, Coventry was treated with elaborate respect and told that "notwithstanding the conference the King's business should be dispatched though they sat up till ten a clock in the night."[44] This visit to the Commons stemmed from the earlier appearance in the Lords of an even more unexpected visitor, the King.

To appear without notice in parliament during a session was very unusual, and James began his speech with a defense of his presence. "I heard that it was told you by Sir Edward Coke at the conference with the lower howse that I alwayes sitt in this place amongst you by representacion, and theirfore I conceive I may much more come personally when I will." Coke apart, the lower house was praised for showing "more respect unto their kinge" than any of its predecessors. Yet James had not come to pass out sweets. He sought to drive a wedge between the two houses, reminding the Lords that "you . . . are neerer to me than they, unto you." To accomplish this a proper mood had to be set, and so James asked Bacon to report what had passed at the conference two days before. Of course, the King already knew "by relation" what had transpired, but he wanted to flatter the Lords by observing custom as well as make sure that they were accurately apprised of the situation.

There is little doubt that Bacon, like the rest of the peers, was genuinely surprised by this visit. The diaries suggest confusion and stumbling. He was unprepared to give a detailed report and had to resort to reading his notes, a practice altogether uncommon to him. Also, he spoke "so low he was not well to be heard."[45] Given the increasingly ambiguous position of his Lord Chancellor, the King probably felt it was neither fit nor necessary to consult with him on such a move.

After hearing Bacon's summary James spoke at length of his hatred for "projects and projectors" and of the cares he had taken to protect his people from monopolies. Buckingham was here singled out for praise; the referees, however, were callously offered up. "As for the thinges objected against the Chancelor and the Treasurer, I leave them to answere for themselves and to stand and fall as they acquitt them selves, for if they cannot justifie themselves they are not worthie to hould and enjoy those places they have under me." Mompesson, by comparison, was eulogized. "I will say nothinge of Sir Gyles Mompesson having wronged me and himselfe in the execution of these Patents, but I conceave he laboured for my profitt and soe few have I about me that doe trewly regard it as I must not discourage nor give creaditt untill I find just cause against those I ymploy." On the question of the Lords' judicial powers, James tried to force his wedge further.

> Now my Lords, I have somewhat to say to you: you neede not search presidents whether you may deale in this business without the lower howse for there is no question yours is a house and a court of Record. You neede not stick uppon it, for the lower howse, they are but a howse of customes and orders and their house hath come from yours, for though heretofore a long tyme since you were but all one house, yett uppon the division all the power of judicature went with your howse.

Not surprisingly he was furious at Coke for the precedents the latter had used to argue his case, and actually commanded the Lords to consider punishing him. "I thinke him an enemie to monarchy and a traytor to me that menciones my actions with such kings [Henry VI and Richard II] as I have tould you." Turning to Buckingham once more, James asked the Lords to view him not as a man adorned with honors, "but as he was when he came to me as pore George Villiers and if he prove not himselfe a white crow he shalbe called a black crow." Whether or not on cue, Buckingham sank to his knees: "Sir, if I cannot cleare myselfe of any aspercion or imputacion cast uppon me I am contented to abide your Majesty's censure and be called the Black Crow."[46]

Unfortunately this tawdry gesture did not conclude the performance. After a few more words from the King, Bacon rose to protest his innocence of any wrongdoing in the handling of the patents. "And may it please your Majestie, for all my Lord Coke hath said, I hope in futuer ages my acts and honestie shall well apeare before his and my honesty over ballance and waigh his and be found hevier in that scale." Through three decades of simmering hostility he had competed with Coke and often lost out. Now it appeared that Coke was bent on ruining him altogether. Characteristically, he applied to posterity to defend his reputation; at the same time, however, he was ready to have his actions judged by his peers. Following Bacon's lead, Lord Treasurer Montagu then made a more obsequious denial, and a moment later Buckingham once more begged the King to believe that he was indeed a white crow. James finally stopped the round robin confession with a strict charge to the Lords to consult with the judges on the legality of patents and to leave their "conveniency" to his discretion. Mompesson they might play with, "but consume not millions of dayes in those things which have enterveyned since the Parliament began, and were not the cawses of calling of it."[47]

As with virtually all of James's speeches, the political and the personal got tangled together. The defense of himself and Buckingham almost overshadowed the distinction he sought to make between punishing persons and examining the legality and "conveniency" of the patents. Likewise the attempt to undercut the new-found amity between the houses was muddled by the attack on Coke. The King was willing to place himself on the side of reform if his prerogative was not challenged. Indeed, such a strategy might ultimately gain him larger rewards from parliament's purse. To cast off his Lord Chancellor and Lord Treasurer in the process did not cost James. Buckingham, though, was another matter. The Commons might have their reform, the Lords their prestige, and the King his money, if none pressed their demands too far. It was a dangerous game to be caught in the middle of, for each of the players was armed with a very passionate sense of self-sanctity. Bacon, always congratulating himself on being aloof from passion and totally dependent on the King for his position, would be an easy victim of this contest, particularly since the King was not likely to separate self-interest from friendship.

At the conference that afternoon Crew and Finch did not forget the referees. Already embarrassed by the King, and naturally anxious to defend themselves, Bacon and Montagu replied out of turn to the charges. Coke then asked the Lords present whether these personal vindications were to be taken as an expression of the upper house. The Lords answered in the negative. The slap was administered again at the next session of the upper house on Monday, March 12, when Pembroke censured the "2 greate Lords" for speaking without permission. Montagu justified himself by pleading that his honor had been touched. Southampton brushed off this defense, "the honour of the House is to be preferred to any particuler mans honour," and pressed for an apology. Spencer was even more severe.

> Noe greate Lordes. Tooke excepcion that any shoulde be called greate Lords. We are Pares, here be noe grandes.[48]

40

Cold words could be used on those who had lost the King's favor. Bacon's justification was poignant, but irrelevant.

> The orders of the House are to be observed. Yt is trewe that at a conference to heare, we ought to be sylent, but that the first committee may speak somwhat briefly at the conclusion of the conference. That I dyd erre in saying more. Yt is Humanum.[49]

And how prudent was it to match Latinisms with one's accuser?

The King's speech also set an example for the favorite, who the following day ran afoul of the same point of order at a conference with the Commons. Although not a member of the delegated committee, he suddenly appeared at the conference and tried to speak, only to be immediately silenced by Southampton. He then rushed back to the upper house, had himself appointed to the committee, and returned to the conference. The speech he finally gave explains his impulsive conduct.

> He said that as the House had done him right in acquainting [probably "acquitting" in the original] him so he would endeavor to do anything might be for the good of the King and the commonwealth which cannot be severed. And now I know what parliaments are I will be a scholar and learn to do my King and country service. There are two brothers of mine in question. I will make no apology for them, but when it comes in question I will tell the truth and leave them to the censure of the House. And if they be faulty, the womb that bare them hath also borne one that will seek to have them punished.[50]

Self-interest worked another dismal betrayal. Buckingham was now swimming furiously. At the conclusion of the conference he stormed back to the Lords and demanded censure of those who had originally silenced him. An acrimonious debate ensued, but softer voices finally prevailed and the matter was allowed to drop. Nevertheless, the incident demonstrates how tempers were shortening as the players scrambled to occupy center stage in the pageant of reform.

The bill against monopolies had been introduced by Coke on March 12, and two days later it was read a second time. On March 15 the charges against Mompesson were carried in their final form to the Lords, and another conference held. Coke spoke at length on monopolies at this conference, making sure not to bruise the prerogative. The referees were given a perfunctory glance; their error preserved the King's honor. Coke closed his remarks with some attempts at levity, and succeeded at least in entertaining the Prince.

> The prince said that he was never wearie with heareinge Cooke, he mingled mirth with busines to so good purpose. If it please your grace, said, Cooke, ther is no danger in a merrie man, but a sullen and Melancholye, as Caesar feared not pleasant Brutus but pale and sad Cassius.[51]

Whether Coke had simply forgotten Brutus's role (or thought the Prince had) cannot be known, but some explanation should be offered for his high humor, as well as for his failure to emphasize the referees's sins.

Success is the likely answer to both. The Commons had won their point on monopolies. The King had admitted their baseness and indicated a willingness to see corrective measures taken. Buckingham's obscene attempts to take a lead in the crusade also testified to success on this matter. How important, then, would the referees be once the bill on monopolies passed? Did the past need further stirring up, particularly since the present offered so many opportunities for the sharp ax of reform? Moreover, to have further hounded the referees would have ensnarled the Commons in the very matter they knew the King was most sensitive to: the prerogative. As he had indicated on March 10, James might be prepared to give up his Lord Chancellor and Lord Treasurer. But for the Commons to have actually accused them before the Lords for doing something (advising the King) that was the essence of their function could have started a quarrel and split the two houses. The original reluctance even to name the referees at the conference of March 8 suggests that few men relished a skirmish so close to the King's prerogative. Also, Buckingham was not to be touched, especially since he had gone so far to clear himself, and this could not have been avoided if the attack had continued. In brief, the question of the referees was really too volatile a matter to press. And since monopolies were now in their death agony, what would have been gained?

Coke's humor may have also sprung from a more private gladness, for on this same day (March 15) Phelips, reporting from the committee inquiring into abuses in the courts of justice, raised the bribery charge that led directly to Bacon's impeachment.

Established at the opening of the session on the recommendation of Cranfield, this committee of the whole house had been meeting on Wednesday afternoons to labor for a reformation of the courts. It was a popular cause and subcommittees were soon formed to handle the avalanche of petitions that poured in from the disgruntled and disenchanted. Chancery, as a court of equity, predictably received careful scrutiny from the practitioners of the common law. Bacon, though, did not feel particularly threatened by this, and offered his full support to the committee. He would "thanke any man that would propound the meanes of Reformeing his Courte."[52] Even when the court's Registers were condemned on February 28 for forging orders to augment their fees, the Lord Chancellor did not blanch; the censure of Registers did not personally touch him. The committee session of March 14, however, saw more hazardous issues raised. Cranfield, supported by Coke, bitterly attacked bills of conformity, which were actions filed in Chancery that sought to force creditors to accept a reduction in the debt(s) owed them.[53] The practice of accepting these actions had been initiated by Bacon, and, besides angering merchants, they were construed by the common lawyers as a sinister attempt to amplify equity at the expense of the common law. But it was the petitions of Christopher Aubrey and Edward Egerton, charging Bacon with accepting bribes, that inflicted a mortal wound. Each man claimed to have presented a sum of money to Bacon through intermediaries before his case was judged in the hope of winning a speedy and favorable judgment. As it happened, Bacon decided against both men, and was probably in no way influenced by the gifts. Nevertheless, accepting a present while a case was pending, instead of after a judgment was rendered, could not be condoned even by the vague judicial standards of the seventeenth century.[54]

The accusations did not come as a complete surprise. Two to three weeks before, Bacon had been told of Aubrey's intention, and on the morning of the fourteenth he had been warned about Egerton. Despite some efforts to quiet Aubrey, Bacon seems in both cases to have believed that his denial of any wrong-doing would suffice to dismiss the charges.[55] The letter he wrote to Buckingham on the evening of the fourteenth illustrates his attitude.

I know I have clean hands and a clean heart; and I hope a clean house for friends or servants. But Job himself, or whosoever was the justest judge, by such hunting for matters against him as hath been used against me, may for a time seem foul, specially in a time when greatness is the mark and accusation is the game. And if this be to be a Chancellor, I think if the great seal lay upon Hounslow Heath, nobody would take it up. But the King and your Lordship will, I hope, put an end to these miseries one way or other. [14.213]

He obviously felt himself a political victim, a man guilty by virtue of his place and other men's ambitions, rather than by his own conduct. Job was to function as his personal emblem in the weeks ahead. Innocent of intentional wrong-doing, he believed himself "clean" and presumed that only a partisan motive could have inspired the charges. He was partially right. Coke and Cranfield despised him (as he did them) and this feeling emboldened the investigation, but there is no evidence that they conspired with Aubrey and Egerton to set a trap for the Lord Chancellor.[56] Attacks on Chancery were commonplace, and the search for corruption involved a logic independent of personal gain. The petitions of Aubrey and Egerton were individual acts of resentment, and were noticed by Phelips and the committee because they exposed precisely the kind of disease the parliament had set itself to cure. Cranfield's own Court of Wards, it should be remembered, also came under very sharp attack by the committee

Having just escaped the tumult over the referees, Bacon naturally became apprehensive and immediately assumed a plot. But an anxious man's observations, especially those of a man who for years believed himself unappreciated and kept back by lesser men, ought to be viewed skeptically. Indeed, the unreliability of Bacon's judgment on the matter is evidenced by the self-serving appraisal made in his request for protection. The King's speech of March 10 had made it clear that James was unwilling to protect a tarnished servant against the righteous wrath of parliament. Bacon was correct in suggesting how worthless the Great Seal would be if the King did not protect *it*, but intimating that the seal could only be protected by the King's defending *him* bordered on the naive. James simply did not consider the person of his Lord Chancellor to be worth a constitutional tussle, and Bacon's personal guilt, if confirmed, would keep the Seal from losing its value, let alone its attractiveness to others.

Phelips's speech to the Commons on March 15, briefing the members on the accusations against the Lord Chancellor, was skillfully done. The charges were listed in detail, the tone was modest, and no rough words were aimed at "a man so endued with all parts both of nature and art as that I will say no more of him because I am not able to say enough." The house was requested to continue investigating the charges and then to send them on to the Lords. Permission to let "further inquisition be made" was granted, and in the afternoon the case was again discussed in committee. Phelips hoped to persuade the house to set aside other business and have all other committee meetings canceled until Bacon's case was finished. This motion was unacceptable to the other members. Although the case was granted precedence, the other committees continued to meet.

The next day the carefully nurtured alliance between the two houses almost came apart. The preceding afternoon, at the recommendation of Southampton, the Lords had agreed that witnesses in the monopoly cases should be sworn when they appeared in the upper house. When this decision was delivered to the Commons on the morning of the sixteenth, it touched off a fierce debate over privilege since some of the witnesses were members of the lower house. Having determined monopolies to be sin, and styled themselves as judges, the members (including Coke) rebelled at the prospect of being sworn before the Lords. "It hath never been precedented," cried Sir James Perrot, "it's a disparagement to the gentlemen, and we shall never shake it off."[57] Even Phelips, the originator of the alliance, was shocked at this request. Yet he would not believe that the Lords would infringe on the Commons' privileges, and offered an explanation intended to turn the members' minds along other paths. A deliberate scheme had been worked up. "But he rather thinks that some one rather maligning the good correspondency of both houses and wishing an interposition in this buisines rather then the desire of the lords have cast in this Bone."[58] This line of argument, however, failed to abate the anger of the lower house.

Weeks of patient effort now seemed in vain and the specter of another sterile parliament rose up. Only a brilliant speech by Sir Edwin Sandys brought the members back to their senses. He argued that since the Commons had petitioned the Lords for punishment and that this might involve the taking of life, the peers were justified in requesting an oath, particularly since the lower house had not the power to administer one. The desire of the Commons to look upon themselves as judges, and therefore above an oath, was dismissed almost rudely when it was pointed out that judges of the assize could be sworn. Sandys's peroration dispelled the mood of suspicion by forcing the members to see what they were jeopardizing with their traditional prejudices.

> We have seen two of the joyfullest days that ever were in parliament. The one in the ready, free and joyful presenting of the subsidies to his Majesty and his reciprocal love and kindness to us. The other in the happy conjunction of both Houses. I will not think that this is a bone of contention cast in among us. I pray God we make it not a bone. They have no means, they say, to direct their judgments. Let us therefore signify unto them that we hope that they have no intent to break our privileges. Therefore observing our ancient liberties we are content to yield to them.[59]

The speech led to a compromise: members might voluntarily take an oath, but no one would be ordered to do so. Sandys very likely knew that it was Southhampton, rather than a conniving courtier, who had made the motion for oaths; the Earl was his patron and a fellow director of the Virginia Company. Indeed, Sandys was eagerly waiting for a detailed discussion of trade problems. Like Phelips, he had sat in James's two previous parliaments and probably wanted something more than an heroic failure out of this one. The incident should remind us not only how tenuous was the alliance that ruined Bacon, but that contingency and prejudice, rather than plots, moved the business of parliament. If there was a conspiracy to destroy Bacon, the argument over oaths was hardly calculated to advance it. The very unwillingness of the Commons to accept Phelips's explanation under-lines this point. To suggest a plot was the surest way to salvage the future, as Phelips possibly realized.

The next day, March 17, the Commons resumed discussions of the charges against Bacon. A desire to tread warily was evident. One member, George Moore, was rebuked for some discourteous remarks he had made in committee about Bacon the day before. Phelips kept a respectful tongue as he delivered the committee's report. After surveying the evidence gathered thus far, he sought to convince th house of the "great weight" of the charge. "For if the fountains be muddy, what will the streams be. If the great dispenser of the king's conscience be corrupt, who can have any courage to plead before him." There was no alternative but to take the case to the Lords; the Commons could not bring a peer of the realm to their bar, and, in addition, had no power to examine witnesses upon oath. Besides, there was precedent for such an action.[60]

The debate that followed was unusually modest in tone. There seemed little enthusiasm for undoing the Lord Chancellor and some uncertainty as to procedures, although the house was not about to accept Secretary Calvert's suggestion to bring the case before the King.[61] Christopher Neville might speak of "such a Minotaur as gormandizeth the liberty of all subjects whatsoever," but most members, sensing the inconclusive nature of the evidence, were uneasy with the charges. For each accusation of bribery depended on but a single witness, the men who had delivered the money to Bacon. Both men, therefore, were *participes criminis*.[62] Perhaps there was a latent fear of royal intervention. Or perhaps it is unsettling, even for reformers, to admit that the very highest authorities *are* corrupt. In any event, Phelips's recommendation was finally accepted by the house, and it was decided to request a conference with the Lords for Monday, March 19.

On Monday morning the King sent gracious messages to the Commons through Sir Thomas Edmondes, Treasurer of the Household, and Calvert. He expressed pleasure over the last reading of the subsidy, "as ye not only gave it but your hearts with it also," and left it to the members to determine when they would rise for the Easter vacation. James also noticed the complaints against Bacon, "for which he was sorry, for it hath always been his care to have placed the best but no man can prevent such accidents." Desiring, he said, to speed the investigation along, he proposed that a commission of six lords and twelve commoners—chosen by the houses themselves—be appointed to examine the case during the recess. He wished, however, to hear the opinion of the lower house before advising the Lords of this proposal, and expressed hope that "the Lord Chancellor will cleare himselfe, but promises to doe him iustice."[63] Perrot and Alford immediately approved of the plan. Coke was not so eager, worrying lest the commission "hinder the manner of our parliamentary proceedings." Backed by Sackville he moved that the King be asked to send the proposal to the Lords and that the two houses then jointly give him their answer. This motion was accepted by the house and Calvert went off to the King. He returned shortly with a message that the King had already sent "a Noble Lord" to the upper house. Whether James actually sent the message is doubtful, for there is no record of the Lords having received it, no mention of the proposal at the conference that afternoon, and, indeed, no further mention of the proposal at all.

Why such a plan, and why so swift a withdrawal? James appears to have been maneuvering for a position where he would not be embarrassed by the charges against Bacon, and, indeed, where he might even gain some credit for his fall. The Lord Chancellor, after all, was the King's servant, and it was the King's justice that had allegedly been sold. Some demonstration of royal effort and concern beyond merely blessing parliament's inquiry was to be expected. But James was not about to step in and snatch his Lord Chancellor out of the hands of his accusers; his reiterated promises to punish the guilty were public knowledge, and had won for him a measure of acclaim.[64] Moreover, he had himself acknowledged the Lords' judicial powers, believing, no doubt, that with his influence over the bishops and many of the peers, as well as his power over the legal officers and judges who advised the Lords, he could effectively control their proceedings.[65] What James was anxious to prevent was the common lawyers establishing themselves as public prosecutor, or the two houses growing more friendly—his speech of March 10 clearly articulated his distaste for seeing either precedent established. He therefore withdrew his proposal for a commission at the very point when it seemed that it might serve to bring the two houses closer together. The Belasyse Diary neatly suggests this when it summarizes the statements made by Sackville and Coke on the King's proposal.

> Since ther hath bene a marvailous and happie union betwene us, Lett us take care not to Divorce it but that both maye conferr together to give one unanimous answere.[66]

Precisely what the King wished to forestall.

●

48

Bacon meanwhile had taken to his bed, "all swollen in his body." Throughout his career ill health had touched him when he found himself in political trouble. Chief Justice Ley was appointed on March 18 to preside over the Lords in his absence. The King dispatched Buckingham twice to visit him, and on March 20 the Marquis reported to the Lords that on his second visit he found the Lord Chancellor much improved. He also carried back a letter written by Bacon the day before explaining his absence. In it there was a plea for time, "according to the course of other courts," to answer the charges against him and for the opportunity, "according to the course of justice," to challenge the witnesses against him. Pointing out that other petitions might be brought against him, he asked the Lords not to let themselves be prejudiced against "a Judge that makes two thousand decrees and orders in a year" (14.215-16). Bacon was not distressed about having his case tried in the Lords; his main concern was that the Lords should hold him in "good opinion, without prejudice, until my case be heard." But his letter reads also like a lecture, instructing the peers how to conduct themselves as a court. Several times he carefully informs them of how "the rules of justice" support his requests for certain procedures. Shocked, of course, by "some complaints of base bribes," he sounds more embarrassed by the anomaly of the legal situation than anguished by the crime or nervous about the outcome. "Yt seemes," Chamberlain huffed, "he doth either dissemble or not feele the ignominie that hangs over him but carries himself as he was wont."[67] A fair trial would establish his innocence because he was obviously the victim of a conspiracy.

The Lords' reply to this letter, proposed by Southampton, was terse. The Lord Chancellor would be treated "according to the right Rule of Justice," and it was hoped that he might "clear his Honour." Meanwhile, he was "to provide for his Defence."[68]

At the conference on March 19 the charges against the Lord Chancellor had been formally delivered to the Lords. In the next few days more petitions, as Bacon had feared, were received by the committee and passed on to the Lords.[69] Phelips conducted the investigation smoothly, keeping both houses well-informed of the charges and working to prevent any further misunderstandings.

Amity had to be preserved. On March 20 the King sent a message to the Commons expressing his dislike for bills of conformity and requesting advice on the best way to recall them. Pleased by the King's concern, the Commons replied that a "proclamation [was] fittest for present, and by bill for the future." At a conference between the houses two days later it was agreed to recess on March 27. Also, notice was taken of "the good Concurrence betwixt the Howses, being such as former tymes cannot match and future will remember."[70] Nonetheless, good feelings were not to slow business. On the twenty-fourth the Commons, at the suggestion of Phelips, ordered those members "who stay in town this Cessation" to be formed into interim committees to receive petitions, examine grievances, and investigate further abuses in the courts of justice. The upper house matched this enthusiasm by appointing three committees to meet during the recess and examine the growing list of witnesses against Bacon. Writing on March 24 to Carleton, Chamberlain expressed his wonder at the busyness of parliament, as well as at the King, who "never shewed himself more forward to redresse what is amisse."[71] A reformation was now in high stride, a new harmony prevailed as King and people worked together.

On March 25 Bacon wrote to the King through Buckingham. By this time the accusations against him were public gossip, and, according to Chamberlain, "many indignities are said and don against him, and divers libells cast abroad to his disgrace not worth the repeating as savoring of too much malice and scurrilitie."[72] He still could not fathom, however, the reasons for "such a tempest"; his dealings with men had been honorable, and his relations with the two houses of parliament friendly. "And for the briberies and gifts wherewith I am charged, when the books of hearts shall be open, I hope I shall not be found to have the troubled fountain of a corrupt heart in a depraved habit of taking rewards to pervert justice; howsoever I may be frail, and partake of the abuses of the times." This famous sentence has often been taken as proof of Bacon's openness as well as his innocence. It might better be read as an example of his naiveté. For he was being investigated precisely because of his participation in the "abuses of the times." Reformers despise what was once acceptable, not what has always been insupportable, and men bent on reform were not likely to differentiate between carelessness and corruption.

Reflections on a deeper honesty were irrelevant. Bacon ended his letter with a personal plea to James.

> I have been ever your man, and counted myself but an usufructuary of myself, the property being yours: and now making myself an oblation to do with me as may best conduce to the honour of your justice, the honour of your mercy, and the use of your service, resting as clay in your Majesty's gracious hands. [14.225-26]

James never answered this note.[73]

The next morning James came to the upper house to address the peers before the Easter recess. His purpose was to convince the Lords of his good faith in serving under the banner of reform. "I come . . . to express My readiness to put in Execution (which is the Life of the Law) those Things which ye are to sentence." He protested that if he had been aware of the grievances before parliament he would have handled them promptly. "(For I confess) I am ashamed (these Things proving so, as they are generally reported to be) that it was not My good Fortune to be the only Author of the Reformation." A tasteless witticism at Bacon's expense followed. "But, because the World at this Time talks so much of Bribes, I have just Cause to fear the whole Body of this House hath bribed him [Prince Charles], to be a good Instrument for you upon all Occasions; he doth so good Offices in all his Reports to Me, both for the House in general, and every one of you in particular." He acknowledged the Lords to be "the Supreme Court of Justice" and assured them of his respect by noting "that I have done you the Honour to set My only Son amongst you." He did not forget to mention how well the House of Commons had treated him, but was careful to emphasize his own good treatment of the Lords. Buckingham was also singled out as one who had done the Lords "good Offices." Having advertised his sincerity to the gathered peers, he gave stunning proof of it. The patents for inns, alehouses, and gold and silver thread were to be canceled by royal proclamation.[74] He then reiterated the theme of his embarrassment, managing with a homely metaphor to excuse himself and cast Bacon adrift.

> I have looked upon many of My Coppices, riding about them, and they appeared on the Outside very thick and well grown unto Me; but, when I entered into the midst of them, I found them all bitter within and full

of Plains and bare Spots; like an Apple, or Pear, fair and smooth without, but, when ye cleave it asunder, you find it rotten at the Heart: Even so this Kingdom, the external Government being as good as ever it was, and I am sure as Learned Judges as ever it had (and I hope as honest), administering Justice within it.

James finished his speech with a caution to the Lords to be impartial in their judgments and to "take hold [only] of the guilty." But they were to "spare none" whom they found just cause to punish.[75]

The King's speech was a triumph. It put him momentarily at the head of the reform. His professed ignorance of grievances would not require scrutiny because he had shown proof of his conversion. The absence of either chastisements or any talk of subsidies contributed to the good effect. James had impressed the Lords, as well as almost all contemporary observers, that he was a King who cared for his people's welfare.[76] And when a committee of the Lords went to thank their sovereign early in the afternoon, they were treated to a second serving of tender words.

While James had been charming the Lords, the Commons had been making an assault on Chancery. Questions of jurisdictional responsibility were raised and Cardinal Wolsey's errors remembered. The common law would not bear interference. Coke insisted, however, that Bacon himself was not the prime target. "[I speak] not, because the now Lord Chancellor under a Cloud; for sorry for it; but, as a Free Man, who knoweth what he speaketh."[77] The debate was interrupted when the lower house was summoned to hear the verdict (in absentia) on Mompesson. Not since the days of Henry VI had the Lords sat in formal judgment on a citizen accused of corruption. The Commons found them equal to the task however. Still in their robes, and doubtless fortified by the King's speech, the peers, with Chief Justice Ley as their speaker, found Sir Giles guilty of "many heinous Crimes against the King's Majesty and against the Common Wealth." The sentence was harsh. The arch-monopolist was degraded from the order of knighthood, outlawed during his life, and ordered to be imprisoned if he ever returned to England. Moreover, his property was to be forfeited to the King, and he was to be "excepted out of all General Pardons" and to be forever "held an infamous person." The King, desirous of keeping up his part, later added perpetual banishment to what he had already termed "the just proceedings and sentence of . . . his high Court of Parliament."[78] If casting out fiends would rid the commonwealth of evil, both King and parliament had shown their mettle. So pleased with the day's activities were the Lords that they set aside March 26 to be celebrated thereafter as a sermon day throughout the land. The Earl of Arundel also moved that a statue be erected to the King and Prince.

The last day before the recess, March 27, was spent by the Commons in praising the King and congratulating themselves. Mompesson's punishment and the King's speech had climaxed a period where seemingly a new respect had been fashioned. Together the King and parliament might make a reformation. Who would have predicted such an outcome seven weeks before? In his speech to the Commons that afternoon at Whitehall, James voiced the appropriate sentiment.

> In former Parliaments there was noe true understandinge betwixt my subiects and me. Wee were like the Builders of Babell, where one called for Morter, another for Stones, whereby we could not receave contentment and sattisfaccion from eache other. But hereafter I hope all things wilbe soe cleare betwixt us That without any Orations our hearts shall speake for us.

The King also made it clear that while he hoped the lower house, upon its return, would not bog itself down with investigating "patents that concerned but particular persons," he would not block its inquiry into those who had abused the commonwealth. "Noe mans place or greatnes should move us, for he wold leave the greatest that had oppressed his people to there owne iustification."[79] Reviewing that morning the accomplishments of the past two months, a very cool Phelips had announced the benefits of acquiescence.

> Kinge hoped this would bee the happyest parliament that ever England had. Surely wee the best commons. If wee gave forme, hee would geve lyfe. The kinge now perceyved himself by this parliament to be at ease and an happy man, fre from sutes and trobles. And that could Buckingham witnes also.[80]

There was indeed nothing to be gained from protecting a Lord Chancellor whose sins, although not great in themselves, were so compromising in the present circumstances. The larger question of the King's control over his ministers, assuming that James gave it much thought, would not have seemed relevant. Even if such sophisticated motives had inspired the attack on Bacon, they were now so charged with the rhetoric of reform as to render any help given him suspect. Besides, the precedent established would not be dangerous. To let parliament attack a judge for corruption was not the same as allowing them to question the fitness of a counselor, especially in the eyes of a King who used his Lord Chancellor almost exclusively as a legal instrument. Bacon would have to defend himself because the King could neither afford to intervene nor saw much need to. And James's personal feelings created no ambivalence.

During the vacation Bacon was busy trying to explain to himself, the King, and posterity how guiltless he was. The papers we have from this three-week period show a confused man trying to conceal his bitterness. On April 10 he drew up a brief will in which he bequeathed his soul to God, his body to an obscure burial, and his name "to the next ages, and to foreign nations." Sir John Constable, his brother-in-law, was to be his literary executor and was to decide which of his unpublished works were to be published. "And in particular I wish the Elogium I wrote *In felicem memoriam Reginae Elizabethae* may be published" (14.228). How proper that Bacon should single out for mention a sketch fourteen years old eulogizing a queen dead even longer! For his recollection of her varied skills and prudent policies shaped his judgment to a remarkable degree. On the same day as he wrote his will, Bacon composed a prayer. Although it confesses a thousand sins and ten thousand transgressions, the prayer reads as a protestation of interior innocence because it would separate deed from intent. In statement and tone it parallels his letter of March 25 to the King.[81]

Nevertheless, Bacon did not forget that parliament was to reassemble on April 17 and that witnesses in his case were being examined by three subcommittees of the Lords during the recess. However pure his heart, his deeds were being closely investigated. He therefore spent time looking up cases resembling his own. The review was heartening: in most instances the punishment meted out had been very light. He also requested an interview with the King. James, obviously wishing to keep himself clear from any suspicion of favoring

Bacon, only granted the request after consulting with the lords who sat on the council. Two sets of notes prepared by Bacon before the audience, which took place on April 16, as well as the report of the interview made to the upper house the next day by the Lord Treasurer, have survived. All three reveal that the Lord Chancellor no longer hoped to prove himself completely innocent, but that if he was permitted to see the actual charges leveled against him, and given a fair trial, he might clear himself of much. He was also anxious to have the King know of his willingness to go on serving him, if only with his pen: "I think of writing a story of England, and of re-compiling of your laws into a better digest." James, rigorously neutral, referred Bacon's request for a list of the charges to the upper house. Pleased by this stance, the Lords asked the Lord Treasurer to give their thanks to the King. They then swore in more witnesses.

On Thursday, April 19, the three committees made their reports, and the examinations taken thus far were read to the assembled peers. Afterwards, it was resolved that the three committees should "meete and make one briefe" of all their materials. At Lord Say's recommendation, the committees were also to continue "to receave complaintes and to contynewe the takinge of examinacions." The Lords then adjourned until the following Tuesday. The next day, however, James spoke to both houses, and urged them to be about their business since the long summer vacation was approaching. In his speech he once again made it clear that he would not protect "bribing judges," but that his prerogative should be left alone. "Try the persons complained of and take away the ground and cause of the complaint, not by abridging the courts but by purging the abuses out of them, as exorbitant fees, multitude of causes, chamber orders, etc. And when you have done all, I will add to it if I can."[82]

The same day Bacon wrote a letter to the King thanking him "for vouchsafing me access to your Royal Person." He hoped the Lords would show themselves merciful, and that "as your Majesty imitateth Christ . . . [they] will imitate you." As yet uninformed of the precise content of the charges against him, for he could only know what they were once the brief was compiled and a formal accusation made, he still showed traces of his typically whimsical confidence. "I shall without fig-leaves or disguise excuse what I can excuse, extenuate what I can extenuate, and ingenuously confess what I can neither clear nor extenuate" (14.240). Overnight, however, he changed his mind, and the next day wrote again to the King. This time, after tediously describing how ill he had been the past three days, he explicitly asked the King to intercede. "This I move with the more belief, because I assure myself that if it be reformation that is sought, the very taking away the seal, upon my general submission, will be as much in example for these four hundred years, as any furder severity." He suggested to the King "the means" for accomplishing this, and, "because he that hath taken bribes is apt to give bribes," reiterated his desire to "present your Majesty with a good history of England, and a better digest of your laws" (14. 240-42).

Why did Bacon suddenly decide not to defend himself and beg the King's mercy? It may be that a friend had brought him a copy or summary of the examinations which had been read on the nineteenth, and that Bacon realized how futile any defense would be against the numerous charges. But it is also possible to see Bacon at this juncture reacting instead to the King's speech of the twentieth. If James really intended to permit his Lord Chancellor to be tried it would not matter how extensive the charges were. Indeed, the very willingness of the King would virtually ensure conviction. That realization may have shocked Bacon into writing a letter which desperately employed flattery and appeals to pity and self-interest to alter the King's mind. Unmoved, James never answered this plea, and on April 24, while commending the Lords on their efforts to rid the commonwealth of grievances, emphasized that he would "prefer no Person whomsoever before the Public Good."[83]

The submission itself, written on April 22 and presented to the Lords by the Prince on the twenty-fourth, was inept. Bacon began with a "professing of gladness" that his example would serve the commonwealth. Thereafter the "greatness" of no man would offer "sanctuary . . . of guiltiness," and "judges will fly from any thing that is in the likeness of corruption." Comparing himself to Job, he did not conceal his sin: "It resteth therefore that, without fig-leaves, I do ingenuously confess and acknowledge, that having understood the particulars of the charge, not formally from the House, but enough to inform my conscience and memory, I find matter sufficient and full, both to move me to desert the defence, and to move your Lordships to condemn and censure me." He would not trouble the Lords with questioning those particulars he deemed unjust, nor raise "scruples touching the credits of the witnesses," nor plead extenuating circumstances. Leaving behind this rhetorical device calculated to show innocence, Bacon asked for mercy while quietly insinuating that he was skeptical of the tribunal's credentials. "Your Lordships are not simple Judges, but Parliamentary Judges; you have a further extent of arbitrary power than other courts; and if your Lordships be not tied by the ordinary course of courts or precedents in points of strictness and severity, much more in points of mercy and mitigation." Two examples, quoted from Livy, were used to show the Lords that "the reformation of justice" might be achieved without actual punishment, "for the questioning of men of eminent place hath the same terror." Nevertheless, he was ready to give up the seal in "expiation of my faults." He only hoped the Lords would show a compassion fitting their station, and remember "that there are *vitia temporis* as well as *vitia hominis.*"

> And therefore my humble suit to your Lordships is, that my penitent submission may be my sentence, and the loss of the seal my punishment; and that your Lordships will spare any further sentence, but recommend me to his Majesty's grace and pardon for all that is past.[14. 242-45]

Convinced of his essential innocence but not prepared to defend it, Bacon set himself above his judges while practically demanding mercy. "Penitent" was scarcely the word to describe his submission. Why did he address his accusers in such tones? The answer probably lies in that sublime confidence so characteristic of him. The Lords *must* recognize that he was really innocent. Bacon's political career was dependent on his capacity to persuade men to his way of thinking. This fatally predisposed him to think that all men are always susceptible to skillful management. Thus, absolutely cynical about character, he time and again misread the feelings of others, and so damaged his own political fortunes. In this instance he failed to understand that his strong sense of guiltlessness meant little to anyone but himself, and that it certainly could not be manipulated into a bargain with men extraordinarily conscious of their own rectitude.

Bacon saw deeply into the manners and morals of some men, but his range was narrow.

The Prince delivered the submission to the upper house on the afternoon of the twenty-fourth. It was bound to fail. Constant flattery by the King—that morning he had again praised the peers for their reform efforts—and the general deference shown by the Commons had puffed feelings of self-importance. Earlier in the day the question had arisen whether to sit the next morning because of a Star Chamber case. Normally the Lords, as a matter of course, did not sit on such days; now the question was magnified into a case of privilege. After a long debate it was finally decided that they would not sit, "provyded that yt be not drawn into any president, as if this supreem Courte were to attend any other inferior courte."[84] A new sense of pride, and thus power, had come over the Lords.

The submission was read twice, once by the clerk and once by the Chief Justice. The next entry in the day's journal is eloquent. "Noe Lord spake to yt, after yt was reade, for a longe tyme."[85] Pembroke ultimately posed the natural question: "Whether this submission be sufficient to ground your Lordships' judgment for a censure without further examination." The peers quickly concluded that the submission was inadequate and rejected it unanimously. A month before, Lord Say added, it would have been satisfactory, "but coming nowe after the examinations and proofes yt comes to late." Literary allusions and vague concessions of weakness could not take the place of a contrite statement of guilt. Southampton noted that here was "noe worde of confession of any corrupcion," while Suffolk scorned the easy penalty Bacon had set himself. The next question was whether to insist that the Lord Chancellor appear before the bar of the house to answer the specific charges, or to send him a copy of the charges and allow him another written submission. There was less agreement on this question. Buckingham urged that the charges be sent to Bacon, and received support from the Prince, Pembroke, Arundel, and Southampton. Say, Huntingdon, and Suffolk pressed for an appearance. In the course of this discussion Viscount Wallingford gave the most temperate exposition not only of what was wrong with Bacon's submission, but what his case meant.

He hath herde the charg and submission, which is too shorte; and he lymitts his punishement by us, and he ymputes all to *vitia temporis non hominis.* That he may come hither to the barr to his answere. Comends his person, and respect to that. But we entending a reformacion, the opener yt is the better.[86]

It was finally decided to send a copy of the charges—twenty-eight in all, involving forty-one witnesses—to the accused, along with a message scoring the inadequacy of his first submission and requesting "his answere with all convenyent expedicion."

How much sympathy and respect Bacon had squandered by his original submission cannot be known. But now the Lords themselves as a body had been given a sample of that insensitivity to other men's self-esteem, amounting to a kind of blindness, that marked his career. Less pride on this occasion might possibly have saved him from spending his last years in frustrating retirement.

Bacon continued his indiscretions the next day. His verbal reply to this last message was that "he would return the Lords an answer." At the same time he sent a letter to Chief Justice Ley. This infuriated the Lords: the Lord Chancellor was now responsible to the whole house and had no business addressing a letter to a person who, though sitting on the woolsack, had a place in the upper house only by virtue of a writ of assistance.[87] Accordingly, the house promptly voted to take no notice of the letter, and its precise contents are therefore not known. Ley was, however, allowed to "open the substance thereof," and his summary, together with Bacon's failure to give a substantive answer to their first message, suggested to many that the Lord Chancellor was now going to make a defense.[88] Was then his previous submission a mere sop? Had he or had he not taken bribes? The Lords were baffled, and growing angry. The question was raised again whether to order Bacon before the bar. Finally, it was decided to send another message.

We have receaved a doubtfull aunswere, and therefore we sende unto him to knowe of him, directly and presently, whether he wyll make his confession or stande uppon defense. Bycause the LL. conceave some doubte of his aunswere, their Lordships require his Lordship to send present answere whether hee will make his confession or stand uppon his justificacion.[89]

The Lords may have lacked the legal qualifications to conduct a proper trial, but they did not want in that self-regard and seriousness conspicuous amongst judges and reformers. To many it must have seemed that Bacon was either stalling for time, or, even worse, toying with them. His reply to the second message did not entirely clear him of either suspicion. This time he at least responded in writing.

> My Lord Chauncelor will make no manner of defens to the charge. But meaneth to acknowledg corrupcion, and to make a particuler confession to every poynt, and after that, an humble submission. But humbly craves libertie that, where the charge is more full then he fynds the truth of the fact, he may make declaration of the truth in such partiulers, the charge being briefe, and conteyning not all circumstances.[90]

Five days were then granted him to prepare a second submission.

This was delivered to the Lords on the morning of April 30 and ordered to be read aloud. Its opening paragraph displayed a more appropriate tone. "I do plainly and ingenuously confess that I am guilty of corruption; and do renounce all defence, and put myself upon the grace and mercy of your Lordships." Each charge was then discussed. Although he frequently justified his actions, Bacon made it clear at the end that he would not have his explanations understood as extenuations. The Lords, he hoped, would show mercy and "be noble intercessors for me to his Majesty likewise, for his grace and favour" (14.252-62). Their immediate reaction was to appoint a committee to go to the Lord Chancellor and verify his signature. Bacon's response to the committee's query is famous, but eloquence could not replace the credit already exhausted. "My Lords, it is my act, my hand, my heart. I beseech your Lordships, be merciful to a broken reed." The Lords next asked the Prince to move the King to sequester the Great Seal. Charles agreed and brought back a favorable answer that afternoon.

> His Majesty most willingly yielded; and said, He would have done it, if He had not been moved therein.[91]

Once more James would not let himself appear backward in the hunt. The following day a committee fetched the Seal from Bacon.

> We founde the L. Chancellor very sick, and delyvered our message unto him; whose answere was, when we wyshed yt had been better with him,

he aunswered, the worse the better, & c. By the Kinge's greate favour I
received the great Seale; by my owne greate faulte I have loste yt & c.[92]

There remained only the sentencing, which was set for the
morning of May 3. The preceding afternoon Southampton moved
that Bacon be present to hear it, but he was found to be still too sick to
attend. The vote taken on his guilt was unanimous. The house then
debated punishment. Prince Charles opened the question by asking
what precedents for punishing Lord Chancellors existed. Spencer,
revealing that he had listened carefully to the King's speeches, turned
the question around. "The Kinge sayd he would make yt a pressident
to posterity. Not to trenche to lyfe, bannishment." Southampton
agreed, and proposed degradation and banishment from court.
Although Buckingham urged leniency for a man "soe syck that he
cannot lyve longe," the Lords were not feeling charitable. The
sentence finally agreed upon was severe: Bacon was to pay a fine of
£40,000, be imprisoned at the pleasure of the King, held incapable of
holding any office in the state, excluded from parliament, and
forbidden from coming within the verge (twelve miles) of the court.[93]
Buckingham alone dissented on the vote. The Commons were then
sent for, and the judgment formally announced.

Bacon's fall from power was not unlike his rise. Circumstances
and his own character, rather than conspiracies, were his undoing.
Amongst the lower house Coke, and perhaps Cranfield, were not
unhappy to see him destroyed, but they did not initiate the alliance
that made his destruction possible, nor were they in a position to
advise the King to desert him. There were some in the upper house
like Suffolk, Say, and probably most of all Southampton, who did not
cherish the Lord Chancellor, but they were a tiny minority. Nor
would it be correct to presume that Bacon was primarily a victim of
the King's efforts to ingratiate himself with parliament. However true
that may be, it should also be evident that Bacon might still have
salvaged much if he had adopted a less sanctimonious tone with the
Lords. Caught in a unique situation, where a desire for reform had
transmuted familiar elements, Bacon was unable to adapt. And
because he knew himself not to be corrupt of heart he assumed that
other men would make the same distinction, and that they would
recognize how unjust it would be to punish him. Here he made a

mistake, one that he often committed: he presumed that men could be persuaded to perform the parts that his own self-interest assigned them. This habit not only contributed to his fall in 1621, but damaged his entire political career.

# Chapter 2
# *Suitor, 1561–1603*

ntil his return from France after his father's death in February 1579, Bacon's life is virtually a blank. Scraps of information are available, which suggest an alert mind and (more often) a fragile constitution,[1] but it is the two well-known stories indicating his precociousness, told first by William Rawley and repeated by all subsequent biographers, that have formed our opinion of his boyhood. At a very early age, so the first story goes, Bacon so charmed Queen Elizabeth with his conversation that she often referred to him as "the young Lord-keeper." The other tale is more famous. "Whilst he was commorant in the university, about sixteen years of age, (as his lordship hath been pleased to impart unto myself), he first fell into the dislike of the philosophy of Aristotle."[2]

Although regarded as holy texts, both stories should arouse skepticism. Rawley, who served as Bacon's chaplain from 1618 to 1626 and thereafter dedicated himself to editing his works, composed the short "commemoration" to raise Bacon's fame among his countrymen. Like any other memoir, therefore, that mixes apology with flattery, the *Life* is something less than objective reporting. Rawley's devotedness, however, is not the only cause for doubt, since the memoir relies primarily on Bacon's perception of himself—note the stated source for the latter tale. It is based less on what Rawley observed than on what Bacon told him and what the admiring chaplain found in the surviving letters, most of which had been selectively saved by their author.

All this might not cause a problem if Bacon were a reasonably dependable observer of himself. But just the reverse, as will become clear, is the case. Whether commenting on the present or reflecting on the past, his statements habitually, if not always intentionally, solicit the world to see him as he would have liked, at the moment, to be seen. The specific content of these two stories from his childhood makes the point. They neatly portray the child performing the roles—respected  counselor to princes and creative philosopher —which the adult ardently hoped to play. By transferring to childhood his adult aspirations, Bacon has induced the reader (and himself) to believe that he was innately fit for great things. No man, of course, is an impartial judge of himself, and memory invariably serves present interests. But for too long the charm and detached quality of Bacon's style have won him undeserved credibility. In addition, the two stories support the seductive myth of a man torn always between the contemplative and the active life. How many are the biographers who have used that tension as their central theme!* In point of fact, although Bacon himself was inclined to advertise that dilemma when he was not getting ahead, as solace for failure, his basic ambition was always political.

When Bacon returned home from Paris (never again to leave England), he resumed the study of law at Grays Inn, where he had first been admitted in 1576. As a student he would have been expected to learn cases, argue in moot courts, and attend readings. No doubt he occasionally found the work tedious and escaped to either his favorite authors or the pleasures of London. Nevertheless, the law came easily to him, for its characteristic modes of reasoning appealed to his intellect.

Basically, English legal reasoning engages the mind's ability to discover similarities and differences between instances, no two of which are identical. Whether applying a rule of law derived from one case to another, or revealing an inconsistency between the rule and cases cited by one's opponent, the competence of the individual legal

---

*The fact that this tension characterizes Spedding's commentary to Bacon's works undoubtedly influenced later writers. In particular, the seven volumes containing the "Letters and Life," though an admirable piece of editing, form one of the most voluminous and persuasive briefs ever worked up in support of an historical figure. There have been writers, of course, unwilling to take Bacon (or Spedding) at his word. E.A. Abbott is a notable, though testy, example. But the most recent academic and popular biographies—by Fulton Anderson and Catherine Bowen— suggest that Bacon continues to be judged on his own terms.

intellect is judged on its capacity for analogical reasoning.[3] This is clearly evidenced in Bacon's earliest surviving legal writing, *A Brief Discourse upon the Commission of Bridewell*, which consists almost entirely of a listing of cases presumed to make for his argument. "I do note one special statute made in the said 42nd of Edward the 3rd, the which if it be well compared with the said Charter of Bridewell it will make an end of this contention"(7.513). Years later Bacon would say of himself, "I found that I was fitted for nothing so well as for the study of Truth; as having a mind nimble and versatile enough to catch the resemblances of things (which is the chief point), and at the same time steady enough to fix and distinguish their subtler differences" (10.85).

The law also encourages a reductive frame of mind. Beginning with an opinion or principle—which may or may not involve a personal sense of truth—the lawyer searches for evidence that will support his position. Necessarily he will extend to old principles and old phrases (new) meanings that fit his needs. Precedents are used to establish authority, and the legal mind develops a special sensitivity to the possibility of *implicit* meaning and intent. The proof of a lawyer's skill, then, lies not only in his memory of cases but in his ingenuity in finding the right interpretation of the "words, sense, matter, and meaning" of a document.[4]

How quickly Bacon became expert in the law is seen in two honors he received in 1588. In the spring of that year he gave his first reading at Grays Inn, a series of eight lectures on Advowsons.[5] Later, in December, he was appointed to a choice committee of sixteen lawyers, four from each of the inns of court, who were to review existing statutes in preparation for the upcoming parliament.[6] Appointed by the council, these "gentlemen of the Innes of Courts learned in the lawes" were to meet with the judges once a week to determine which laws might be amended or repealed. Bacon's selection, a fact hitherto unnoticed by his biographers, indicates that he had already gained some reputation as a legal mind by the age of twenty-seven, since the other fifteen men were all many years his senior.[7] It also provides us with the first evidence of his lifelong interest in the reform of the law, a concern probably inherited from his father,[8] and one that Elizabeth, and particularly James, would hear about.

While engaged in learning the law Bacon began soliciting help from his uncle, Lord Burghley. The young man was eager "to lay forth the simple store of these inferior gifts which God hath allotted unto me," and felt no compunction about requesting favors that he admitted to be "rare and unaccustomed." He felt that his father's "precedent should be a silent charge" to dedicate himself to the Queen's service, for both "the use and spending" of his life.[9] Already in the early letters there are signs of an unusual self-consciousness and a conviction of unique integrity. "I am not yet," he tells his aunt, Lady Burghley, in September 1580, "greatly perfect in ceremonies of court, whereof I know your Ladyship knoweth both the right use and true value. My thankful and serviceable mind shall be always like itself, howsoever it vary from the common disguising" (8.12).

Bacon did not receive whatever office he was a "humble suitor" for. Still, Burghley was inclined to help his nephew. A seat was provided in the parliamentary session of 1581 and again in 1584, although on the latter occasion Bacon chose to take a place offered by his godfather, the Earl of Bedford. His uncle also eased his progress through Grays Inn.[10] More significant are the signs of appreciation of Bacon's genius for language. In December of 1580, during the visit of the Duke of Alençon to England, Bacon was employed as a translator.[11] And it is possible that the earliest political tract assigned to him, the 1584 *Letter of Advice* to Elizabeth, which analyzes the methods of dealing with England's "factious" subjects and foreign enemies, was commissioned and overseen by Burghley.[12]

No one familiar with Bacon's works can be indifferent to his remarkable gift for expression. Nor can one fail to recognize how thoroughly trained and brilliantly used that gift was. In an age that worshipped rhetoric, where school, work, and culture so decisively depended upon one's sense and command of language, Bacon stands out. In fact, from whatever angle his life is viewed, it will be seen that the arts of persuasion had to be a dominant concern. Whether we come upon him arguing a case in a law court, speaking on a question in parliament, or penning the endless memoranda of advice, it is clear that words—to reverse his own dictum—rather than matter necessarily played the crucial role in his life. And even in science, his greatest contribution would prove to be not his own haphazard efforts but his various engaging summonses to other men.

Whether Elizabeth ever saw the *Letter of Advice*, or was persuaded by it if she did, is not known. The work displays, nonetheless, the characteristics of Bacon's mature style: arguments are well-ordered and their subordinate parts clearly marked; sentences loosely periodic are juxtaposed with sentences symmetrically balanced; images occur infrequently but always with effect. In brief, language is used with a deliberate care to imprint thought. "To make them [Papists] half-content, half-discontent methinks carries with it as deceitful a shadow of reason, since there is no pain so small but if we can we will cast it off; and no man loves one the better for giving him a bastinado with a little cudgel" (8.48). Evident also is the Renaissance (and legal) practice of using history as precedent, to see in the past parallels that describe and confirm the present. The Romans provide the best examples, whether one is generalizing about governments ("The poison of all government, . . . [is] when the subject thinks the prince doth anything for fear. And therefore the Romans would rather . . . .") or suggesting a specific plan whereby all children of Catholic parents might be taken from their homes and educated as "hostages" near the court, "a notable strategem used by Sertorius in Spain" (8. 48,50).

There is nothing unusual in this mode of argument, and Bacon here seems to have been relying heavily on Machiavelli for his rules.[13] But habits of culture can be exaggerated in individual minds, or what might seem but a standard rhetorical device can involve deeper needs than the search for eloquence. Such is the case with Bacon, who, by nature and training, was disposed to perceive experience as if it conformed to knowable rules, or might be made to. His mind continually seeks to mold what it sees into patterns, to codify its observations. Randomness and contradiction are customarily dismissed or ignored, and thus his prose always exudes a special confidence and penetration. That Bacon should depend on other authors for rules in a youthful work is natural, but there is already evidence in the *Letter of Advice* of a willingness to assemble his own. Arguing that the French pose no real danger to England, he declares that they are "generally poor and weak, and subject to sickness at sea" (8.53). The latter conclusion presumably dates from his observations while crossing the channel, and foreshadows the tendency to inflate his own experience into general theorems.

Considering his rhetorical talents, it is understandable that Bacon should begin writing propaganda.[14] In the parliament of 1589 he was charged with composing a section of the preamble to the subsidy bill, the purpose of which was to justify the unusual request for two subsidies and to allay any fears that a precedent had been established. Although the draft (which has not survived) was eventually replaced with one indited by Burghley, Bacon's selection by the large committee formulating the bill denotes respect for his pen. In the same year, probably, he drew up a letter addressed to a French official and signed by Walsingham that explained the Queen's religious policies. In it Elizabeth was defended against the accusation, made by men of "superficial understanding," that she was a "temporizer in religion." In reality, Bacon insisted, her policy was grounded upon two "principles": consciences were to be won by persuasion, but should causes of conscience grow "to be matters of faction," force was allowable.

The letter is convincing propaganda. It is brief and well organized,[15] unrelenting in its insistence on the humane logic of royal policy, and colored in black and white. The ambiguity and tragedy of the situation are evaded by neat (and unreal) formulations. "The causes of conscience, when they exceed their bounds and grow to be matter of faction, lose their nature; and . . . sovereign princes ought distinctly to punish the practice or contempt, though coloured with the pretence of conscience and religion" (8.98). Particularly noteworthy is the summary comment on the Queen, which sketches her as possessing the disinterested mind of a judge. "It is not the success abroad, nor the change of servants here at home, can alter her; only as the things themselves alter, so she applieth her religious wisdom to methods correspondent unto them; still retaining the two rules before mentioned" (8.101). Bacon obviously knew what he was doing, a conclusion reinforced by a note he wrote to Archbishop Whitgift that apparently relates to the above letter.

> I have considered the objections, perused the statutes, framed the alterations, which I send; still keeping myself within the brevity of a letter and form of a narration; not entering into a form of argument or disputation: For in my poor conceit it is somewhat against the majesty of princes' actions to make too curious and striving apologies; but rather to set them forth plainly, and so as there may appear an harmony and constancy in them, so that one part upholdeth another. [8.96]

A final work from 1589, *An Advertisement Touching the Controversies of the Church of England*, although always assumed to have been a personal, unsolicited effort, may actually have been commissioned and intended for publication, perhaps by Burghley.[16] Written at the height of the Marprelate controversy, it urges an end to "this immodest and deformed manner of writing lately entertained," and examines "the accidents and circumstances of these controversies, wherein either part deserveth blame or imputation." The immanent concern of this tract, though, is not to lay blame but to persuade peace, for the fanaticism and intolerance of some of the bishops, as well as of the more radical Puritans, threatened to tear apart a church well-grounded and to open seams in civil society. "I trust what hath been said shall find a correspondence in their minds which are not embarked in partiality, and which love the whole better than a part. Whereby I am not out of hope that it may do good" (8.95). The work is unquestionably effective—not least because Bacon himself follows the advice he lays down in his argument for sound preaching, still another form of persuasion. A preacher, he states, should concern himself with "ordering the matter he handleth distinctly for memory, deducing and drawing it down for direction, and authorizing it with strong proofs and warrants" (8.91). He knows his task is to cool passions while explaining error, and so his tone is always detached yet concerned. At the same time he seeks to minimize the real importance of the controversies, to make it seem as if they were really only squabbles over angry words. "If we did but know the virtue of silence and slowness to speak, commended by St. James; our controversies of themselves would close up and grow together" (8.75).

To see Bacon as a publicist is to raise an obvious question: To what extent do these works reflect his personal views? They flow from his pen, but his pen is for hire, just as his legal talents will be. This question intrudes itself because so many of his writings belong to his role as advocate. The answer, for the moment, must take a negative form: men are not asked to prepare arguments for positions they basically disagree with, or at least not for very long. For sympathy, as well as skill, is assumed by those who set such tasks. On the other hand, do Bacon's own feelings then color his propaganda? Does the portrayal of Elizabeth's religious policy, for example, magnify her logic and moderation because his own religious convictions were watery, because he writes as a "politic man," from his brain, "without touch or sense of his heart" (8.76)? How much, after all, did Bacon actually know about the Queen's government, how close was he to the decisions and minds of those that mattered?

Before he was thirty Bacon had a deserved reputation for being learned in the law and proficient with his pen. If he was to rise in the world he would need to put these talents (and his family connections) to good use, since land, wealth, physical beauty, or a martial spirit were denied him. In return for his efforts thus far he had received from his uncle the remainder right to the office of Clerk of Star Chamber. Valued at £1600 a year and executed by deputy, the office would have been a sweeter plum if he had not had to wait twenty years for the picking. As it was, Bacon grew increasingly dissatisfied with what he deemed an embarrassing lack of progress. The assumption that he should have been doing better was predicated on an unshakeable confidence in his abilities, and spurred by the memory that his father had held the Solicitorship of the Court of Augmentations when he was but twenty-eight. "I wax now," he would write in 1592, still without office or honor, "somewhat ancient; one and thirty years is a great deal of sand in the hourglass." He was clearly not anxious to spend his days practicing the law; it was not until January 1594, and then only to gain some quick experience in his pursuit of the Attorney-Generalship, that he argued his first case in the King's Bench. Yet to sit in Grays Inn reading and daydreaming was frustrating, and expensive. An empty pocket now began to goad ambition.

In this frame of mind he wrote (1592) the famous letter to Burghley pronouncing "all knowledge to be my province." Tirelessly quoted and praised as a declaration of intellectual independence, the letter is more plausibly construed as an attempt by Bacon to justify himself and press his uncle to live up to the title of being "the second founder of my poor estate." He claims to want only "some middle place that I could discharge" and dismisses the often heard objections—age, health, arrogance—to his advancement. It is not really for himself, however, that he makes his suit. Instead, he would use the leisure office would give him, as well as the "wits" it might enable him to employ, to advance his "vast contemplative" projects. "This, whether it be curiosity, or vain glory, or nature, or (if one take it favourably) *philanthropia*, is so fixed in my mind as it cannot be removed." If Burghley ignores his suit, he will become "some sorry book-maker, or a true pioner" in the search for truth. Periodically in his life Bacon made the same threat: if civil advancement did not come soon, he would retire to his books. After all, he was not "a man born under Sol, that loveth honour; nor under Jupiter, that loveth business (for the contemplative planet carrieth me away wholly)" (8.108-9).

There is, of course, no question that his intellect had a highly speculative character, and so for Bacon to persuade himself that he was meant for contemplation required minimal self-deception. Yet it is odd, considering that his bluff was often called, how later writers should so readily swallow this convenient assessment of himself. For the consuming desire to put his mark upon life, intimated in the confession of his inability to distinguish between "curiosity," "vain glory," "nature," or "*philanthropia*," always prevented voluntary retirement from the only place (in his day) where a man might become the center of his world.[17] But brilliance has never ensured success, and Burghley, who may never have actually seen this letter,[18] probably felt that he had thus far not done too badly by his nephew.

This letter also marks the period when Bacon was turning his talents and allegiance to the service of the Earl of Essex, already the Queen's favorite. The frustrated suitor obviously envisioned some "worldly advancement" resulting from the connection. With Leicester, Walsingham, and Hatton dead, and Burghley grown ancient, common sense demanded that Essex be courted. But we do Bacon an injustice to see calculation as the sole motive for his attachment. The Earl was more than a pretty boy; he was intelligent, well-read, and generous, and in his ingenuous way probably made clear to Bacon how much he admired his great parts. Moreover, Bacon was inclined throughout his life to be drawn to men older or younger than himself, where respect and admiration came more immediately and easily to relationships. Burghley, Thomas Egerton, Essex, Buckingham, Tobie Matthew, and Rawley, these are the men he felt comfortable with, at least for a time.

Early in 1592 his older brother Anthony returned to England

after a thirteen-year stay on the continent. For much of his time abroad he had supplied Walsingham and Burghley with intelligence estimates, and now, in ill health and precarious finances, he joined his brother in the latter's lodgings at Grays Inn. Henceforth Burghley was to have a second Mr. Bacon as a suitor, and one with a better claim on his favors. Soon, however, Anthony lost patience with his uncle and staked his future completely on Essex, even going so far as to move into the Earl's house and establish an intelligence network for his benefit. The younger brother was more circumspect: while looking more and more to Essex, he never completely turned his back on Burghley and his fast-rising son Robert. In the 1597 essay, "Of Faction," he would prescribe his personal practice for later genera-tions. "Meane men must adheare, . . . yet euen in beginners to adheare so moderately, as he be a man of the one Faction, which is passablest with the other, commonly giveth best way." Such supple-ness, though, has a way of engendering distrust.

Also in the same year (1592) Bacon composed *The Conference of Pleasure*, a quartet of orations that may have been delivered by Essex before the Queen on the anniversary of her accession. The two which have survived in their entirety, *In Praise of Knowledge* and *In Praise of the Queen*, clearly point to later and more familiar statements on the same subjects. The former piece, for example, with its condemnation of "the knowledge that is now in use," anticipates with an almost studied arrogance Bacon's later critiques of contemporary knowledge. "Words" and "experiments" are deemed fatal to "the philosophy of nature"; they are, as he had earlier told his uncle, "the two sorts of rovers" that had to be purged from "all knowledge." Here already is the critical stance Bacon will adopt toward every subject: he conceives of himself as working in an area midway between unlimited specificity and unencompassable vagueness, free from the superstitions and idols that hobble other men. A feeling of disengagement and confi-dence in a special capacity to perceive the order inhering in things mark this speech as they will mark all his pronouncements as a philosopher. "Is there any such happiness as for a man's mind to be raised above the confusion of things, where he may have the prospect of the order of nature and the error of man?"[19] Indeed, that

self-assured sense of perspective permeates also his writings on law
and politics, and regularly marks his portrayals of the prince and the
judge.

*In Praise of the Queen*, a far longer speech, was designed to be the
last and most important of the four encomiums. Praise for the
benefits of Elizabeth's "politic, clement, and gracious government"
was not stinted, nor could Bacon speak enough of the "excellencies of
her person." Yet his speech is not just wisps of flattery. For in every
subsequent description of the Queen done by Bacon will be heard
clear and detailed echoes of this oration; it is the ur-text of his real
opinions. What we are dealing with is an idealized, imagined portrait,
one that depends partly on what other men had said or written about
the Queen—note the references to events Bacon, because of his age,
could not have known about at first hand—and partly on what his
own notions told him a prince ought to be. He tips his hand on the
latter point when he spends more than half a page extolling her "rare
eloquence"—a virtue certainly present in Elizabeth but enlarged by
the writer because of his own talents. More importantly, listen to what
he says of her wisdom:

> Observe the prudent temper she useth in admitting access, of the one
> side maintaining the majesty of her degree, and on the other side not
> prejudicing herself by looking to her estate through too few windows;
> her exquisite judgment in choosing and finding good servants . . . ; her
> profound discretion in assigning and appropriating every of them to
> their aptest employment; her penetrating sight in discovering every
> man's ends and drifts; her wonderful art in keeping servants in
> satisfaction, and yet in appetite; her inventing wit in contriving plots and
> overturns; her exact caution in censuring the propositions of others
> [for] her service; her forseeing [of] events; her usage of occasions.
> [8.139]

Those are the words of a propagandist, to be sure, but they are also
the words of a believer, and one whose small acquaintance with the
Queen at this time would hardly have made him privy to her mind or
her methods. And anyone familiar with Bacon's multitudinous political advices will recognize here his customary stress on foresight, on
seeing clearly (and early) into the nature of men and events. Bacon is
showing us a flattering portrait, but it is done to his *own* tastes. Later in

life, therefore, when he consciously uses the Queen and her strategies as a touchstone for political wisdom, he will be relying on an estimate of her government that in itself was faulty.

The 1592 device was not to be the last of Bacon's dramatic efforts. In 1594 he wrote for the Christmas festivities a set of five speeches on "the scope and end" of government, and in 1595, to commemorate the Queen's Day, he composed four speeches on the subject of love and self-love.[20] To the modern ear neither of these efforts is theatre; they are too close to formal debate. But forensic pageant held a great appeal for the Elizabethans, and Bacon undoubtedly felt at ease busying himself with such trifles.[21] Almost two decades later, in 1613, he would prudently arrange two far more ambitious (and expensive) wedding masques, one to celebrate the marriage of Princess Elizabeth, the other the nuptials of the Earl of Somerset.[22] These "toys," as he would term them in his 1625 essay, "Of Masques," clearly amused him; he enjoyed the contemporary fondness for pomp and display more than he would always acknowledge.

In February 1593 Bacon once more took a seat in parliament. Returned for the county of Middlesex, he sat on several committees, reported a conference with the Lords, and spoke his mind when it pleased him. By now he understood, as he intimated when recommending a codification of the laws, the nature of a parliament. "The cause of the assembling of all Parliaments hath been heretofore for Laws or Money; the one being the sinews of Peace, the other of War" (8. 214). He felt comfortable in the House of Commons, perhaps too comfortable, since it is in this parliament that he made a mistake in judgment of the kind that bedevilled his career. The need for money had been the chief reason for summoning parliament, and in its eagerness to see a subsidy bill passed quickly the government showed itself clumsy. Instead of having the Commons introduce the measure, Burghley pushed it from the Lords. Bacon and several members of the house, including minor court officials like Robert Beale, opposed this unprecedented strategy and won their point. A decision, nevertheless, had still to be made on the amount of supply, and a motion for raising three subsidies in four years was pressed. Both the sum and the payment schedule shocked Bacon and he spoke vigorously against them. Rich and poor would feel the squeeze, he argued, "and as for us, we are here to search the wounds of the realm and not to skin them over." Furthermore, so stiff a tax would "breed discontentment" and set an ominous precedent. Overriding Bacon's concern—and it seems as if he was the only member to protest—the Commons passed the bill.

What appears to have been a noble fight cost Bacon dearly. Elizabeth was furious at his opposition, the more so because he had long been a suitor for favor. Access was immediately denied; she would not endure a seeker after popularity. Word of her displeasure came through Burghley, and thus it was to his uncle that Bacon wrote, within a week of his "offensive" speech, the first defense of his actions. Significantly, it is also the first of his letters preserved through his own care (8.233). The tone was far from apologetic. He is prepared to explain anything "misreported" or "misconstrued," but he will not suffer his motives to be impugned. "If my heart be misjudged by imputation of popularity or opposition of any envious or officious informer, I have great wrong; and the greater, because the manner of my speech did most evidently show that I spake simply and only to satisfy my conscience, and not with any advantage or policy to sway the cause; and my terms carried all signification of duty and zeal towards her Majesty and her service" (8. 234). Bacon's sincerity cannot be doubted; the same, alas, cannot be said for his ability to apprehend how others interpreted his actions. The Queen, after all, had been in desperate need of money, and may be excused if she mistook "the discharge of my conscience" for ungrateful insubordination. Bacon's subsequent reluctance to admit a fault only aggravated her displeasure. Not much was ever needed to anger Elizabeth, but those who offended and later apologized lived to see better days. Bacon's conduct in this situation is symptomatic. In 1593 it lost him office for the next decade; in 1621 a similar attack of rectitude and stubbornness helped bury his career.

Ironically, at almost the same time Bacon was crossing Elizabeth and Burghley in parliament, he was lavishly praising them in his study. In late 1592 or early 1593 he composed *Certain Observations Made upon a Libel Published this Present Year, 1592*, which responded to attacks on the policies of the Queen and her ministers, notably

Burghley, made by Robert Parsons, the Jesuit pamphleteer, in his *Responsio ad edictum Reginae Anglica*. It is not clear whether Bacon undertook this lengthy propaganda piece, unpublished in his lifetime, on his own initiative or at someone else's urging, but the rather large number of surviving copies suggests that he might have circulated it privately *after* the blunder in parliament so as to restore his reputation.[23] Whatever the case, the work displays an intriguing feature of Bacon's literary habits: the willingness to use again and again the same images, sentences, and paragraphs. In the *Certain Observations* he includes, with only slight variation, passages from the 1589 letter to a French official and from the 1592 *In Praise of the Queen* (8.97, 143-44). Self-plagiarism in a writer is not a very remarkable trait, although Bacon may be unique for the extent to which he indulged himself.[24] But in Bacon the habit would seem to betoken something more than conscious rhetorical practice (or busyness). Rather, it can be seen as a sign also of an inability to grow, to gather fresh insights. The satisfaction with favorite phrases is a good measure of that certainty of opinion Bacon never questioned.

The quest for the Attorney-Generalship, which began at this time, was ill-starred from the very beginning. Elizabeth did not appoint to important offices men she did not trust. And although she might grant Essex, who diligently and sincerely lobbied for his mentor-friend, whatever he wanted for himself, she was always loath to give his friends anything,[25] especially friends steeped in their own pride. "I will not," Bacon would write to the Queen herself about his conduct, "wrong mine own good mind . . . , when your Majesty may conceive I do it but to make my profit of it" (8. 241). In addition, Bacon's rival for the office, Sir Edward Coke, held trump cards. He was nine years older, well-practiced in the law, and had been Solicitor-General since 1592. Besides his professional skills, Coke had also shown exemplary loyalty and shrewdness as Speaker of the House in 1593.[26] Finally, the oft-repeated charge that Burghley and his son declined simply out of jealousy to help Bacon seems specious—though Bacon (and so, later, Rawley) believed it. For it would have been foolhardy for the Cecils to have energetically sponsored a man—even if he was a relative—whom the Queen sourly told Essex her father "would have . . . banished his presence for ever."[27]

Bacon nevertheless made a serious effort to capture the Attorney-Generalship. Specifically, he sought to cancel the charge that he lacked experience. On January 25, 1594, he made his first appearance in a courtroom, pleading in King's Bench for the heir of Lord Cheney, said to be Sir Thomas Perrot, brother-in-law to Essex, in a land dispute. Two weeks later he argued another case, this time in the Exchequer and with a group of notables specially invited to witness his performance.[28] That Bacon should have thus far avoided the courtroom is not surprising. Then, as now, the study of law was deemed a respectable course for those with uncertain futures. And from scattered comments it is evident that he thought himself superior to the daily practice of law. "To speak plainly, though perhaps vainly," he wrote to Burghley in March 1595, "I do not think that the ordinary practice of the law, not serving the Queen in place, will be admitted for a good account of the poor talent which God hath given me" (8.358). The proviso about serving the Queen indicates, however, his willingness to use a legal career to advance in the world of politics.

Despite these efforts, by March 1594 it was clear that Bacon (not for the last time) had lost out to Sir Edward Coke. Bitterly he wondered how family connections, "the honourable testimony of so many counsellors," and the "obscureness and many exceptions to my competitors," had failed him: "I cannot but conclude with myself that no man ever received a more exquisite disgrace." His rejection was simply against logic: "I am a man that the Queen hath already done for; and princes, especially her Majesty, loveth to make an end where they begin." All too often his biographers have nodded agreement, forgetting that the Queen was neither obliged nor predisposed to conform to someone else's ideas of what she ought to do. Bacon misinterpreted his strengths and weaknesses in this situation; he neglected to consider how others viewed his qualifications. His mind instinctively shied away from problems and situations that might demand unpleasant self-judgments, clinging instead to a logic based entirely on its own desires. As a rebuttal to failure, illness and talk of retirement accompany this "disgrace," as they did every other one. "I will . . . retire myself," he told Essex, "with a couple of men to Cambridge, and there spend my life in my studies and contemplations, without looking back" (8.290-91). Unbelieving, the Earl was already at work trying to obtain the Solicitor-Generalship for Bacon. Passionately convinced of his friend's brilliance, "his parts were never destined for a private and (if I may so speak) an idle life,"[29] he once more began to plague the Queen with his entreaties.

Bacon, meanwhile, set out to show Elizabeth that she had made a mistake. Early in May he argued Chudleigh's Case before the judges assembled in the Exchequer. In a somewhat suspicious-looking coincidence, Bacon took the same side (viz., against perpetuities) that Coke, as Solicitor-General, had taken in an earlier brief, and used the occasion to give a lesson in law throbbing with the resentment of defeat. "I will not bind myself to Mr. Attorney's order, but pursue my own course, which is the order the matter itself more aptly induces for resolution and decision!"[30] Twice more in his argument he scores Coke's competence. "And I confess when I heard Mr. Attorney argue so strongly out of the preamble [to the Statute of Uses], I objected within myself that it was but a fallacy, and that it was the equivocation of the word 'use.'"[31] His opponents in the case, on the other hand, are always treated with great deference. It is, in short, obvious that Bacon is bent on demonstrating who the better man is, and that he is exploiting the case in hand for that end. But his ego is not satisfied just with excoriating Coke; the language and structure of the brief as a whole are calculated to draw attention to the virtuosity of the advocate. Having, for example, previously rejected a precedent cited by the opposition because the case was based on a "palpable error," he gives his auditors a sample of his brilliance. "If this case be well scanned, I say it makes greatly for me, for in truth it was the opinion of this inventor that if the contingent use had been limited to await the alienation consummate, it had come *nimis tarde*; and to mend this, the rising was appointed on the conclusion: and so I repent that I have discredited the case, as it makes for me" (7.620). Similar strutting is evident when he handles the political and social aspects of the case, and Coke is again rebuked. "And these are the bad effects [of perpetuities] besides those of fraud and deceit [Coke's argument]. And I well know a difference between speaking in the Parliament and before the judges in an argument of law" (7.635).

The Queen seems to have been informed of this exhibition. Filing another of his progress reports with Bacon on the suit for the

Solicitor-Generalship, Essex tells his friend that Elizabeth acknowledged his "great wit" and "excellent gift of speech, and much other good learning," but "in law she rather thought you could make show to the uttermost of your knowledge, than that you were deep."[32] Bacon had exceeded the accepted limits on puffery.

Unfortunately, the prolonged suit for the Solicitor-Generalship was even more exhausting than the earlier fight for the Attorney-Generalship. Help in the form of recommendations to the Queen was sought from all the great persons he knew, with the suitor often suggesting tactics to his promoter. "And because *vis unita fortior*," he writes to Lord Keeper Puckering, "I pray your Lordship to take a time with the Queen when my Lord Treasurer is present."[33] But as the months wore on he became dispirited. Was the Queen, he wondered, playing with him? "For to be . . . like a child following a bird, which when he is nearest flieth away and lighteth a little before, and then the child after it again, and so *in infinitum,* I am weary of it" (8.359). Gradually despair and frustration turned into suspicion. Was Essex, perhaps, more a liability than an asset? "For against me she is never peremptory but to my Lord of Essex." Puckering was openly accused of "crossing" him, and then reminded that he owed better service to the son of the man who was responsible for his own rise. Bacon even began to think that his cousin, Robert Cecil, was actively blocking his path, but soon apologized to his uncle for being "too credulous to idle hearsays." And still he defended the unforgotten subsidy speech. "That which I . . . spake in difference was but in circumstances of time and manner, which methinks should be no great matter, since there is variety allowed in counsel, as a discord in music, to make it more perfect" (8.362). By raising the individual case to a generalization sweetened with a metaphor, Bacon sidesteps the issue as it was felt by the Queen; rather than admit imprudence, he offers a new vindication. Even in defeat, and by October 1595 it was clear that he had lost again, he seems bent on concealing from himself the failures he had experienced. "If I had been an ambitious man, it would have overthrown me. But minded as I am, *revertet benedictio mea in sinum meum*" (8.369).

The failure to gain office during this three-year period was not, however, entirely a consequence of past errors or habits of personality.

To some extent Bacon *was* a victim of the larger ambitions and strident behavior of Essex, who sought to solidify and advertise his position, and thus his honor, by placing his followers where he could. "Upon me the labour must lie of his [Bacon's] establishment, and upon me the disgrace will light of his being refused."[34] But to badger the Queen was to annoy her and reinforce her natural ambivalence. Essex realized that his persistence in the suit made the Queen "passionate against" the appointment, but he evidently also imagined that his battering strategy would ultimately prove successful (8.289, 297-98). So, apparently, did Bacon, who ever urged the Earl to speak for him. Later, Essex would say that he had "hurt" his friend rather than "done him good."[35] But it is not likely that he ever gave the speech attributed to him in Bacon's later defense, the 1604 *Apology in Certain Imputations Concerning the Late Earl of Essex*: "I know you are the least part of your own matter, but you fare ill because you have chosen me for your mean and dependance" (10.144). For every speech in that self-justifying brief is suspect, and, in this case, the words suspiciously resemble those Bacon had written to his brother in January 1595: "My conceit is, that I am the least part of mine own matter" (8.348).

Though Elizabeth was not ready to give him a significant office, she still had work for him. Having evidence of his legal skills, she began employing him regularly as a member of her legal counsel in the summer of 1594.[36] Bacon did not receive a patent for this subordinate office, which was perhaps the Queen's way of reminding "a tired sea-sick suitor" that real favor depended on much more than ability. His task was to assist the Attorney-General and Solicitor-General in their many duties, and for the next several years his activities can be traced through the State Papers and the minutes of the privy council. Primarily he was involved in examining prisoners and searching out conspiracies, though at times he was used to referee disputes between parties bringing their suits to the Crown. It was a position of small honor, yet it gave its holder much experience in discovering the cankered hopes and plots of men.

At the same time Bacon's talents as a publicist did not go to rust. In 1594 he wrote *A True Report of the Detestable Treason Intended by Dr. Roderigo Lopez*, presumably at the request of Essex, who was anxious lest it not be believed that the Queen's physician had sought to poison her.[37] As an attempt to piece together a conspiracy from evidence that was, at best, spotty, the *True Report* is brilliant. By the time he is finished Bacon has set out the "order and form" of a treason "which mought be proved to be not only against all Christianity and religion, but against nature, the law of nations, the honour of arms, the civil law, [and] the rules of morality and policy" (8.275), and succeeded in portraying a frightened old man as the most cunning of conspirators. The same cleverness is evident in *A Letter Written out of England to an English Gentleman in Padua*, composed in the winter of 1598-9 to present the government's case in the so-called Squire Plot.[38] Once more he creates villains with deep-laid plans. "This Walpoole [a jesuit], carrying a waking and waiting eye upon those of our nation, to discover and single out fit instruments for the greatest treasons, observed this Squire."[39] This tract was published immediately, and a hint of Bacon's effectiveness as a propagandist is to be found in Chamberlain's comment to Carleton, "the letter of Squires conspiracie is well written."[40] What specific qualities Chamberlain had in mind cannot be known, but certainly any reader would have to be impressed with Bacon's ability to create forceful—if not exactly real— characters. Placing himself inside the heads of his traitors, he shows his readers why they acted as they did. As a result, the traitors become something more than two-dimensional figures. Ultimately, of course, all the men and women (including those on the government side) in these tracts are caricatures since Bacon must make his people operate solely on the basis of what it is necessary to prove about them. But unless the reader is indifferent to the subject or possesses additional information, the technique is extremely persuasive. The unknown is illuminated, and in a way that wonderfully satisfies the preconceptions of the reader.

The unexpected death of Lord Keeper Puckering in late April 1596 and his replacement by Thomas Egerton, Master of the Rolls, meant that Bacon was given another opportunity for advancement. This time he took a softer approach. Essex, busy at Plymouth with preparations for the Cadiz expedition, was to remain silent and instead persuade Egerton (a good friend) and several others to appeal to the Queen. Eagerly, Bacon waited for the prize to fall into his lap.

When he wrote his brother on May 30 he betrayed once more that habit of allowing his expectations to color his perception. "I do find in the speech of some ladies and the very face of this Court some addition of reputation, as methinks, to us both, and I doubt not but God hath an operation in it that will not suffer good endeavours to perish. The Queen saluted me to-day as she went to chapel. I had long speech with Sir Robert Cecil this morning, who seemed apt to discourse with me" (9.37). What is convenient to his interests is what he reads to be true. A more remarkable instance of this quality is the famous letter he drafted to Essex in October of the same year, shortly after the Earl had returned a hero from Cadiz. Complimented for its wisdom even by Bacon's severest critics, the letter deserves attention.

It opens with a long defense of the writer's previous advice. His counsels have been consistent and the Earl has not taken "hurt at any time" by them. Having established his reliability, Bacon asserts that Essex , far from standing in a position of real trust and influence with the Queen, was actually teetering on the edge of an abyss. For deep in Elizabeth's mind *must* lurk dark impressions.

> A man of a nature not to be ruled; that hath the advantage of my affection, and knoweth it; of an estate not grounded to his greatness; of a popular reputation; of a military dependence: I demand whether there can be a more dangerous image than this represented to any monarch living, much more to a lady, and of her Majesty's apprehension? [9.41]

No wonder, then, that the Earl suffered so many disgraces. His estate was "base and low," "your friends and dependents that are true and steadfast" are exposed to "repulses and scorns," "your reputation" besmirched in "odious employments and offices," etc. Essex was clearly the victim of a higher logic. "I say, wheresoever the formerly-described impression is taken in any King's breast towards a subject, these other recited inconveniences must, of necessity of politic consequence, follow; in respect of such instruments as are never failing about princes: which spy into their humours and conceits, and second them" (9.41). Following his statement of the problem Bacon offers a solution. Dissimulation is the key. Essex is told to alter his carriage, not change his ways. For example, his military ambition: "It is a thing that of all things I would have you retain, the times considered, and the necessity of the service; . . . But I say, keep it in substance, but abolish it in shows to the Queen" (9.43). Or, his popular reputation: "The only way is to quench it *verbis* and not *rebus*. And therefore to take all occasions, to the Queen, to speak against popularity and popular causes vehemently; and to tax it in all others: but nevertheless to go on in your honourable commonwealth courses as you do" (9.44).

If we momentarily put out of our mind the escapade of February 8, 1601, the letter should lose some of its glitter, and begin to display its fundamentally imaginary quality. Bacon's view, for example, of Elizabeth's half-conscious fears and how they are "seconded," couched as it is in a grandiose, pseudo-axiomatic formulation ("inconveniences must, of necessity of politic consequence, follow"), discloses a slender faculty for understanding character. For his interpretation suggests how, as a result of his *own* failures, he imagined the Queen felt toward himself; it is not a perceptive analysis of her ambivalent feelings for Essex. Of course there is something to what Bacon says about her fears, but the hyperbole distorts the situation to the point of carica-ture. Moreover, his proposal that Essex should undertake a policy of systematic dissimulation is absurd, and not just because it misconceives the Earl's character and capacities. Rather, it is because this recom-mendation also primarily derives from Bacon's own predicament, his own sense of what was now, after repeated failure, required to get ahead. Having failed (as he would have seen it) with an open countenance, Bacon has now become obsessed with the advantages of dissembling. The letter, in brief, represents a fundamentally solipsistic view of Essex's situation. Those who lament the Earl's not following this advice should note that he may never have seen the letter.[41]

Meanwhile the search for office, quickened by sagging finances that made inevitable the common practice of law, went on. More than ever success must have seemed to depend on personally impressing the Queen. But aside from avoiding words and deeds that might vex her, what could be done? Bacon had already shown his talents in the courtroom, and had dutifully performed as a member of her legal counsel. Would these and glowing recommendations from friends eventually open the royal fist? He could not be sure. Beset with uncertainty, he sent her in January 1597—or at least proposed to—a set of legal maxims,[42] hoping to convince her that he *was* "deep" in the law. What probably precipitated this gesture was "the gracious usage and speech" he had "received during the Christmas holydays, from her majesty."[43] If he could suitably impress her at a time when she was seemingly inclined toward him, "good words" might finally sprout "some princely real effects."

Bacon obviously believed that his "sheaf and cluster of fruit" would appeal to Elizabeth. Had she not ordered a commission set up in 1588 to look into the matter of law reform (to which, as noted above, Bacon had been appointed); had not the Lord Chancellor "published . . . from your royal mouth" in the last parliament a continued interest in such a project (to which speech Bacon had immediately offered an echo); and, finally, had not the Queen herself since then presumably told him of her interest "these many years" to see "a general amendment" of the laws? Thus, his dedicatory epistle—by far the longest he ever composed—is something more than customary flattery. While seeking to persuade Elizabeth to undertake "one of the most chosen works, of highest merit and benificence towards the subject, that ever entered into the mind of any king" (7.316), he attempts at the same time to portray himself as an "obeying subject and servant" who is both learned and respectful. "I conceived the nature of the subject, besides my particular obligation, was such, as I ought not to dedicate the same to any other than to your sacred Majesty; both because, though the collection be mine, yet the laws are yours; and because it is your Majesty's reign that hath been as a goodly and seasonable spring weather to the advancing of all excellent arts of peace"(7.316-17).

Of course, self-promotion cannot by itself 'explain' the *Maxims*; motive and substance must be distinguished. But if Bacon's writings are always a true expression of his interests and thoughts, there is also evidence—recall the Queen's reaction to his first legal argument—that the "fruits" of his tongue and pen were apt to be skeptically appraised by contemporaries just because his ambition was so manifest. The several protestations of modesty in his preface to the *Maxims* suggest an awareness of this aspect of his reputation. "I have in all points . . . applied myself, not to that which might serve most for the ostentation of mine own wit or knowledge, but to that which may yield most use and profit to the students and professors of our law."[44]

Given the persistent need to call attention to himself, we should not be surprised that the content of a work of Bacon's, as well as the occasion, was influenced by ambition, nor that his contemporaries sometimes misjudged or mislaid his efforts. Whether, as in the present instance, Bacon (hurriedly) assembled pages already on his worktable,[45] or wrote out an entirely new piece, it is important to consider the specific personal context of his compositions, and not, as is usually the case, read them solely as products of an Olympian intellect.

The preface to the maxims eloquently states their purpose while displaying the attitudes and categories of criticism that will subsequently be applied to all "sciences."[46] Each man, Bacon insists, is obliged to work his profession honestly and preserve himself from "the abuses" common to it. But he also should attempt to "visit and strengthen the roots and foundation of the science itself; thereby not only gracing it in reputation and dignity, but also amplifying it in perfection and substance." His own task is to deduce the "rules and grounds dispersed throughout" the confusion of the laws so as to create a rational and predictive approach.

> Hereby no small light will be given, in new cases and such wherein there is no direct authority, to sound into the true conceit of law by depth of reason; in cases wherein the authorities do square and vary, to confirm the law, and to make it received one way; and in cases wherein the law is cleared by authority, yet nevertheless to see more profoundly into the reason of such judgments and ruled cases, and thereby to make more use of them for the decision of other cases more doubtful; so that the uncertainty of law, which is the principal and most just challenge that is made to the laws of our nation at this time, will by this new strength laid to the foundation somewhat the more settle and be corrected. [7.319]

Clearly manifest in the above quotation is the desire for certitude and utilitarian procedure that Bacon, in both the 1592 letter to his uncle and the *Praise of Knowledge,* had given notice was to inspire his rebuke of existing knowledge. "Chance" alone, he earlier argued, had been responsible for those few inventions (printing, artillery, compass) that had thus far benefited man. Significant progress could only come when a method was developed that was more certain than "vain notions and blind experiments." To argue that Bacon's concern for certainty came from his study of the law and was then applied to every other field of knowledge would be too mechanical. As with his capacity for analogical reasoning, it would seem that the law refined and reinforced primary needs. The passion—and the word hardly exaggerates Bacon's concern—for certitude runs so strong through all the writings that the reader often feels as if he is dealing with a demand of the personality as well as a goal of the intellect.[47]

How Bacon conceives of the maxims themselves further demonstrates the feeling for a common method. The *legum leges*, as he calls them, are not themselves law, but aid in the understanding and application of the law. They form a middle ground between specific cases and lofty generalizations, an area whose reality is not always clear to the reader but whose terrain Bacon would spend his life exploring.

> For as, both in the law and other sciences, the handling of questions by commonplace, without aim or application, is the weakest; so yet nevertheless many common principles and generalities are not to be contemned, if they be well derived and deduced into particulars, and their limits and exclusions duly assigned. For there be two contrary faults and extremities in the debating and sifting out of the law, which may be best noted in two several manner of arguments: some argue upon general grounds, and come not near the point in question; others, without laying any foundation of a ground or difference or reason, do loosely put cases, which, though they go near the point, yet being put so scattered, prove not; but rather serve to make the law appear more doubtful than to make it more plain. [7.320-21]

Whether he is discussing law, philosophy, or politics, Bacon will invariably formulate the same schema to represent the mistaken methods of other men. Rhetorically it is a very compelling critique —who has not read about the ants and spiders of knowledge? But that perhaps is its problem. For it is a schematization founded on theory, and thus its relevance to particular "matter" is often either unclear or too simple.

Bacon set the maxims in the form of aphorisms, henceforth a favorite style of "delivering . . . knowledge" because they leave the "wit of man more free to turn and toss, and to make use of that which is so delivered to more several purposes and applications." Each maxim is declared in Latin and followed by an exposition in English that specified the instances in which it held or did not. Whether the situations cited (the positive or negative instances) were used in formulating the maxim, and not simply created afterwards to justify it, is a moot point. Bacon informs us that "ancient wisdom and science was wont to be delivered in that form," but that it is actually the precedent of the civil law which persuaded him to it. Indeed, he assumes a close proximity between the common law and the civil law, for both are the product of the "same reason" inhering in all men. Any diversities that exist do so "in regard of accommodating the law to the different considerations of estate" (7.321). Once again we can see that instinctive urge to find common denominators.

While unquestionably adept in the sources and procedures of the common law, Bacon's ambition as a legist centered on establishing greater order and method in the law itself. The mere practice of law was unsatisfying and insufficient. Rawley's comment, which obviously reflects Bacon's own feelings, is apt: "He wrote several tractates upon that subject [law]: wherein, though some great masters of the law did out-go him in bulk, and particularities of cases, yet in the science of the grounds and mysteries of the law he was exceeded by none."[48] And so in offering a project to "settle a certain sense of law which doth now too much waver in incertainty," Bacon was serving his intellectual inclinations as well as his career.

Bacon's first published work, *Essayes. Religious Meditations. Places of perswasion and disswasion*, appeared in February 1597. He had not intended to publish "these fragments of my conceites," he explains in the dedication to his brother, but someone had tried to steal the "fruit" of his labors, thereby forcing his hand.[49] To Anthony he repeats the common refrain, although now the whole world is meant to hear it. "I haue preferred them to you that are next myself, Dedicating them, such as they are, to our loue, in the depth whereof (I assure you) I sometimes wish your infirmities translated uppon my selfe, that her Maiestie mought haue the seruice of so actiue and able a mind, & I mought be with excuse confined to these contemplations & studies for which I am fittest." No doubt when he penned those words he meant them; the wishes of "sometimes," however, had a way of quickly evaporating. And even as he mused on this occasion, he kept an eye on his worldly chances. For why, it must be asked, did he not dedicate the book to Essex, his devoted patron? The answer, that he had nothing to gain and very possibly something to lose, indicates that pronouncments of ambivalence, while sincere (and virtually *de rigueur* for intellectuals of that era), were really only that: pronouncements.[50]

Too little attention—mostly confined to style—has been paid to this famous volume. This is regrettable because the three works contained therein vividly summarize basic attitudes and habits of mind. The ten essays, easily the most familiar portion, form the best example. Built up from aphorisms, many of which are variations on sentences written down over the years in commonplace books, the essays both individually and as a group seem to be only a collection of random thoughts. Actually, the intensely autobiographical character of the essays supplies them with a unity of perspective, emotional and literary.

In 1597 Bacon wrote as a private man bitterly disappointed in his hopes. His topics were those necessarily helpful to other men wishing to rise in the world, and their order of presentation recapitulated the life sequence of the common scenario. The guarded and, at times, almost compulsive shrewdness of these essays witnesses their author's mood. "If sometimes you dissemble your knowledge of that you are thought to know, you shall be thought another time to know that which you know not." Fifteen years later he writes as Solicitor-General and has solid hopes of going much higher. Accordingly, he lifts his eyes and directs the essays, both old and new, to advising the King. Domestic topics are included but "business" is his primary subject, and the tone is more relaxed, less hortatory.[51] Finally, in 1625, still dreaming of a possible return to favor but preoccupied with establishing a firm reputation with posterity, he extends their range to include any subject that might enhance his fame. "I have enlarged them both in number and weight; so that they are indeed a new work."[52] Yet while successively altering his perspective, he never cuts out what has been previously said except to forestall foreign complaints or avoid verbal obscurity.[53]

The autobiographical element in the 1597 edition is readily apparent. Earlier letters often provide almost parallel statements, as when he speaks of friendship.

> To be gouerned by one is not good, and to be distracted with many is worse; but to take aduise of friends is ever honorable: 'For lookers on many times see more than gamesters, And the vale best discouereth the

hill.' There is little friendship in the worlde, and least of all betweene equals; which was wont to bee magnified. That that is, is betweene superiour and inferiour, whose fortunes may comprehend the one the other.

Compare this to what he had said to Essex four years before.

And for the free and loving advice your Lordship hath given me, I cannot correspond to the same with greater duty, than by assuring your Lordship that I will not dispose of myself without your allowance; not only because it is the best wisdom in any man in his own matters to rest in the wisdom of a friend (for who can by often looking in the glass discern and judge so well of his own favour, as another with whom he converseth?), but also because my affection to your Lordship hath made mine own contentment inseparable from your satisfaction. [8.235]

More often, though, we can only use his letters as explanations for what he says. A particularly good example of this is the essay "Of Sutes," which in subsequent editions will be titled "Of Suitors." Directed exclusively at suitors, the 1597 version informs them what they can expect from those who serve as middlemen, "undertakers," in suits. The outraged letters of the previous four years provide chapter and verse for virtually every statement.[54] At the same time a glance at the introductory sentences of this essay, as composed in 1597 and then in 1625, reveals how the changing circumstances of the life shift the perspective of the thought.

[1597] Manie ill matters are vndertaken, and many good matters with ill mindes. Some embrace Sutes which neuer meane to deale effectually in them.

[1625] Many ill matters and projects are undertaken; and private suits do putrefy the public good. Many good matters are undertaken with bad minds; I mean not only corrupt minds, but crafty minds, that intend not performance.

In 1597 Bacon went on to describe the falsities engaged in by those who "undertake" suits. In 1625, however, he is clearly talking about the problems encountered with suitors, not undertakers. This new point of view, which is absent from the 1612 edition, results from his having sat a long time on the other side of the bench; the bitterness of the disappointed suitor has been superseded by the scorn of the man too often bothered. But because Bacon will not disown anything he has said before, the reader is constantly (and not always comfortably) aware of the two perspectives striving for his attention.[55]

The essays insist on their usefulness. Bacon believes his observations can have "medicinable" effects on men's "manners" and understanding. His method, however, raises doubts. To what extent can advice knotted to specific personal experiences, no matter how inflated by didactic periods, serve other men? Indeed, so personal are certain remarks that the "wit" of the reader is *not* "free to turn and toss, and to make use of that which is so delivered to more several purposes and applications," but is locked in place, compelled to watch the man speak his own disappointment. "Suters are so distasted with delaies and abuses, that plaine dealing in denying to deale in Sutes at first, and reporting the successe barely, and in challendging no more thankes then one hath deserued, is growen not only honourable but also gracious." The imperative tone of these essays, a consequence of their aphoristic form and Bacon's accustomed didacticism, gives them an abrasive urgency.

Another, and more serious, problem with the method can be seen in the essay "Of Faction." In the 1597 edition Bacon is thinking of factions as they existed at Elizabeth's court.

> Manie have a newe wisdome, indeed, a fond opinion; That for a Prince to gouerne his estate, . . . according to the respects of Factions, is the principal part of pollicie. Whereas contrariwise, the chiefest wisedome is either in ordering those things which are generall, and wherein men of severall Factions doe neuerthelesse agree, or in dealing with correspondence to particular persons one by one.

Nevertheless, Bacon says, factions are not to be neglected, and so he devotes the essay to analyzing their make-up and advising how they are to be dealt with. Always his point of departure is court politics. Slight changes occur in 1612, but in 1625 there is a general overhauling that includes three fresh sentences at the end.

> Kings had need beware how they side themselves, and make themselves as of a faction or party; for leagues within the state are ever pernicious to monarchies: for they raise an obligation paramount to obligation of sovereignty, and make the king *tanquam unus ex nobis*; as was to be seen in the League of France. When factions are carried too high and too violently, it is a sign of weakness in princes; and much to the prejudice both of their authority and business. The motions of factions under

kings ought to be like the motions (as the astronomers speak) of the inferior orbs, which may have their proper motions, but yet still are quietly carried by the higher motion of *primum mobile.*

The phrase "or party" signals a problem: Bacon must now confront a very different political situation, one where the term "faction" cannot retain the same value it had twenty-five years before. (The complete phrase, "of faction or party," translated into *factioni alicui subditorum suorum* of the 1638 posthumous edition at least nods at the problem by blurring the distinction and employing the previously unused word, "subjects.")

The essay is really about two different—though not unrelated—phenomena: court intrigues, and divisions within the country. This becomes apparent when we realize that Bacon makes precisely the same point about princes and factions with precisely the same example of Henry III and the Catholic League in the 1625 version of the essay, "Of Seditions and Troubles." Indeed, the very nature of the example suggests that Bacon was not overly sensitive to a changing reality. "Faction," although a word still in vogue, cannot articulate the times. Even within the court what would be described by the word involves people and problems very different from those of twenty-five years before, while outside the court the divisions in the country reflect a far more complex situation than that existing in the 1580's. Small men as well as great are questioning assumptions and institutions, albeit tentatively, and in the process redefining the bases of political life. Unlike the patchwork essay on suitors, where additions do not necessarily interfere with the substantive validity of what has been said earlier, the essay on faction comes unravelled.

It is important to realize that the anachronism at the heart of this essay arises inevitably from a mind predisposed to enlarging its own experiences and perceptions into general rules, and unable to admit error. Is it any wonder that the essays kept growing, that Bacon refused to censure any observations once thought worthy? How could the man unlearn what he had once experienced? All men, of course, use the self as the prime reference point for analyzing the world, but not all men are so obsessed with having certain knowledge.

The *Meditationes Sacrae* formed the second section of Bacon's first book. Twelve in number, they resemble much more in form the essay as we know it. But if the reader should anticipate a sampling of Bacon's piety he is soon disillusioned, for the writer's purpose was to demonstrate common errors that plague men in their spiritual exercises. The set of his mind, moreover, is unfailingly temporal. "Now the heresies which spring from this source [denial of God's power] appear to be more heinous than the rest: for in civil government also it is a more atrocious thing to deny the power and majesty of the prince, than to slander his reputation" (7.253). Bacon did not lack religion, but it did not take up his time or disturb his thoughts.[56] And the high intellectualizing that characterizes all his religious writings, though it can inspire a piece as luminous as the *Confession of Faith*,[57] betrays an inability to comprehend how men give themselves to God or other men—his strictures on human love are well known—for he is incapable of the first requirement: forgetting self. Thus there is an easy confidence in providing definitions, whether one is distinguishing the "faithful workman of God" from the "impostors" and "hypocrites," or determining the kinds and "degrees" of heresies. And there is a tendency to resort to a quibble, as when he proves that atheists do not exist by insisting that the biblical phrase, "The fool hath said in his heart there is no God," purposely used "said" rather than "thought." "Of Earthly Hope," the longest piece in the *Meditationes*, further attests to an unfinished sensibility; the failures of the preceding four years cannot entirely account for so jaundiced an outlook. "But in hope there seems to be no use. For what avails that anticipation of good?" (7.247). Answers are offered to the question, but they lack sufficiency. To measure feelings by 'use' is to bleed them of their essence.

*Of the Colours of Good and Evil*, the concluding piece in the collection, indicates Bacon's abiding fascination with the arts of persuasion. Inspired, he says, by the "best book of Aristotle,"[58] he appears to have been collecting colours—as he had legal maxims—for several years. Bacon meant by colours propositions that men assume to be always true but which are just as likely to be false:[59] 'The evil that a man brings on himself by his own fault is greater; that which is brought upon him from without is less.' His procedure is to state the colour and then, drawing upon a variety of sources ranging from Aesop's fables to spring flowers, demonstrate "in what cases they hold, and in what they deceive." The exercise flattered his sense of himself as the polymath uniquely fitted to free men's judgment. "The discovering and reprehension of these colours . . . cannot be done, but out of a very universal knowledge of the nature of things" (7.77). Bacon sought to convince his reader of how the mind itself —independent of any particular subject—was prone to being mesmerized by the "persuaders labour." He was, of course, perfectly suited by training, experience, and inclination to compose such a grammar of fallacies; indeed, on no other subject was he so well qualified to advise. Whether he was instructing men on the rules governing effective speech, as in the 1597 essay "Of Discourse" or in the *Discourse Touching Helps for the Intellectual Powers* addressed about the same time to Sir Henry Savile, or providing them with defenses against rhetoric, Bacon speaks as an expert.

In the months following this first book Bacon continued to seek the Mastership of the Rolls. It was all for naught, though, since Egerton, in a rare display of the Queen's favor, was allowed to retain his old position.

Dwelling on how Bacon struggled for office, however disagreeable it may appear, is necessary: lifelong suitorship had consequences. He himself recognized that a man who turned the "same things over and over in his mind," who was suspended "in the same circle of cogitations," would be consumed by them (7.247). Bacon was always searching for position and reputation, and much of what we have from his pen, as should be apparent by now, either played a direct part in his strategies or witnessed the effects of the struggle. Repeated failure, moreover, tended to magnify certain traits. The thrust to position and influence becomes a racking desire to have the world recognize and reward his genius. But since he must continually rationalize failure, he gradually forges a persona that will, appropriately, deny the primary ambition. The philanthropic urge to reform knowledge, used by virtually all his biographers to give an acceptable meaning to what often seems a soiled life, and which was first enunciated by himself, becomes increasingly a self-justifying formula.

Suitorship also largely accounts for Bacon's posture in the House of Commons after 1593, as he endeavors to declare his loyalty and skill. To watch him perform, for example, in the session of 1597, when he sat for Southampton,[60] is to see a man straining to be recognized. On the first working day he prepared two bills, one against the depopulation of towns and houses of husbandry, the other for the maintenance of tillage. He argued forcibly that the "former moth-eaten laws" on depopulation would have to be revived despite the inconvenience they might bring to "lords that enclosed great grounds." A savage depression lay on the land and Bacon had seen at first hand some of its consequences when, as a member of the legal counsel, he had participated in the examinations of certain Oxfordshire rebels.[61] Pragmatic *sententiae* were offered to those who might choke on the cure. "For in matters of policy ill is not to be thought ill which bringeth forth good" (9.82). Whether Bacon was acting in this matter as an official spokesman of the Crown has never been definitely determined, but the absence of any letters or memos indicating contact, the fact that he was the first member to speak, the hurried following motion by Sir John Fortescu, Chancellor of the Exchequer (who may be presumed to have known the council's plans), to have the bill put in committee instead of being read, as Bacon hoped it would be, and the phrases used to introduce the two bills ("drawn [not] with polished pen but with a polished heart, free from affection and affectation"), suggest that Bacon had decided to push himself forward as the exponent of a needful and popular—at least with the common people and the government—measure.[62] From being about the court he would have been aware of the government's desire to introduce some sort of social legislation, and probably decided that to initiate discussion with "his two children," as he is reputed to have spoken of the two bills, would draw favorable attention. After all, had he not done the same thing in the last parliament when he stood up the first day to talk about legal reform, a subject he knew was close to the Queen's heart? In any event, a large committee worked on the bills and they were eventually passed with extensive changes.

On the subsidy question Bacon further proved his loyalty. Significantly, the speech he gave, or at least thought he gave, for we cannot be certain whether the version we have was written out before or after the event, is the only one of his parliamentary speeches from Elizabeth's reign that he bothered to preserve. This time, unlike 1593, if there was any misunderstanding of his words or intentions, there was to be a copy to check. That he intended his speech even more for the Queen's ear than for the Commons' was to be expected. How else to correct the impression made four years before? The same tactic will be used in 1601 and in the parliamentary sessions of the succeeding reign until he becomes a member of the official party. As he had used the law courts for his advancement, so too was he willing to use the House of Commons. His acquiescence in this parliament to an even stiffer subsidy bill than had passed in 1593 also sets a precedent: never again on an issue will he take a position that might seem to cross royal interests. But aside from being an exercise in ambition, the speech is a good example of Bacon's oratory, and suggests the source of his influence and reputation as a parliamentarian.[63]

His remarks followed a series of speeches by court officials, a point that he gladly noticed in his introduction to justify his own effort. "But because it hath been always used, and the mixture of this House doth so require·it, that in causes of this nature there be some speech and opinion as well from persons of generality as by persons of authority, I will say somewhat and not much."[64] Resorting to the traditional rhetorical device of saying what you want to say while protesting that you will not, Bacon opened his substantive comments with three paragraphs praising the "benefits" of Elizabeth's "most politic and happy government," the "freedom and ease" of subjects who, compared to those of other countries, make so few "payments to the Crown," and the wisdom in "her Majesty's manner of expending and issuing treasure." He then reminded the members of the "familiar truth, that safety and preservation is to be preferred before benefit or increase, insomuch as those counsels which tend to preservation seem to be attended with necessity, whereas those deliberations which tend to benefit seem only accompanied with persuasion. And it is ever gains and no loss, when at the foot of the account there remains the purchase of safety" (9.86). Concrete examples of this truth were then set forth. "The seafaring man will in a storm cast over some of his goods to save and assure the rest." Softened by such commonplaces, his listeners were ready for the main argument: the increased danger in which the country stood since "the last parliament."

What is particularly striking in Bacon's discussion of the "four accidents or occurrents of state" that imperiled the realm is the method he adopts in explaining "things public and known to you all." Instead of immediately analyzing the dangers themselves—Henry IV's acceptance of Catholicism and the probability of a reconciliation between France and Spain, Spain's capture of Calais, the "ulcer of Ireland," which was bound to attract Spain, and the Cadiz and Island voyages that "have braved" Spain and "objected" her to "scorn"—he first sketches a model.

> For I do find, Mr. Speaker, that when kingdoms and states are entered into terms and resolutions of hostility one against the other, yet they are many times refrained from their attempts by four impediments.
>
> The first is by this same *aliud agere*; when they have their hands full of other matter which they have embraced, and serveth for a diversion of their hostile purposes.
>
> The next is when they want the commodity or opportunity of some places of near approach.
>
> The third, when they have conceived an apprehension of the difficulty and churlishness of the enterprise, and that it is not prepared to their hand.
>
> And the fourth is when a state through the age of the monarch groweth heavy and indisposed to actions of great peril and motion, . . .
>
> Now . . . examine whether by removing the impediments in these four kinds the danger be not grown so many degrees nearer us . . . since the last parliament. [9.87]

As a planned rhetorical device, the model is persuasive; to examine (and resolve) cases with the help of rules induces a sense of greater certainty. But is Bacon fishing principles out of his pocket only as part of a deliberate strategy? Or are we also seeing the penchant for finding the laws that govern the behavior of men and events?

Bacon moves toward his conclusion by reminding his audience of how, since the last parliament, the country had been satisfied in its desire for an "invasive war" against Spain. Brief but colorful summaries of the Cadiz and Island voyages were presented to raise the spirit. "The second journey . . .was like a Tartar's or Parthian's bow, which shooteth backward, and had a most strong and violent effect and operation both in France and Flanders, so that our neighbors and confederates have reaped the harvest of it, and while the life-blood of

Spain went inward to the heart, the outward limbs and members trembled and could not resist" (9.88-89).

A passion for order and a remarkable gift for synthesis and metaphor are the basis of Bacon's parliamentary oratory. Even his brief remarks display these traits, suggesting an extraordinary concern with having the listener grasp and believe (and remember) what is said.[65] Only the dullest wits would have had a problem following his discourse. As in his writings, there is always an explicit order to his thoughts; no matter how complex the subject, the audience is carefully guided down a clearly marked path. "The course that I will take in the relation of that part of the speech which is committed to me shall be by division; for that will be the safest for my memory and readiest for your understanding."[66] Equally considerate are the images and examples that so deftly (and sometimes deceptively) bring the complicated or the ambiguous into focus. "The gentlemen," he complains in 1593 of the subsidy bill, "must sell their plate and the farmers their brass pots ere this will be paid. And as for us, we are here to search the wounds of the realm and not to skin them over."[67] Besides making him a pleasing speaker, Bacon's rhetorical abilities, especially his genius for summarizing other men's thoughts, ensured his selection as a spokesman for the Commons and a reporter of committees. Rawley's observation is appropriate: "I have often observed . . . that if he had occasion to repeat another man's words after him, he had an use and faculty to dress them in better vestments and apparel than they had before; so that the author should find his own speech much amended, and yet the substance of it still retained."[68] Yet we should be careful not to let our admiration for his obvious skill, or even the praises of contemporaries like Ben Jonson, persuade us that Bacon generally won the minds of his listeners. The very brilliance and facility of his speeches might well have annoyed those who knew themselves less talented or believed themselves more serious.[69] Nor should we assume that his use as a spokesman or reporter was a sign of the Commons' great respect for his person and his politics. In fact, the house was taking advantage of his talents, and he seems not to have been always happy with their "silent expectations" (10.347).

During these years, and, indeed, throughout his life, Bacon resided mainly at Grays Inn. The little self-contained world of lawyers and students was comfortable to him, and later, when he was Attorney-General, he would think of dedicating a volume of his "weighty and famous" pleadings to "my loving friends and fellows." Something, however, other than the law probably tied him to the place: perhaps its orderliness, perhaps its scholastic character, perhaps even its cheapness. Whatever the reason(s), he lived an insulated life, more acquainted with the law and court politics than with England or the world beyond.[70] Except for the years when he was Lord Chancellor, he seems to have always been busy in the Inn's affairs, and from 1608 to 1617—an unusually long tenure—he held the Treasurership. "Few men," he once said, "were so bound to their societies" as he was to Grays Inn. Certainly nowhere else did he ever find people so submissive to his will or so ready to acknowledge his genius. A similar explanation may lie behind Bacon's passion for gardens.[71] To read his 1625 essay "Of Gardens" is to listen to a man almost beside himself with the joy that comes from balancing and ordering the things of nature. "God Almighty first planted a Garden. And indeed it is the purest of human pleasures." At both Grays Inn and Gorhambury Bacon spent considerable time and money in satisfying this pleasure. Less successful, however, were his grandiose plans for building, which seem also to have sprung from that obsession with putting things in order. A story told by John Aubrey is revealing. "At Verulam is to be seen, in some few places, some remaines of the Wall of this Citie. This magnanimous Lord Chancellor had a great mind to have it made a Citie again: and he had designed it, to be built with great uniformity."[72] In his private pleasures, as well as in his public ambitions, his basic desire is always to achieve control by establishing order, or presuming it.[73]

In the spring of 1600 Bacon gave the Lent reading at Grays Inn on the Statute of Uses, "the most perfectly and exactly conceived and penned of any law in the book," but one that had continually received a "false and perverted exposition!" Chudleigh's Case six years before had initiated "a true and sound exposition," but since then, "as it cometh to pass always upon the first reforming of inveterate errors, many doubts and perplexed questions have risen, which are not yet resolved, nor the law thereupon settled" (7.395-96). Bacon is now the interpreter, not merely the advocate, of this crucial statute, and therefore he seeks to "dispose or digest the authorities and opinions which are in cases of uses in such order and method as they should take light one from another" (7.396). In doing so the philosopher is foreshadowed in a point of method. "The nature of an use is best discerned by considering, first, what it is not; and then what it is: for it is the nature of all human science and knowledge to proceed most safely by negative and exclusion, to what is affirmative and inclusive" (7.398). Bacon had followed this procedure in his argument in Chudleigh's Case—"In my order I will first endeavour to remove all prejudices."—but had presumably not yet thought to elevate a common legal mode of reasoning to a more general usage. Gradually, a method applicable to all "sciences" is being formulated.

The argument also evinces a sophistication not usually found—as Bacon intimates—in a mere lawyer. "I would wish all readers that expound statutes to do as scholars are willed to do; that is, first, to seek out the principal verb; that is, to note and single out the material words whereupon the statute is framed."[74] His manner of undoing the "knots" of language (whether English or Latin) is neat and convincing. The promise to "open the law upon doubts, and not to open doubts upon the law," is the more easily fulfilled because of his sensitivity to the nuances of language. The reductive tendency, too, is very much in evidence. "For the inception and progression of uses, I have, for a precedent of them, searched other laws; because states and commonwealths have common accidents" (7.407). And it is, perhaps, this very tendency that saved him from assuming that English practice derived from Roman law just because there was an analogy between the use and the *fideicommisum*.[75] That is, a mind given to searching for common rules and customs is less apt to be thinking in an 'evolutionary' pattern—unless the nature of the case called for it. And when Bacon provides us with a definition of the use, he gives in one sentence a splendid example of his perspective. "An use is no more but a general trust, when a man will trust the conscience of another better than his own estate and possession; which is an accident or event of human society which hath been and will be in all laws, and therefore was at the common law which is common reason" (7.415).

That same spring found the Earl of Essex back from his disastrous Irish expedition and in the custody of Lord Keeper Egerton at York House. Bacon had encouraged the Earl "to purchase honour" in Ireland and had provided him with occasional advice, but he could not have been surprised when things fell to pieces. "Your Lordship," he had told Essex in March of 1599, "is designed to a service of great merit and great peril; and as the greatness of the peril must needs include a like proportion of merit: so the greatness of the merit may include no small consequence of peril, if it be not temperately governed" (9.129-30). From the moment Essex returned to England Bacon was caught in a dilemma. Was he to serve the Queen, and so his own future, or Essex, a man legally in the wrong and politically in eclipse? For a time he could do both, but when disobedience grew to treason following "the branesik meeting" at Essex House, there was no longer a choice.[76]

Ironically, the downfall of Essex was to provide the greatest opportunity to date for Bacon's talents as lawyer and propagandist. He proved himself eminently worthy.[77] At the Earl's trial he stepped in at a critical moment and saved Coke from thoroughly muddling the Crown's position. The Attorney-General, fitting his argument to the particular facts of the case, had been unable to break down Essex's defense that he had intended no harm to the Queen or to the State, and that a legitimate fear of his enemies had prompted most of his actions on that fatal Sunday. Bacon refused to discuss the actual circumstances of the rising; instead, in a scornful brief profoundly typical of his mind, he aimed a mortal blow. "No man can be ignorant that knows matters of former ages, and all history makes it plain, that there was never any traitor heard of that durst directly attempt the seat of his liege prince, but he always coloured his practices with some plausible pretence."[78] By squeezing Essex into a type—thus bypassing the need for evidence of actual culpability—he is able to turn the Earl's defense into a confession of guilt. Later, Bacon came again to Coke's rescue when it seemed that the Earl was recovering the advantage. How could anyone, he claimed, be so credulous as to believe that "armed petitioners" went only as "suppliants to her Majesty?" Essex might hope to settle the question of intent by reference to conscience, but the law was satisfied to judge by the overt act. Once more the coils of a deadly analogy slipped around the Earl.

> It was not the company you carried with you, but the assistance you hoped for in the City which you trusted unto. The Duke of Guise thrust himself into the streets of Paris on the day of the Barricados in his doublet and hose, attended only with eight gentlemen, and found that help in the city which (thanks be to God) you failed of here. [9.230]

More lethal, if no more accurate, than his first comparison, this allusion climaxed the trial. Essex appears to have not replied to the speech and shortly afterwards was condemned.

Following the Earl's execution Bacon was called upon to write a justification of the government's actions during the long unseemly affair.[79] Provided with the relevant papers, he quickly completed the twenty-five page narrative, *A Declaration of the Practices and Treasons Attempted and Committed by Robert, late Earl of Essex, and his Complices,* and saw it published anonymously along with various supporting documents in April 1601. Two years later, when it became necessary for him to explain his part in the Earl's fall, he would try to dissociate himself from responsibility for the *Declaration* by arguing that he was working under very precise instructions and that his first draft was "made almost a new writing" by "certain principal counsellors."[80] But signs of paternity are not easily done away with. Essex joins Lopez and Squire as one of those traitors who scheme with preternatural skill. "He had long ago plotted it in his heart to become a dangerous supplanter of that seat, whereof he ought to have been a principal supporter; in such sort as now every man of common sense may discern not only his last actual and open treasons, but also his former more secret practices and preparations" (9.248). Bacon was, of course, only working out in detail the mode of argument he pursued at the trial itself. As a result there pervades the *Declaration* the assumption that Essex, whether *he* himself knew it or not, had conformed "to the nature of all usurping rebels" in his treachery. "But my Lord having spent the end of the summer . . . in digesting his own thoughts, with the help and conference of Master Cuffe, they had soon set down between them the ancient principle of traitors and conspirators, which was, *to prepare many, and to acquaint few*" (9.261, Bacon's emphasis). For his efforts as prosecutor and publicist Bacon was assigned £1200 out of the fine of one of the conspirators, the most ample gratuity he ever received from the Queen.

Bacon's Judas-like behavior at Essex's trial has always been regarded as the chief blot on his character. But it is doubtful that he himself ever recognized the moral scruple felt by contemporaries and later writers. Possessed always by a sense of his special fitness to serve the State, he willingly prosecuted Essex because the Earl had become a traitor, the most dangerous of men. No longer did Essex merit sympathy once intemperateness, and then disobedience, grew to disloyalty. The vigor and coldness of Bacon's attack suggest a clear conscience, and he is genuinely shocked when men will condemn his posture as springing solely from calculated self-interest. When he writes the *Apology* he will be telling the truth as he is able to know it; as with his 1593 subsidy speech and his impeachment, he is certain that he has not sinned. The final scene in the relationship of these two men, like so many scenes in Bacon's life, argues a fundamental blindness, not an ignoble character.

Despite his growing reputation as a lawyer,[81] Bacon found the twilight years of the Queen's reign frustrating. There is little evidence that his services were wanted.[82] His brother died in May 1601, a loss that was felt, one hopes, more deeply than Chamberlain implies. "Antony Bacon died not long since but so far in debt, that I thincke his brother is litle the better by him."[83] In the fall of the same year he would once again be a faithful man in parliament, instructing the members as to their duties—"I have been a member of this House these seven parliaments" (10.37)—and earnestly protesting that he did but deliver "my conscience" when defending the prerogative during the monopolies debate. There is eloquence and wit to these speeches, and sometimes much sense, but they also jar in their officiousness and their self-acclaim. The desire to be heard and thought wise is found again the following year, when, during a "dead vacation time," he sends an unsolicited letter of advice to Cecil on how to deal with Ireland. "But if it seem any error for me thus to intromit myself, I pray your Lordship believe, I ever loved her Majesty and the state, and now love yourself" (10.46). Prudent though the advice often is, the reader wonders how Cecil received proposals intended to make him appear "as good a patriot as you are thought a politic," by showing the world "that you have as well true arts and grounds of government as the facility and felicity of practice and negotiation" (10.45).

Perhaps the best index of Bacon's mind during this period is the *De Interpretatione Naturae Prooemium*.[84] Designed to serve as the introduction to some larger work, the *Proem* is an autobiographical fragment that rehearses with greater detail and more feeling the same argument as the 1592 letter to Burghley. Here is the man who believes himself "born for the service of mankind" and "fitted for nothing so well as for the study of Truth"; who was pressured by "birth and education," as well as the "opinions" of others, into a civil career, but who always believed that a "place of honour in the state" would enable him to command talents "to help me in my work"; and who now, realizing "my zeal was mistaken for ambition," has decided to devote himself entirely to advancing knowledge (10.84-87). The *Proem* cannot be faulted for its sincerity; this is undoubtedly how Bacon conceived of his life. But the words also rationalize the sense of failure. Past forty, he knows he has accomplished nothing to be remembered by.

he spring of 1603 was a time of freshened hopes, an opportunity for men—especially those who felt aggrieved or unrewarded—to forget the past. "I find myself as one awaked out of sleep"; Bacon wrote to his young friend Tobie Matthew, "which I have not been this long time" (10.73-74). Expectantly dispatching letters to the new King and the Scots officials close to him, he represented himself as a man "not . . . altogether unseen in the matters of this kingdom." His name, however, was unfamiliar across the border, at least by comparison with his brother Anthony, who had coordinated Essex's secret correspondence with James.[1] Realizing this he tried to appropriate some credit for himself by noting that he had been less "a stranger" to the exchange of letters than it had seemed at the time, and by resurrecting the memory of "my father, so long a principal counsellor in this your kingdom." The living were also called upon for help. To the Earl of Northumberland, a serious rival to Cecil for the Secretaryship, Bacon sent in early April a proclamation he thought the King should issue "to forerun his coming." He had been dissatisfied with the proclamation issued on March 24, which had been composed by Cecil and approved by James prior to Elizabeth's death, for instead of "cherishing, entertaining, and preparing . . . men's affections," it had merely pronounced the rightful succession of James and the readiness of the signers to uphold it. Bacon knew better what was needed. "I have conceived a draught, it being a thing familiar in my Mistress' times to have my pen used in public writings of satisfaction."[2] He even recommended its possible "uses." The Earl might either show it to the King, "which if your Lordship should do, then I would desire you to withdraw my name, and only signify that you gave some heads of directions of such a matter to one of whose style and pen you had some opinion," or hold it back and use it as "a kind of portraiture of that which I think worthy to be advised by your Lordship to the King" (10.67).

Though primarily intended as a ploy for gaining attention, this unnecessary (James's accession, as Bacon himself noted, was met with universal joy) and unsolicited proposal denotes a basic concern in Bacon's career and outlook. Thus far his experience in politics, whether as publicist or parliamentarian, had been confined to the task of persuading people with words. As a result, he had developed a high sensitivity—surely reinforced by his work as a lawyer—to the need for manipulating opinion, and an unrivaled skill in the techniques involved. This, together with his tart view of men and his experience of a Queen surpassed by none in winning hearts with words, predisposed Bacon to see politics as a matter of public relations and to exaggerate the degree to which problems were resolvable by rhetoric. "For although in true value," he would write in the *Advancement of Learning*, "it [rhetoric] is inferior to wisdom, . . . yet with people it is the more mighty: for so Salomon saith, *Sapiens corde appellabitur prudens, sed dulcis eloquio majora reperiet,* signifying that profoundness of wisdom will help a man to a name or admiration, but that it is eloquence that prevaileth in an active life" (3.409). Such an approach in itself did not render him unfit as a counselor, and in the years ahead he frequently offered sound advice. But his advice, significantly, was most often heeded precisely on those occasions when words were what was called for. And even then his concern for "some gracious declaration" was likely to be brushed aside by a King who imagined himself a vice-regent of God, and who (not unlike his predecessor) was inclined to believe that explanations detracted from authority.[3]

Ultimately, however, Bacon has had his revenge on those who would not listen. Because of his persuasiveness, subsequent generations have admired his analyses of events and, in particular, accepted his view that a better public image, attainable through a better public rhetoric, would have gone far to solving the King's complex dilemmas. While James may not have been as admired as his predecessor (although our sources for making such a judgment are limited), and it is probably true that popular sovereigns have an easier time of things, it is questionable whether any monarch (including Elizabeth—how often, after all, would the Golden Speech of 1601 have worked?) could have long evaded or overcome the King's problems by depending on words.

For the next four years, until he obtained the Solicitor-Generalship in 1607, Bacon waged an uninhibited campaign to gain favor. His object was to be employed, like his father before him, as "a principal counsellor in this your kingdom," and not to be regarded as merely an industrious member of the legal counsel whose pen might be occasionally called upon, or as one of the many loyal supporters of the Crown in the House of Commons. To achieve his goal he had to give evidence of his talents, his wisdom, and his loyalty. Unlike the situation that prevailed during his early years, Bacon had now to rely almost entirely on his own efforts; aside from Robert Cecil, his family connections were few and no longer significant. That he so determinedly relied on his pen is not surprising; the precedent had been set in Elizabeth's reign, and greater use reflected an awareness that time was passing him by. How much during these years the King, beleaguered as he was by suitors for "honour, Preferment to place, Credit about my Person, and Reward in matters of land or profit,"[4] actually noticed the small, middle-aged lawyer who lived in semi-seclusion with his dreams, is a moot point. Unmistakable, however, is the suitor's effort to write himself into recognition.

Bacon's first effort was the fragment, *Of the True Greatness of Britain,* a work normally assigned to a later date.[5] By redating it, we begin to sense the urgency of his ambition. Dedicated to the King, its manifest purpose was to inform James of the "forces and power" available to him as a result of the *de facto* joining of the kingdoms. What the King was to do with this potential is never made clear because it was not really a part of Bacon's purpose. He wished only to prepare a survey that would demonstrate his appreciation of some basic "principles" of politics, as well as a specific knowledge of the kingdoms, especially England. What better way was there to introduce his talents to a new king? By "forces and power" Bacon meant those conditions that were "proper to the amplitude and growth of states," those factors that were pertinent to the questions of growth and decline. "Here is no mention of religion, laws, policy. . . . that which is common to their [states] preservation, happiness, and all other points of well-being" (7.49). The "order" of argument is straightforward: "certain immoderate opinions" about the indices of greatness (e.g. largeness of territory, treasure) are reduced to "a true value and estimation"; infrequently cited but more "solid and principal" points (e.g. "fit situation" of territory) are introduced; and, finally, there is a "brief application" of both the corrected and "less observed . . . principles" to "these your kingdoms." Obviously the treatise owes its categories and most of its conclusions to Machiavelli,[6] a debt Bacon vaguely acknowledged. "Neither is the authority of Machiavel to be despised," he says when discounting riches as an accurate index of greatness, "specially in a matter whereof he saw the evident experience before his eyes in his own times and country" (7.55). It is a revealing statement. The reliability of one's own experiences in confirming or making political rules is, as we have seen, fundamental to Bacon. But it is scarcely self-evident that such a method is more certain to achieve truth, for the quality of the observer's perception may be defective. Machiavelli himself is a case in point of the difficulties involved;[7] later we' shall see the particular problems the method raised for Bacon. For the moment, however, we should recognize the feature that distinguishes his argument from Machiavelli's, and that is the copious analogies ("similitudes") drawn from nature that Bacon uses as both illustration and proof of his comments. Indeed, their frequency points to his next writing.

Sometime in late May or early June, Bacon quickly prepared and had published a short tract advising James to move prudently in realizing his dream of union between England and Scotland. What specifically prompted *A Brief Discourse Touching the Happy Union of the Kingdoms of England and Scotland* was a feeling Bacon returned with after first seeing the King. "He hasteneth to a mixture of both kingdoms and nations, faster perhaps than policy will conveniently bear" (10.77). The *Brief Discourse* was palpably designed to impress as well as to persuade a King whose reputation for learning had preceded him to his second throne.[8] Natural philosophy became the vehicle for a discussion of the desired union, since a wise King, the writer imagines, would appreciate "the congruity" existing "between the principles of nature and policy." Centuries ago, Bacon asserts, the kings of Persia had been schooled in magic to observe "the contemplations of nature and an application thereof to a sense politic; taking the fundamental laws of nature, with the branches and passages of them, as an original and first model, whence to take and describe a copy and imitation for government." Such wisdom, unfortunately, had almost disappeared in later times "because of the difficulty for one man to embrace both philosophies." Nevertheless, for a gift to a King "studious to conjoin contemplative virtue and active virtue together," the author attempts "to revive" the ancient practice "in the handling of one particular."

Having proved with several examples a manifest correspondence between "the government of the world" and "the government of a state," Bacon takes up the specific issue of unions. He distinguishes, following the "best observers in nature," between *compositio* and *mistio*, the former being a "putting together of bodies without a new form," and the latter a "putting together of bodies under a new form." Both in nature and politics the effect of *compositio* is strife, while the result of *mistio* is harmony. Vergil is quoted to show how Roman history offers proof that unless a new form, a *commune vinculum*, is created, "the old forms will be at strife and discord." A few words are then said about the components of integration (e.g., sovereignty, language, laws), and the King reminded that the conditions of a perfect mixture are time, "for the natural philosophers say well, that *compositio* is *opus hominis* and *mistio opus naturae*," and the realization that the greater must draw the less, "so we see when two lights do meet, the greater doth darken and drown the less" (10.90-98).

The King did not follow this intelligent advice, and even a less contrived warning would not have changed his mind. But though Bacon's instincts were right, the tract itself betrays a weakness common to his writings and speeches, one that arose directly from his meticulous care to adopt persuasive modes of address. There is simply too much cleverness. Arguments tend to grow woolly, leaving the reader unconvinced and even a little perplexed. Hoping to please, Bacon often ends up posturing.

The argument of the *Brief Discourse* also reflects a philosophical position Bacon was attempting to articulate in several unfinished pieces of the same period. Format was not purely a matter of flattery. He seems to be feeling his way toward a synoptic view of the world, one that would derive rules relevant to all of existence.[9] In the *Cogitationes de Natura Rerum* (1604) he begins to sketch his own version of atomistic materialism, although most of it was borrowed from Democritus. In the *Valerius Terminus* (1603), on the other hand, which was primarily conceived as a summons to men to commit themselves, without fear of "God or priest," to studying nature in order to increase "the power and kingdom of mankind," he suggests that the different "sciences" can aid each other in the "framing or correcting" of "axioms," and that there exists a general set of axioms by which *all* sciences can be individually tested. Thus, when Bacon says "there is a great affinity and consent between the rules of nature, and the true rules of policy" (10.90), he is neither mouthing stale images nor blindly following the lead of his contemporaries, who quite matter of factly saw the world through a web of analogies.[10] He is, instead, trying to move away from the passively descriptive character of such thinking, and hopes to charge it with the task of offering greater certainty. For if a rule is discovered to operate throughout existence it may be said to possess greater validity when applied to a specific part.

"Gracious acceptation" is all that Bacon received from the King for the *Brief Discourse,* unless the knighthood he obtained in July, which seems to have been the work of Robert Cecil, was also meant to be token thanks. His wish, however, to be granted what he sneeringly called this "almost prostituted title" at the Coronation—a splendid chance to be conspicuous—and not "be merely gregarious in a troop" was disappointed. Two days before the Coronation he was knighted at Whitehall along with three hundred other worthies. Nevertheless, he kept his pen at work. In August or September he composed and sent off to the King the *Certain Considerations Touching the Better Pacification and Edification of the Church of England.*[11] Once again he had chosen a timely topic. The accession of a Scottish king had revived Puritan hopes of further reform in the doctrine and government of the Anglican church, a possibility considered anathema by the bishops. After a decade of relative quiet on religious questions, controversy flared again in press and pulpit. Characteristically, Bacon assumes that detachment guarantees wisdom, and employs a favorite image to certify his view. "Finding that it is many times seen that a man that standeth off, and somewhat removed from a plot of ground, doth better survey it and discover it than those which are upon it, I thought it not impossible but that I, as a looker on, might cast mine eyes upon some things which the actors themselves . . . did not or would not see" (10.103). And, unquestionably, there is a temperateness of expression and sanity of viewpoint that is very appealing. His proposals were designed to eliminate grievances that cost more in reputation and influence to defend than they would to abolish, to set the clergy on a better economic footing, and, most importantly, to reduce the sources of conflict between the established church and those pressing sincerely for moderate reform.

Perhaps, however, it is a little too easy for us to admire Bacon's plan "to find out the golden mediocrity, in the establishment of that which is sound, and in the reparation of that which is corrupt and decayed." For the method he employs in discussing "things not properly appertaining to my profession" raises suspicions. From the outset he assumes a parallel identity for church and state, arguing that the "ecclesiastical state" needs to be "purged and restored by good and wholesome laws" no less often than the civil state. Protests against his analogy are quickly smothered in a metaphor.

> But if it be said to me that there is a difference between civil causes and ecclesiastical, they may as well tell me that churches and chapels need no reparations though houses and castles do: whereas commonly, to speak truth, dilapidations of the inward and spiritual edification of the Church of God are in all times as great as the outward and material. [10.105]

Bacon's tidy view of the church as a political entity extends to its very foundations. In his reading of the Scriptures, for example, he finds that God has allowed to church government the same freedom he has to civil government. Only the "general grounds of justice and manners" of civil government are imposed by God, the policies and forms are left to men. "So likewise in Church matters, the substance of doctrine is immutable, and so are the general rules of government, but for rites and ceremonies, and for the particular hierarchies, policies, and disciplines of church, they be left at large" (10.107-108). But it is in the treatment of the "government of Bishops," much the longest section of the tract, that the method of argument breaks down.

Bacon accepts the episcopal form of church government. Nevertheless, there are two corruptions to be rooted out. The first is the bishops' "sole exercise" of their authority, whereby they give orders alone, excommunicate alone, and judge alone, all of which "seems to be a thing almost without example in government." Citing several English examples, Bacon argues that "in all courts the principal person hath ever either colleagues or assessors." Thus, this practice of the bishops simply cannot have been always so; the deans and chapters must "at the first" have served as "councils" to the bishops. How then did this change? "It is probable that the Dean and Chapter stuck close to the Bishops in matters of profit and the world, and would not leese their hold; but in matters of jurisdiction (which they counted but a trouble and attendance) they suffered the Bishops to encroach and usurp, and so the one continueth and the other is lost" (10.110). The ingenuity and even possible correctness of the explanation should not hide from us how Bacon arrives at it. Having first linked the ecclesiastical and civil states, he is able to explain the development of the former by what he knows about the latter. The presumed analogy enables him to fill gaps in his knowledge. In his second objection to the bishops, "the deputation of their authority," Bacon has his method perform even stranger tricks. "The Bishop is a judge," he asserts, "and for experience, there was never any Chancellor of England made a deputy; there was never Judge in any court made a deputy." Once again certain that *ab initio non fuit ita,* Bacon must explain how the practice was born.

> But it is probable that bishops when they gave themselves too much to the glory of the world, and became grandes in kingdoms, and great counsellors to princes, then did they deleague their proper jurisdiction as things of too inferior a nature for their greatness; and then, after the similitude and imitation of kings and counts palatine, they would have their chancellors and judges. [10.111]

As a result, the bishops are reduced, both in action and thought, to a prescribed model.

If we leave aside Bacon's specific recommendations, and look instead at the *Certain Considerations* as a piece of reasoning, we can obtain further insight into his mind. To begin with, it must be recognized that when Bacon presupposes a basic equivalence between church and state he is sincere; the man devoid of religious feeling has no more difficulty seeing the church and its offices as simply another civil institution than he does imagining himself an objective observer. But having forged the analogy Bacon is obliged to explain the unknown (how bishops came to depute authority) solely on the basis of the known (the fact that judges do not). That is, "the examples and rules of government" become his source both for judging the conduct of the church as it exists today, and for knowing its history. The catchword here is "probable." Necessarily Bacon is led to rationalize the past according to what he knows and approves about the present.[12] Thus, we can see how the working life and the bent of his intellect supported one another; what instinctively he was predisposed to do involves a process particularly suitable to the law, if it is not, indeed, a requisite of it. For whether examining the meaning of a statute, where words are one's only source for knowing, or building a case out of a pile of miscellaneous evidence, the opinion in the present is used to shape the past. Indeed, there is no essential reason for knowing what was *really* intended by the framers of a statute,[13] or what *really* happened in a crime. As a man continually, if not always happily, practicing the law Bacon was inevitably engaged in such reasoning. But because it is not a method conducive to discovering what is unknown, particularly where language is either unavailable or irrelevant as a possible medium for knowing, Bacon will flounder when he actually tries to do science, as distinguished from his attempts to establish a method for doing it. Later it will be seen why William Harvey's famous dictum, "He writes Philosophy like a Lord Chancellor," is at least as descriptive as it is pejorative. And what this meant for the writing of history will be made clear in the final chapter.

By the end of 1603 Bacon had failed to gain the King's attention with private advices. Moreover, his quasi-retirement (or exclusion) from the government's legal business prevented him from showing what he could do as an advocate.[14] But the convening of parliament in March of 1604 offered a splendid opportunity for a display of skills and readiness. When, for example, he addressed James while presenting the Commons' petition on purveyance, Bacon went far beyond the needs of the occasion to commend the King's "course of government."[15] Indeed, the common misconceptions as to his role in this session stem, logically enough, from the failure to appreciate how much he desired to convince the King of his worthiness. It is generally thought that Cecil, who now sat in the Lords and who had arranged for a seat at Ipswich for Bacon, systematically used his cousin as the Crown's spokesman in the Commons since only two privy councilors had obtained places in the lower house.[16] As with the assertion that Bacon was the "official" leader in 1597, this interpretation is based on a faulty assumption: because Bacon supports the Crown he is therefore working hand in glove with officials. Hope for advancement, however, could alone account for his outspoken support, since if he was to show the King just what he could do for him, it would be virtually impossible for Bacon *not* to have given the appearance of being an instructed agent. Furthermore, the hard evidence that does exist also supports the conclusion that Bacon was acting essentially independently, even though he and Cecil would obviously have sometimes discussed business.[17]

Equally unconvincing is the argument that emphasizes Bacon's role as a "mediator," as the man who deliberately took it upon himself to preserve a "balance" between King and Commons.[18] Once again appearances are deceiving, for though Bacon undoubtedly tried to reconcile differences that arose, he did so out of a desire to help the King's cause, not out of some principled regard for a nebulous constitutional theory. Besides, the King himself took the lead in seeking compromises. On almost every issue, beginning with the Goodwin-Fortescue election, James backed off with gracious, almost apologetic, words when it seemed he had gone too far, and his decision not to ask for supply underlines that desire to please which had (to date) characterized his actions since his accession. Finally, implicit in such an argument is the still not buried assumption that Crown and Commons were, by 1604, already in "conflict." But unless we are to insist that all quarrels—the very stuff, after all, of politics—be made to walk a path to revolution, we ought to be careful about concluding that either the King or the situation required a "mediator" in 1604.

Subsequent sessions, however, of James's first parliament were to see Bacon actively collaborating with the government. By 1606 he had proven himself useful and faithful, a judgment arising in large measure, perhaps, from his devoted industry in working for the King's greatest desire, union of the kingdoms.[19] In the 1606-7 session he seems to have borne the main responsibility for this project, delivering in the squabble over the post-nati his most famous speech. How typical it was! "Whosoever looketh into the principles of estate, must hold that it is the mediterrane countries, and not the maritime, which need to fear surcharge of people."[20] Whether countering the opposition's case, or advancing his own, Bacon relies on "rules" or "principles" of "estate" sanctioned either by history, nature, or reason. Three years later he will need more than eloquence to uphold the royal prerogative, as the issue of impositions tested the capacities of the best lawyers in the Commons. Now clearly identified as a supporter of the King, he depends often on his long experience as "a parliament man" to find convincing arguments. The memory of Elizabeth's firm handling of parliament emerges, and gradually her government as a whole will set itself in his mind as a precedent. "The advice of the prophet will teach us, *state super antiquas vias et videte quaenam sit via recta et ambulate.*"[21] But even though his speeches were models of learning and wit, it is unclear that they actually moved his listeners to belief. "I was," said John Savile on April 11, 1606, when replying to Bacon's defense of impositions, "by the Speech of the learned Gentleman that first spake . . . almost transported to the other opinion untill I now upon hearing more have further considered on the matter: . . . I remember . . . when I was a Boy I heard them say Mercury was a Thiefe, at which I marvailed in regard they also said he was a God, but since I came to better Judgement I perceive it is meant that Eloquence whereof Mercury was esteemed God, is the Thiefe."[22]

Nor can we assume that because Bacon gradually became one of the government's chief spokesmen in the House of Commons the King prized him as a counselor. Paradoxically, it is likely that his talents, while useful politically to the King, were antipathetic to him in personal terms. For Bacon, whether in speech or on paper, whether addressing the King or his own niece,[23] increasingly sounded the pedagogue as he grew older. Thoughts and recommendations were invariably suffused with a rhetoric of abstractions; the would-be counselor recites more often like a philosopher as he soars from the advice of the moment to the rule that corroborates his opinion. The following comes from the *Certain Articles or Considerations Touching the Union of the Kingdoms of England and Scotland,* an unsolicited memorandum Bacon sent to the King in the summer of 1604 while preparing for the upcoming meeting of the Commission of the Union.

> Not that I am of opinion that all the questions which I now shall open were fit to be in the consultation of the Commissioners propounded. For I hold nothing so great an enemy to good resolution as the making of too many questions; specially in assemblies which consist of many. For Princes, for avoiding of distraction, must take many things by way of admittance; and if questions must be made of them, rather to suffer them to arise from others, than to grace them and authorize them as propounded from themselves. [10.219]

The tone of the statement demands more attention than its possible validity. How did Bacon appear to a man inclined himself to pedantic pronouncements? Did the officious suitor seem to be a "simple schoole-man, that onely knowes matters of kingdomes by contemplation,"[24] the kind of man that James, who prided himself on knowing "both the theoricke and practicke" of kingship, said he scorned? Certainly there is no evidence of intimacy between the two men, a fact which in itself goes a long way to explaining why Bacon never exerted much influence on the King.[25]

In May 1604 Bacon published his *Apology in Certain Imputations Concerning the late Earl of Essex.* The reputation of the Earl—never judged a traitor by the public—as well as the fortunes of his friends, had begun to increase the moment James, on his journey south, had declared his love and respect for "the most noble knight" England had ever raised, and followed his declaration with an embrace of Essex's young son. Soon enough there was sniping at those who had betrayed Essex, as can be seen from the letters in Cecil's correspondence from men desperate to clear themselves of guilt. To James it most likely made no difference where one had stood in 1601.[26] But public gossip and his own small strides undoubtedly persuaded Bacon that Essex had become in death an even more serious obstacle to the progress of his fortunes than he had thought him to be in life.[27]

The *Apology* was composed in the form of a letter to the Earl of Devonshire, formerly Lord Mountjoy, a man presumably in a position to verify the truth of the work because of his close connection with the individuals and incidents involved. Bacon wanted to show that far from bearing any responsibility for Essex's fall, he had always served him faithfully, and had occasionally even sacrificed his own progress in doing so. With the public record demonstrably against him, Bacon was obliged to prove his case by recalling private conversations between himself and the other two principal parties, Essex and Elizabeth. "I have set down as near as I could . . . the very words and speeches that were used" (10.160). The resultant brief is unconvincing, although for generations the conversations have been quoted as if the *Apology* were a reliable historical source. Wherever Bacon's statements can be checked with earlier letters it can be seen that his memory is not to be trusted,[28] while the actual words he puts into the mouths of Elizabeth and Essex, besides their manifest tendency to reflect favorably on himself, too clearly echo his own style of speaking.[29] There is no reason, however, to believe that Bacon deliberately set out to distort the past; his conscience was clear. "My scope and desire is . . . that you may perceive how honest a heart I ever bare to my Sovereign and to my Country, and to that Nobleman" (10.142).

Nevertheless, there is a substantial element of calculation in the *Apology,* and rhetorical embellishment smoothed more than one sharp corner. In defending his actions, Bacon was careful to present himself as a wise and trusty counselor who always offered both Essex and the Queen prudent advice. "I never," he protests when registering his disapproval of Essex's going to Ireland, "in any thing in my life-time dealt with him in like earnestness by speech, by writing, and by all the means I could devise. For I did as plainly see his overthrow chained as it were by destiny to that journey, as it is possible for any man to ground a judgment upon future contingents" (10.146). Elizabeth, too, proved obstinate; she would not follow Bacon's advice to recall Essex to a position of high favor at court, "which course, . . . if it had been taken, then all had been well" (10.147). Gradually the impression is gained that when Elizabeth and Essex disregarded the author's advice they suffered, and when they followed it all went well. Indeed, Bacon depicts himself as a man at the very center of business, a self-aggrandizing portrayal that might aid present hopes but which the facts do not support. And by a clever device he continually reminds the reader of his loyalty. In every conversation reported with Essex the Earl is cautioned about his friend's order of allegiance, that he would "forsake his King [a revealing substitution] rather than forsake God, and forsake his friend rather than forsake his King" (10.141-42). How persuasive all this ingenuity was with Bacon's contemporaries is not known, although the work was obviously popular since it was printed twice in 1604 and once in 1605.[30] The only contemporary reference, admittedly opaque, suggests it was read as sport. "I have sent you Sir Francis Bacon's apology to serve you for an hour's recreation. Kinge the fool calls it the philosoter [*sic*] of his wit."[31]

The last and greatest work to come from Bacon's pen before he acquired office was the *Advancement of Learning,* which went on sale in late October 1605. While it has been recognized that political ambition influenced him to undertake the book,[32] the text itself is still read and admired as if it were untainted by mundane considerations. This particular oversight, like so many others, stems from the desire to separate the good philosopher from the worldly politician, a separation that Bacon wished to believe himself, and which the commentators, beginning with Rawley, have consistently reproduced. Not surprisingly, a letter accompanying a presentation copy of the book to Sir Thomas Bodley struck the familiar chord.

> I think no man may more truly say with the Psalm *Multum incola fuit anima mea,* than myself. For I do confess, since I was of any understanding, my mind hath in effect been absent from that I have done; and in absence are many errors which I do willingly acknowledge; and amongst the rest this great one that led the rest; that knowing myself by inward calling to be fitter to hold a book than to play a part, I have led my life in civil causes; for which I was not very fit by nature, and more unfit by the preoccupation of my mind. [10.253]

In years to come Bacon will frequently employ this line from Psalm 120 as a tag of identification.[33]

If we read the first book of the *Advancement* closely, remembering the context in which it was written, we cannot fail to hear the author persistently urging his worthiness. "There belongeth to kings from their servants both tribute of duty and presents of affection. In the former of these I hope I shall not live to be wanting, according to my

most humble duty, and the good pleasure of your Majesty's employments" (3.261). Still dissatisfied with his lot, Bacon uses learning—as
he had law and parliament—as a platform to air his hopes and
frustrations. This is not to insist that the *Advancement* is merely
self-advertisement; to impugn the interest in learning or deny the
excitement and eloquence of the work would be foolish. It would be
equally foolish, however, to ignore the symptoms (and tactics) of
chronic suitorship.

The first book was given over to a defense of learning in which
Bacon first refutes the accusers of his client and then summons his
own witnesses. Much of the argument was sacked from earlier
fragments, and the posture is that of the lawyer-orator speaking to a
single judge, in this case the King.[34] Nowhere in the entire work, in
fact, does he address himself to a wider audience, a curious oversight
considering his desire to "ring a bell to call other wits together."

The cross-examination of the complainants often strays into
self-recommendation. It is not learning per se, but learned men
whom Bacon conceives to be under attack, and the thrust of the attack
is that too much learning leaves a man unfit for civil life. Bacon's
object is to reverse that argument, to show that learning is indispens-
able to the business of life. What he says recalls the preface to the
*Maxims of the Law:* the empiric man, whether as physician or lawyer,
knows only cases out of his "experience," and therefore lacks the
understanding that would make him truly effective. "So by like reason
it cannot be but a matter of doubtful consequence, if states be
managed by empiric statesmen, not well mingled with men grounded
in learning."[35] Each of the common slanders against learned men is
examined and shown to be wrong. For example, far from being
slothful, "only learned men love business as an action according to
nature, as agreeable to health of mind as exercise is to health of body,
taking pleasure in the action itself, and not in the purchase: so that of
all men they are the most indefatigable, if it be towards any business
which can hold or detain their mind."[36] Nor will he accept the opinion
that learning softened the mind for business. "For if by a secret
operation it make men perplexed and irresolute, on the other side by
plain precept it teacheth them when and upon what ground to
resolve; yea, and how to carry things in suspense without prejudice till

they resolve" (3.271). Particularly heated is his defense against the accusation that learned men are unreliable as servants because they are too concerned with their own well-being. The charge was better brought, he insists, against the "corrupter sort of mere politiques, that have not their thoughts established by learning in the love and apprehension of duty, nor never look abroad into universality" (3.279). It hardly needs saying that Bacon was here responding to charges he had often heard leveled at himself.[37]

Having dismissed ignorant opinions, Bacon begins assessing "the true value" of learning "by testimonies and arguments divine and human." Only a few pages are spent consulting "divine" testimony, and they are organized into a brief historical survey showing the basic respect for knowledge operant in God's plans for the world and regularly appearing in his servants. Turning to human proofs the same method is used. History shows that "under learned princes and governors there have been ever the best times." The reason is that such rulers possess "those notions of religion, policy, and morality" that keep them from "errors and excesses." Attached to this theorem is a self-regarding corollary. "And senators or counsellors likewise which be learned, do proceed upon more safe and substantial principles than counsellors which are only men of experience; the one sort keeping dangers afar off, whereas the other discover them not till they come near hand, and then trust to the agility of their wit to ward or avoid them" (3.302-303). This sentence summarizes neatly the image of himself that Bacon offered in the *Apology;* the model he proposes as the kind of counselor kings should seek describes his own sense of himself. Foresight and "principles," as might be expected, were for him two aspects of the same condition of knowing. If a man had knowledge he necessarily (if his mind, like Bacon's, was predisposed to expanding fact into rule) had principles. And since principles reflected inherent order, the capacity for both foresight and predictability necessarily followed. Over the years Bacon will make foresight the prime index of political wisdom, and continually applaud his own example.

Except for a brief, flattering mention of Elizabeth, the human examples used by Bacon in this argument are all taken from antiquity. Repeating Machiavelli and foreshadowing Gibbon, he recounts the several virtues of the good Antonine emperors, "all learned or singular favourers and advancers of learning." He then backtracks and takes a more extended look at Alexander the Great and Julius Caesar. Both men were great favorites of the King, who had recommended them to his son in the *Basilikon Doron*.[38] Bacon uses the recorded words of each man to show that learning helped to make them more able, and the lessons he finds in their words echo his own.

> Weigh also that excellent taxation of an error ordinary with counsellors of princes, that they counsel their masters according to the model of their own mind and fortune, and not of their masters; when upon Darius' great offers Parmenio had said, 'Surely I would accept these offers, were I as Alexander'; saith Alexander, 'So would I, were I as Parmenio.' [3.310]

Years before he had often told Essex that he would not "frame you best to mine own turn," but give advice as he thought best for the Earl; the same point had also been at the heart of the *Apology*. Bacon's choice for his last example from antiquity is perhaps most revealing of all. It is Xenophon, from whom we hear no words, but whose story conjures up Bacon's dream.

> This young scholar or philosopher, after all the captains were murdered in parley by treason, conducted those ten thousand foot through the heart of all the king's high countries from Babylon to Graecia in safety, in despite of all the king's forces, to the astonishment of the world, and the encouragement of the Grecians in time succeeding to make invasion upon the kings of Persia; as was after purposed by Jason the Thessalian, attempted by Agesilaus the Spartan, and achieved by Alexander the Macedonian; all upon the ground of the act of that young scholar. [3.313-14]

The writer of that carefully constructed passage, where the rising clauses act out the journey of Xenophon,[39] was himself no longer young, and scarcely a soldier, but he had dreamed all his life of performing similar feats.

In May 1606 Bacon finally married. A bizarre combination of pomp, wit, and ambition marked his wedding day as it did his whole life.

> He was clad from top to toe in purple, and hath made himself and his wife such store of fine raiments of cloth of silver and gold that it draws

deep into her portion. The dinner was kept at his father-in-law Sir John
Packington's lodging . . . where his chief guests were the three knights,
Cope, Hicks, and Beeston; and upon this conceit (as he said himself)
that since he could not have my L. of Salisbury [Cecil] in person, which
he wished, he would have him at least in his representative body.[40]

The young wife, Alice Barnham, a girl of no more than fifteen years
and the daughter of a deceased London alderman, brought with her a
dowry of over £200 a year as well as £1000 in cash which Bacon used
in designing and building himself a house at Gorhambury.[41] The
marriage itself was less productive. No children, no evidence of
affection (the two lived apart much of the time), and a codicil to
Bacon's last will revoking, "for just and great causes," all that he had
earlier granted to his wife. Her remarriage eleven days after his death
to a gentleman usher in the household at Gorhambury suggests the
cause. Rawley, however, supposed the marriage to have been marked
by "much conjugal love and respect." Since then silence has covered
the domestic side of Bacon's life. But if we have few facts, we have the
essay "Of Marriage and Single Life" to suggest its sterility.

On June 25, 1607, the long struggle for office finally bore fruit:
Bacon was appointed Solicitor-General. At the age of forty-six he had
finally arrived. The office was granted for services rendered and
anticipated, though the question of what those services were might
have received very different answers from the parties involved. Bacon
was brought inside "the door" for his legal and rhetorical skills; it was
assumed that his opinions were in sympathy with the King's. In
addition to the issue of the union, the recent and still unresolved
squabble over the jurisdiction of the Council in the Marches, for
which he had drawn up papers suggesting arguments the Crown
might employ, had demonstrated not only his forensic skills but his
respect for a strong prerogative.

> The King holdeth not his prerogatives of this kind [to establish a court
> of equity] mediately from the law, but immediately from God, as he
> holdeth his Crown; and though other prerogatives by which he
> claimeth any matter of revenue, or other right pleadable in his ordinary
> courts of Justice, may be there disputed, yet his sovereign power, which
> no Judge can censure, is not of that nature; and therefore whatsoever
> partaketh or dependeth thereon, being matter of government and not

of law, must be left to his managing by his Council of State. And that this is necessary to the end of all government, which is preservation of the public, may in this particular appear.[42]

Bacon was, logically enough, raised to the Solicitor-Generalship so that he might be used more advantageously by a government increasingly in need of a talented advocate.

The man himself, however, had finally the taste of power on his tongue. Haughty confidence oozes from even the occasional letters of this period. "The great and daily travels which I take in his Majesty's service," he informs Sir Vincent Skinner, an officer of the Exchequer (and an "ancient" acquaintance) who had delayed paying out a small grant to Bacon, deserve "due respect." Small perquisites such as requesting and receiving a knighthood for his brother-in-law, John Constable, are now his for the asking.[43] And what pleasure it must have given him to pen the following words to Cecil at New Year tide. "Having no gift to present you with in any degree proportionable to my mind, I desire nevertheless to take the advantage of a ceremony to express myself to your Lordship; it being the first time I could make the like acknowledgment, when I stood out of the person of a suitor" (11.12). There were also large visions of future services. He writes to Henry Perse, secretary to the Deputy in Ireland, requesting to know "how things pass in that kingdom," and to an old friend, Sir John Davies, Attorney-General in Ireland, thanking him for a "discourse" on recent problems in that troubled kingdom. "I would be glad," he tells Davies, "to hear often from you, and to be advertised how things pass, whereby to have some occasion to think some good thoughts" (11.6). The object of these soundings is to be able to advise the King.

> I know your Majesty shall not want the information of persons expert and industrious, which have served you there and know the region: nor the advice of a grave and prudent council of estate here, which know the pulses of the hearts of people, and the ways and passages of conducting great actions. . . . Yet notwithstanding in a thing of so public a nature it is not amiss for your Majesty to hear variety of opinion.[44]

Translated, Bacon is urging his familiar cautions. Beware the advice of "empirics," in this instance those who know only Ireland, and "rationalists," those, like the privy council, who are so "busied with a world of affairs" that they could give only theoretical advice. What the

King needs instead is a man with a uniquely balanced outlook like himself, and a sure understanding of the principles of politics.

In the same summer that he became Solicitor-General Bacon composed the *Cogitata et Visa,* one of his more admired demolitions of the old learning. Though never published during his life, the work was passed around to friends for their approval, and it is perhaps best understood when viewed together with two other unpublished works, the *Temporis Partus Masculus* (1603) and the *Redargutio Philosophiarium* (1608). Each work has the same purpose: to disclose the errors and stupidities of the traditional schools of philosophy, and to point out a new (though as yet obscurely marked) path in which learning can advance. The same complaints voiced often in the same language appear in all these tracts, though some modern commentators discern a more acute historical sense operating in the later works. This is probably an illusion stemming from a change in format, rather than a sign that there had been any serious reconsideration of views already announced in 1592;[45] rhetorical ends, not philosophical, are being served. A brief look at these formats is revealing.

The *Temporis Partus Masculus,* a work that embarrasses Bacon scholars on account of its excessively abusive treatment of past philosophers, is composed in the form of an oration addressed by an older man to a person, obviously younger, whom he continually refers to as "son." Although structured, like the first book of the *Advancement of Learning,* as an oration, the criticism is imbued with the outlook of a prosecutor. Censuring the traditional ideas, the older man hopes to prepare his "dear boy" (*fili suavissime*) to accept new truths, from which shall come salvation. "Take heart, then, my son, and give yourself to me so that I may restore you to yourself."[46] The echo of Jesus is not surprising in this early work since Bacon had taken special pains in the *Valerius Terminus* (1603) to show that God actually encouraged man to acquire knowledge of nature, "a work truly divine."[47] And the speaker's benevolent tone when speaking to the boy contrasts sharply with his harsh indictment of the old philosophers. "I shall hand on to you, with the most loyal faith, out of the profoundest care for the future of which I am capable, after prolonged examination both of the state of nature and the state of the human mind, by the most legitimate method, the instruction I have to convey."[48] Much less emotional is the *Cogitata et Visa,* which consists of nineteen identically structured paragraphs. Each stands as a self-contained discourse, while the argument as a whole moves from revealing the causes for the failure of traditional philosophy to predicting the omens and suggesting the methods for the philosophy that will replace it. The curious aspect of the format is the third person mode of address. *"Franciscus Bacon sic cogitavit"* are the opening words of the first paragraph, and each succeeding paragraph begins *"cogitavit et illud"* and ends with *"Itaque visum est ei"* or some slight variation thereof. As a result, the reader's attention is fixed more on the thinker than on the thought. The format of the *Redargutio Philosophiarium* is more imaginative. A brief preface introduces the reader to a scholar working at a noble task. "I am preparing a refutation of philosophies but know not how to begin." The scholar then mentions a recent visit by a friend just back from France, who assured him that he was not alone in his labors. For while in Paris the friend heard a lecture given by a man unidentified but described as having a "peaceful and serene air, save that his face had become habituated to the expression of pity." The remainder of the tract is taken up with the unidentified lecturer's criticism of traditional philosophy.

Beyond the sameness of their argument, all three tracts are characterized by the manifest centrality of the speaker. This in itself might be thought unworthy of notice since Bacon was obviously trying out different formats to express the same set of ideas. But something more than rhetorical experiment is involved, for both the orator of the *Temporis Partus Masculus* and the lecturer (not to mention the man speaking in the preface) of the *Redargutio Philosophiarium*—as well as the father who will appear later in the *New Atlantis*—are examples of what Bacon believed the true philosopher ought to be.[49] Compassion for mankind is his identifying mark. Furthermore, this figure is quite obviously a literary formulation of how Bacon always presented himself when speaking of his "vast contemplative ends."[50] To place these tracts side by side with the 1592 letter to Burghley and the *Proem* of 1603 is to see an argument become a person—undoubtedly a logical transference in a man burdened with an extraordinary self-consciousness.

Equally intriguing is the *Commentarius Solutus,* a lengthy set of reminders and advices to himself dating from the summer of 1608. The memoranda, jotted down from July 25 to August 6, included artful strategems to advance his political fortunes and schedules of scientific projects to be taken up in the future, as well as a review of his financial situation (which had measurably improved since obtaining the Solicitor-Generalship) and *"memoriae valetudinis,"* (giving the lie to Rawley's protests that he did not indulge in physic) (1.17). Obviously not intended to be scanned by any eyes but his own, the political notes have been the object of execration ever since they were first published. They reveal a man very anxious to make his name and not, it seems, very scrupulous about his methods. To win the King is the common theme; Bacon speaks now to himself as he used to speak to Essex.[51]

> Keeping a cowrs of accesse in the begynnyng of every term and vacac. w^th a memoriall, the one being a tyme of execution, the other of praeparacion. To attend some tyme his repasts and to fall into a cowrse of famil. discowrs. [11.41]

Strategies were also needed for clearing away those blocking his path.

> To have in mynd and use y^e Att. weakenes^s . . . the exorbitant assur. to y^e Cytye, in w^h so great estate was ingaged as y^e K could not help himself by any other assur. . . . weak in Gunters cavse. . . . To full of cases and distinctions. . . . No gift with his penne in proclamacions and y^e like.[52]

The indignation, however, at these entries is misconceived because it turns our mind to the wrong questions.

Actually, there is nothing in the *Commentarius Solutus* that any modestly ambitious politician would be ashamed to recognize in himself. How many, though, would need, or be willing, to write down such thoughts? Further, why do these private notes, whose declared purpose was "for better help of memory and judgment," both reverberate with the advice Bacon was wont to give others, and cast their author in relation to their intended reader precisely as Bacon himself stood to the world? It is as if his mind were totally intellectualized, totally in control of its reality; a mind incapable, therefore, of seeing deeply because it lacks the capacity for feeling its way to knowledge; a mind that sincerely believes itself always right because it takes in only what fits its self-inspired categories; a mind for which 'double-think' is habitual.[53] Is it any wonder that Bacon can imagine that his play-acting will convince others?

> To corresp. w[th] Salsb. [Cecil] in a habite of naturall but nowayes perilous boldness, and in vivacity, invention, care to cast and enterprise but with dew caution, for this maner I judg both in his nature freeth ye standes, and in his ends pleaseth him best and promiseth most use of me. [11.52].

Or that other men must have seen through his wiles so easily? There is, in brief, something naive, something disturbingly obtuse about the *Commentarius Solutus*.

At about the same time as Bacon was penning these reminders to himself he composed the *In felicem memoriam Reginae Elizabethae*, a work that has served intentionally or otherwise as the model for every praising portrait done since. It was intended to defend Elizabeth's reputation against the attacks of Catholic pamphleteers, and contains little that had not already been said in the propaganda written during her reign. Bacon passed the memorial around for friends to see and even tried to get De Thou to use it in his history.[54] Although it was never published during his lifetime, in the spring of 1621, as we have seen, when he thought himself dying, this was the one work singled out in his hurried will for posthumous publication. All this makes for an intriguing irony: despite his failure to gain Elizabeth's favor Bacon always admired her skill, and increasingly used her methods of government as a yardstick by which to measure her successor. That his memory often played him false, and that his original understanding of her methods was, as noted above, based on casual contact and influenced by his own imagination, made it easier for him to create a convincing (and idealized) portrait. In part, the apotheosis of Elizabeth is attributable to Bacon's inability to adapt himself to changing ways, a characteristic seen early in James's reign. Writing to Cecil in 1603 of his "quenched" ambition he notes that "in the Queen's, my excellent Mistress's, time the *quorum* was small: her service was a kind of freehold, and it was a more solemn time. All those points agreed with my nature and judgment" (10.80). And so it is also that he does not hesitate recommending to James, as early as the *Certain Considerations*, that he imitate policies of his predecessor (10.124). What Bacon has seen work for Elizabeth he never doubts will work for

James; once his mind has imprinted upon it an image or idea, it never afterward rejects it. Moreover, from the evidence available to us, it would seem that Bacon felt (or imagined he did) a closer affinity to the Queen than he ever did to either his mother or his wife. The very undertaking of the *In felicem memoriam Reginae Elizabethae* would suggest a sense of duty. Be that as it may, there is a poignant truth to the comment often made to James, "I do yet bear an extreme zeal to the memory of my old mistress Queen Elizabeth."

The years as Solicitor-General were not easy. The work was hard—Bacon later, and not unjustly, told the King it was "one of the painfulest places in your kingdom, specially as my employments have been"—and the rewards small for a man seeking more than wealth. He performed his tasks well and continued to impress the King with his forensic skills,[55] but he felt unfulfilled. It was simply not enough to prepare and conduct the Crown's cases, or sit on royal commissions, or draw up advices for the privy council. Bacon craved instead a position of decisive influence in the government, where he might realize finally his as yet unappreciated potential.[56] Advancing age, moreover, as well as the world's obstinacy threatened to keep him from power, an eventuality that only reinforced the pressure on his pen. "And I must confess," he tells Tobie Matthew in the summer of 1609, "my desire to be, that my writings should not court the present time, or some few places, in such sort as might make them either less general to persons, or less permanent in future ages" (11.135).

In this frame of mind he published toward the end of 1609 the *De Sapientia Veterum* and dedicated it to Cambridge University. The work consists of brief summaries of thirty-one ancient fables together with Bacon's interpretation of their meanings. These reflect his own opinions and interests, although in the preface he attempts to convince the reader that his glosses only follow the obvious meaning of the story.

> For who is there so impenetrable and that can so shut his eyes to a plain thing, but when he is told that after the *Giants* were put down, *Fame* sprang up as their posthumous sister, he will at once see that it is meant of those murmurs of parties and seditious rumours which always circulate for a time after the suppression of a rebellion?[57]

What is more obvious is that Bacon, in discovering the meaning of a fable, is going through the same mental gymnastics as when he is finding the intention of a law. A well-developed sense of the "probable," working almost entirely on linguistic evidence, always manages to discover a wisdom consonant with its assumptions.[58]

Despite the pleasure it offers its readers, the *De Sapientia Veterum* has provoked controversy. Does it belong among the literary or the philosophical works?[59] Since the work is almost evenly divided between those fables with a civil and those with a philosophical interpretation, the question would appear insoluble—or irrelevant, for Bacon seems to have quite purposely mixed his categories. Two prefatory letters, one to his cousin Cecil, now Lord Salisbury, the other to Cambridge, introduce the work. Since Salisbury was chancellor of the university there was formal cause for including him in the dedication. But actually the letters are more tightly connected by a theme that virtually precluded either of them not appearing. To his cousin Bacon speaks of his desire "to give some help toward the difficulties of life and the secrets of science." Philosophy may be the key. "Even the art of politics, wherein you are so well approved both by faculty and by merits, and by the judgment of a most wise king, springs from the same fountain, and is a great part thereof" (6.689). The obverse of the argument is offered to Cambridge. "The inventions of the learned" may receive some contributions from a man acquainted "with affairs." "Certainly I am of opinion that speculative studies when transplanted into active life acquire some new grace and vigour, and having more matter to feed them, strike their roots perhaps deeper, or at least grow taller and fuller leaved" (6.691). In other words, both worlds, the experiential and the philosophical, are in themselves incomplete. Luckily the author, schooled in both, has gained the vision to perceive the respective natures of each more clearly than do their inhabitants. Like the Orpheus described in one of the fables, he could, "by the harmony and perfect modulation of a lyre," beget order in either philosophy or human affairs. By analyzing, therefore, "stories invented" by men who had "in their thoughts natural philosophy," as well as by men who had "civil affairs," Bacon declares once again the distinctive value of his mind.

Though James might show himself oblivious to his servant's higher ambitions, he was not willing to lose so clever a lawyer. To

Bacon's request early in 1611 for some assurance that he would "succeed (if I live) into the Attorney's place," there came back an affirmative reply, and this was followed in June by appointment as one of the two judges in the newly created Court of the Verge.

But it was Cecil's death in May 1612 that seemed to hold far more than promises and small favors. Bacon regarded it as the occasion for finally reaching the promised land, and we have from his pen at this time several letters (not all of which were probably sent) pleading his worthiness to the King. "Your Majesty may have heard somewhat that my father was an honest man, and somewhat you may have seen of myself, though not to make any true judgment by, because I have hitherto had only *potestatem verborum,* nor that neither."[60] Cecil and his policies were dismissed. "He was a fit man to keep things from growing worse but no very fit man to reduce things to be much better." If the King wanted a proper servant he must look for one able to "give a frame and constitution to matters." More specifically, he advised James to summon a parliament, "for the supply of your estate" and "for the better knitting of the hearts of your subjects," and he offered to draw up "some preparative remembrances" for it. Was he not, after all, the ideal person, a "perfect and peremptory royalist," as well as a man respected by parliament? "Every man makes me believe that I was never one hour out of credit with the lower house" (11.280). The King, however, may be forgiven if he was skeptical of how fruitful and loyal this "ancient and honourable remedy" would prove to be. And perhaps we should be skeptical of Bacon's claims about the influence and respect he enjoyed in the Commons. Insensitive always to what did not reward his self-esteem, he is hardly the best judge of what other men felt about him. In addition, the last two sessions (1610-11) of James's first parliament, with the King's power of taxation surfacing as the critical issue, had indicated that the old rules and methods governing the management of parliaments might no longer work.

Bacon did not rely entirely on naked appeals to the King. Short and unsolicited proposals on various subjects were also sent forward. From this period date the advice on Sutton's Estate and a paper dealing with the Court of Wards. With each Bacon hoped to show cause "whereby," as he said in a letter to James, "you may think it fit for your service to remove me to business of state."[61] Also, as a member of a subcommission appointed in the summer of 1612 to confer on ways of replenishing the Treasury, Bacon followed his usual practice of sending a private report of the business to the King. "So that besides the joint account which we shall give to the Lords, I hope I shall be able to give your Majesty somewhat *ex proprio*." The desire always is to establish special rapport. The King, as it turned out, was not unappreciative of these efforts, at least those dealing with the Court of Wards, "which it pleased you to say were no tricks nor novelties, but true passages of business," and he asked his Solicitor-General to think about the feasibility of converting Crown lands into fee farm rents. This was enough to embolden Bacon to draw up, in September 1612, a more general letter of advice "upon this subject of the repair of your Majesty's means." Aside from damning Cecil for his futile attempt to reach a compromise with parliament through the Great Contract, and preaching patience to the King, Bacon could offer only a largesse of words.

> Your Majesty's recovery must be by the medicines of the Galenists and Arabians, and not of the Chemists or Paracelsians. For it will not be wrought by any one fine extract or strong water, but by a skilful compound of a number of ingredients, and those by just weight and proportion, and that of some simples which perhaps of themselves or in over-great quantity were little better than poisons, but mixed and broken and in just quantity are full of virtue. [11.312]

What did James make of this? The wordy vagueness suggests that Bacon, as yet, had few concrete ideas. But that he should choose to set the problem in his familiar analytical mold—"repair" will come through neither one encompassing tactic nor a plethora of particulars—reveals again that tendency to examine situations (especially those he is unfamiliar with) according to prescribed categories. And when he repeats a favorite phrase at the end of the letter, "I know these things are *majora quam pro fortuna*: but they are *minora quam pro studio et voluntate*," he is simply justifying his windy ignorance of the matter in hand.

On the threshold, as he undoubtedly saw it, of gaining real influence, it is appropriate that Bacon should bring out a new edition of the essays in the fall of 1612. The world, and particularly the King, could witness the superior political intelligence of a man who labored as a lawyer and occasionally wrote as a philosopher. Of the thirty-eight essays in the volume, nine dated from the original 1597 edition. No explanation has ever been offered for why Bacon left out the 1597 essay "Of Honour and Reputation," or why he did not include "Of Seditions and Troubles," known to have been already composed.[62] The reason for these omissions is very possibly tied to the purpose that generated this edition.

As pointed out above, the 1597 set of essays was intended to pass on to a man of the world various observations that would be of value to him. The 1612 collection was aimed deliberately at a more select audience: kings, and particularly James. Bacon undertook the task of showing the real nature of politics, of bringing greater certainty into a realm where man's knowledge was vague. (His title for the posthumously published Latin edition, *Sermones Fidele, sive Interiora Rerum,* more explicitly reveals his conception of what he was doing.)[63] With this in mind, it is a fair guess that Bacon left out the two essays to spare himself possible embarrassment with the King. In "Of Honour and Reputation," for example, his list of the degrees of sovereign honor would have put James in the lowest category. On the other hand, the entire argument of the essay "Of Seditions and Troubles" was apt to disturb. "So when any of the four pillars of government are mainly shaken or weakened (which are Religion, Justice, Counsel, and Treasure), men had need to pray for fair weather." Bacon was always careful to minimize or suppress the unpleasant, and even more careful now considering the stakes. In the letter recently sent to the King on the repair of his estate an entire paragraph had been devoted to making sure "these cogitations of want do not any ways trouble or vex your M's mind. . . . It is no new thing for the greatest kings to be in debt" (11.312-13). Bacon sought in this new edition to demonstrate his value, and he was not prepared to risk his chances by frightening or angering the King.

Words of toneless piety marked the dedication to his brother-in-law, Sir John Constable. "Missing my Brother, I found you next; in respect of bond of near alliance, and of straight friendship and society, and particularly of communication in studies." Constable had not been his original choice however. What was he to do with advice meant for princes? The intended, and logical, recipient had been Prince Henry, whose death shortly before had checked the display of "devoted affection." Fortunately the draft of the intended dedication has survived, providing a succinct explanation of what Bacon thought he was accomplishing in these essays.

> And although they handle those things wherein both men's lives and their pens are most conversant, yet (what I have attained I know not) but I have endeavoured to make them not vulgar, but of a nature whereof a man shall find much in experience, and little in books; so as they are neither repetitions nor fancies. [11.340]

Rules grounded in experience they certainly are, though, as in 1597, they stand or fall on the validity of Bacon's perception of his experience, as well as the experience itself. When he writes about deformity, for example, he is not writing about the phenomenon but about his cousin.

> Againe in their superiors, it [deformity] quencheth ielousie towards them, as persons that they think they may at pleasure despise; and it layeth their competitors and emulators asleepe: as neuer beleeuing they should bee in possibility of aduancement, till they see them in possession.

His contemporaries caught him out at this. "Sir Fraunces Bacon hath set out new essayes, where in a chapter of deformitie the world takes notice that he paints out his late litle cousin to the life."[64] Nevertheless, the purpose of the essays was to persuade James of his wisdom so that he might be employed as a counselor. Thus, essays such as "Of Seeming Wise," "Of Ambition," "Of Wisdom for a Man's Self," and, obviously, "Of Counsel," demonstrated those qualities which were to be looked for and those avoided in a counselor; the essays "Of Dispatch" and "Of Cunning" discussed the best methods for doing "business"; and, finally, perennial problems of statecraft were discussed in "Of Empire," "Of Religion," "Of Nobility," "Of the Greatness of Kingdoms," etc. Presumably the man who had knowledge of the qualities, habits, and ideas of a good counselor was himself prime material. And the last words of the last essay, "Of the Greatness of Kingdoms," exuded that confidence in the manageability of things that Bacon had already pressed on the King, and would continue to.

> But certainly in the great frame of Kingdomes and Commonwealths, it
> is in the power of Princes or Estates by ordinances and constitutions,
> and maners which they may introduce, to sowe greatness to their
> posteritie and succession. But these things are commonly left to chance.

In politics, no less than in philosophy, "chance" had for too long kept
men from realizing their potential.

The publication of the *Essays* did not mark the end of Bacon's
extra-curricular efforts to win the Attorney-Generalship. Sometime in
1612 or early 1613 he drew up the brief memorial, *In Henricum
Principem Walliae Elogium.* If he had any purpose in mind other than
pleasing the grief-stricken King it is not known. As long ago as the
*Commentarius Solutus* he had shown no qualms about exploiting the
King's well-known love for his children. "M$^d$ the poynt of y$^e$ 4 shyres
and to think to settle a cowrse in it; but to listen how y$^e$ K. is affected
in respect of y$^e$ prince, and to make use of my industry in it towards
the Pr."[65] A more joyous occasion gave him another opportunity. In
February 1613, as noted above, he organized and directed a masque
celebrating the marriage of Princess Elizabeth and Prince Frederick of
the Palatinate. Unfortunately the King was exhausted from the recent
round of festivities and had the production stopped so that he might
go home to bed. "These things are but toys," Bacon wrote knowingly
in the 1625 essay "Of Masques and Triumphs," "to come amongst
such serious observations. But yet, since princes will have such things,
it is better they should be graced with elegancy than daubed with
cost."

He did not, however, neglect more weighty services. By the
spring of 1613 it was becoming clear that another parliament would
have to be summoned. Rising costs and kingly extravagance had
increased the debt far beyond a level the sale of lands and honors
could conceivably reach. Outraged though he had been at the
opposition encountered in 1610-11, the King had no alternative.
Bacon now saw a splendid opportunity to impress James. No man
around the court with the exception of Coke had his experience in
parliament, and probably no one had his confidence in what might be
accomplished. In June, therefore, he drew up a long and "private"
letter to the King, outlining the reasons why greater success would

attend a new parliament and suggesting measures to be taken to ensure that success.

"The matter of Parliament is a great problem of estate, and deserveth apprehensions [understanding] and doubts." Thus Bacon sets out the subject for the King's understanding, simultaneously talking to him as the servant who yearns to have charge of the business and as the philosopher with special knowledge of the phenomenon. Old grievances, he asserted, were "dead and flat," like the minister chiefly responsible for previous failures. He further assumed that the opposition of 1610-11 was in disarray, although many listed as "yours" would be found in 1614 to be still factious. Turning to the courses "I wish to be held," Bacon expressed his displeasure at the King's appearing in "the person of a merchant and contractor"—there were to be no more projects like Cecil's Great Contract. He begged James to proportion his "demands and expectations" and to be content with receiving less money but more goodwill. The King was advised to follow the "more ancient form" of parliament by making it appear less obvious that money was the only reason for the summons. Let the causes "given forth *ad populum*" be the plantation of Ireland, "the opening or increase of trade," or "the reducement and recompiling of laws"—Bacon's old favorite. It should also be given out that the King did not lack other remedies to help his estate. Finally, Bacon cautioned against using underhanded electioneering practices since they would only increase "animosities and oppositions," and create an "evil conceit" among the people about what was eventually done in parliament (11.368-73).

In the working papers that formed the basis of this letter Bacon concisely stated the vital question. "I conceive the sequel of good or evil not so much to depend upon Parliament or not Parliament, as upon the course which the K. shall hold with his Parliament" (11.366). That course, as can be seen from the letter, was based on a somewhat naive understanding of both men and events. Could James, or any sovereign, expect to obtain his will by resorting to an elaborate set of pretenses? Through instinct, education, and experience Bacon had come to see political problems as soluble through a kind of verbal management, and having little respect for the minds of other men he was inclined to exaggerate the effectiveness of dissimulation. A favorite phrase, "until your Majesty have tuned your instrument you will have no harmony," expresses that sublime confidence in manipulation that marks his career. Whether he speaks to Essex on wooing the Queen, to James on working a parliament, or to himself on winning favor, Bacon never doubts the potency of words. No doubt more tact might have gained James better results; several of Bacon's cautions were prudent. But by 1613 the insubordinate temper of parliament, which Bacon thought arose *"ex puris naturalibus"* or "out of party" (viz. ambitious factions), represented a widespread and complicated network of thwarted interests and emerging powers.[66] The fight over impositions in the previous session had set a distinctly new tone to the disputes between King and Commons, for the extension of the taxing power of the King raised the specter of unlimited exploitation. Grievances debated in earlier sessions, like wardship and purveyance, were noxious, but at least they were known and defined. Favors, offices, and smooth words, however, could not have quashed the anger and fears of men who rightly surmised that elemental questions of power were at stake. Indeed, in the last parliament Bacon himself had received a lesson in the limits of persuasion. "These reasons and persuasions," wrote an anonymous diarist in the Commons on May 14, 1610, after hearing Bacon attempt to soothe the Commons' anger on an important procedural matter, "(though delivered by an excellent speaker and with all advantage that wit, words or eloquence could add to them) moved the House no whit."[67]

In August of 1613 Bacon was made Attorney-General. As the recent Whitelocke Case had demonstrated,[68] he was the best legal advocate the Crown had. Nevertheless, there is no evidence that he had begun to enjoy the King's confidence in political matters. Content to work his servant's pen and tongue, James found little use for his ideas. Significantly, in the parliament which met in April of 1614, the King was happy to include in his opening speech some points touched on in a memorial given him earlier by Bacon,[69] but seems not to have consulted with his Attorney-General on whatever strategy he may have had in mind for the session itself. As it was, Bacon almost found himself without a seat, for a quarrel at Cambridge came close to canceling his election, and at the very beginning of the session the question was raised whether an Attorney-General should sit in the

Commons at all.[70] There is no evidence that Bacon himself was the cause of the Commons' worry, but the assumption that any man holding office was *prima facie* unsympathetic symbolizes the suspicion that now existed in the house and which Bacon imagined words could dispel.[71] Their limited value should have been even clearer two months later when the parliament was dissolved. For in his final appearance in the House of Commons, Bacon was at first ineffectual and then, during the last wild weeks of the session, simply disappeared from the record. His plea for supply on April 12 fell on deaf ears; his introduction of four bills of grace on May 2 was met with silence; his long rebuttal on the same day against the charge of undertaking was not believed; and his defense on May 10 of Sir Thomas Parry—whose treatment by the King foreshadows events of 1621—was disregarded.[72] On the last occasion, moreover, he was mockingly introduced in the *Commons Journal* as "the heir apparent of eloquence."

When Bacon spoke of parliament he was thinking of "the Parliament in Queen Elizabeth's time, in whose reign things were so well settled and disposed, as if she demanded anything it was seldom denied, and if she pretended any it was never inquired" (12.177). In the several advices on calling and handling parliaments that he will give to James in the next six years, it is clear that he is trying to resurrect that somewhat mythical "ancient" relationship. All it will take will be golden speeches and dexterous tactics. There is no recognition that circumstances, not just counselors, have changed, that there was no longer even the tenuous majority sentiment, based on the war with Spain and the repression of Puritans and recusants, that had existed in Elizabeth's later parliaments.

That Bacon was thinking of the Elizabethan pattern has often been recognized,[73] although the emphasis is usually placed on James's failure to continue that pattern rather than on Bacon's faulty perception. Never asked is why so presumably astute a man should not identify the changing nature of the problems faced by the sovereign he so fervidly wished to serve? It could, of course, be argued that Bacon only demonstrates how human he is by reading reality according to guidelines formed early in life, that he shares the instinctive conservatism of the species.[74] However true that answer may be, it is still insufficient to account for his desire to see the old ways restored.

> Now therefore I will proceed to an affirmative concerning those wishes and advices which I have thought of for a future Parliament, which I do not less in heart than for form's sake submit to his Majesty's better judgment. And although perhaps they may seem *antiqui moris,* yet I persuade myself they will master the time, and be far more effectual than those counsels which may seem more agreeable to the modern arts.[75]

Nor does it altogether account for the continued outbursts against his cousin's efforts to formalize the fiscal arrangements between King and parliament and ensure a steady source of supply. Whether or not the Great Contract was a feasible alternative, it is obvious that the much-maligned Cecil—how much has Bacon's view of his cousin, like so many of his judgments, shaped our view?—was searching for a policy more in line with contemporary realities.[76]

Bacon's insistence on handling parliament in the old way must in part be attributed to the particular character of his mind. Given to casting his experiences and perceptions into usable principles, he had clearly come to think of parliament as a phenomenon controllable through certain rules, in this case derived from his own early observations. To depart from those rules, as had been done in 1610-11 and again in 1614, was to guarantee failure. Thus, because of his essentially static view of the institution, Bacon can be confident that a simple return to the old methods will see "that great council" restored to its "natural use and ancient dignity and splendor." He tells the King in 1615 that "the notation of those errors carrieth in itself by rule of contrary a kind of direction or platform, what course is now to be held. For I do not think there can be a more true or compendious advice how to carry things concerning a future Parliament than this—to do just contrary to that that was last done" (12.183). His mind refuses to see freshly, for to do so would be to deny those learned rules which are vital to its well-being; and so there is always a discrepancy between its notions of the 'scientific' approach and its own practice.[77]

Sometime not long before becoming Attorney-General, Bacon began sketching out two brief, complementary works on the heavens, the *Descriptio Globi Intellectualis* and the *Thema Coeli*. Neither fragment has merit whether considered as a document intended to advance science or even as a statement of what was known about astronomy in its author's day.[78] Simple ignorance cannot alone explain their inadequacy, or, put differently, some defect besides sloth accounts for Bacon's ineptitude. As with all subjects, Bacon comes to astronomy as a self-styled devil's advocate, automatically challenging whatever has been hitherto accepted. "Nothing extant . . . satisfies me." And, predictably, his criticism is leveled at the "calculations" of astronomers, which he contends are wrong or unimportant, and the "opinions" of philosophers, which are "full of error and confusion." Once again the old errors, "particulars" and speculations; this time corrupting the study of celestial bodies. Astronomers and philosophers, he declares, have both "scorned to follow nature." His solution is no less familiar than his critique. "Let it then be arranged, if you will, between philosophy and astronomy, as by a convenient and legitimate compact, that astronomy shall prefer those hypotheses which are most suitable for compendious calculation, philosophy those which approach nearest the truth of nature" (5.557). Always there is the assumption that the middle way provides the best method; every subject is analyzed from the same vantage point, defined by the same categories.

Unfortunately Bacon's distaste for mathematics and its possible accomplishments, "for it is not merely calculations or predictions that I am at, but philosophy," an aversion that seems to have arisen from his scorn for "generalities," necessarily disqualified him from making any contribution to astronomy.[79] His reliance instead on straight analogical reasoning doomed him to failure.

> For he who knows the universal passions of matter and thereby knows what is possible to be, cannot help knowing likewise what has been, what is, and what will be, according to the sums of things. Therefore the best hope and security for the study of celestial bodies I place in physical reasons; meaning by physical reasons not such as are commonly supposed, but only the doctrine concerning those appetites of matter which no diversity of regions or places can distract or dissever. [5.512]

Implicit in that statement is the belief that the whole universe obeys a unitary system of rules, and that as a result we can learn about celestial bodies and space from what we know about matter here on earth. "All bodies by the manifold consent of things are endued likewise with many motions, some ruling, some obeying, and some also lying dormant unless exerted" (5.556). By straightforward inference, then, we can discover knowledge. Obviously such a method can bring positive results, and so, for example, Bacon has been praised for being an early advocate of the theory that celestial bodies are no more perfect than worldly bodies. "Between heaven and earth, as regards constancy and change, there is not much difference." But the method is inherently unable to discover very much because it has only logic as a tool and can never break from its first assumptions about things.

> It would seem therefore that all tumult, conflict, and disorder take place only in the confines of heaven and earth; just as it is in civil matters, in which it is commonly found that the border land of two kingdoms is troubled by continual inroads and violence, while the interior provinces of both countries are in the enjoyment of long peace, and are not disturbed except by the more serious wars, which happen rarely. [5.532]

To dismiss such a comparison as being merely descriptive tinsel, or to wink, for example, at an addition to the 1612 version of the essay "Of Regiment of Health," "For it is a secret both in nature and state, that it is safer to change many things then one," is to miss the peculiarly synoptic bent of Bacon's mind.[80]

Another fragment, the *De Fluxu et Reflexu Maris,* which dates probably from the same period,[81] underlines the reason for Bacon's failure as a scientist. Once again he must reject all previous work before setting out his own ideas. "The consideration of the causes of the ebb and flow of the sea, attempted by the ancients and afterwards dropped, taken up again by the moderns and yet by variety of opinions rather unsettled than discussed, is commonly by a light conjecture referred to the moon" (5.443). Following a view earlier advanced by Pandulpho Sfondrato, Bacon argued that the tides were produced by the American continent's interference with the general tendency of the ocean to move from east to west. Unlike Sfondrato, who attributed this tendency to the influence of the sun, Bacon conceived of the problem in universals. "I judge that the motion of rotation or conversion from east to west is not properly a celestial but quite a cosmical motion; a motion primarily belonging to the great fluids, and found from the summits of heaven to the depths of the water; the inclination being always the same, though the degrees of velocity vary greatly; varying, however, in a regular order, so that the swiftness of the motion diminishes the nearer the bodies approach the earth" (5.449). It is not plausible, he insists, that the movement of the sun and moon "have dominion over those motions of the sea," despite appearances. Instead, "these correspondences arise out of the universal passions of matter, and the primary combinations of things," and "both emanate from the same origins and fellow causes" (5.448). If, as Bacon claims, it was "veneration for the heavenly bodies" that disposed men to view the correspondence between heavenly bodies and tides as a cause and effect relationship, it was his own penchant for the "true nature of reality" that disposed him to misinterpret phenomena by straining to find their explanation in higher, totally inclusive, laws. And the logic in this fragment, based as it is on the assumption that nature, like the law, is rational, is rather vulnerable. The mind that saw a "regular order" of diminution in the velocity of east-west motion as "bodies approach the earth" will persist in using simple patterns of inference. Consider, for example, his objection to Gilbert's belief that the earth is a magnet. "It is impossible that things in the interior of the earth can be like any substance exposed to the eye of man; for with us all things are relaxed, wrought upon, and softened by the sun and heavenly bodies, so that they cannot correspond with things situated in a place where such a power does not penetrate" (5.455). Or, his way of calculating the distance covered in a day by the east-west movement of water.

> For if (to estimate this) you take some of those shores which are least mountainous or depressed, and are contiguous to an open sea, and if you take a measure of the distance between high and low water mark, and if you multiply this distance by four on account of the four tides a day, and again double the product on account of the tides at the opposite shores of the same sea, and add something more on account of the height of coasts, which are always somewhat raised above the level of the sea; this calculation will give the distance which a globe of water, if it were free from all obstruction and always moved in a circular progression round the earth, would travel; and certainly it is not a great one. [5.456]

What finally is apparent is that Bacon, for all his lip service to experience and induction, is restricted to an essentially deductive method when he does science. Simple extrapolation from hastily conceived laws often at variance with the work of other men is at the heart of this exquisitely verbal science. And the mode of reasoning, as well as the expectation of results, is distinctly reminiscent of his mind when it applies itself to law.[82]

Until the *Novum Organum* there will be no more science; indeed, there will be no more unofficial writings of any kind. The steady climb in the King's service will not require such aids; and Bacon will need to devote all his energies to business. "And for industry," he informs James around the time of receiving the Attorney-Generalship, "I shall take to me in this procuration not Martha's part, to be busied in many things, but Mary's part, which [is] to intend your service; for the less my abilities are the more they ought to be contracted *ad unum*."[83] Tobie Matthew might note that "no day can pass, wherein you give not liberty to your wise thoughts of looking upon the works of nature," but just such a contemplative acquaintance was inclined to result in that superficial knowledge of contemporary science which Bacon has been so often criticized for.[84] And appropriately enough it will be as a lawyer, not as a counselor or philosopher, that he will gain greater standing with the King.

In the early months of 1615 several important cases— Peacham's, Owen's, and St. John's—took up his time. Each involved verbal assaults on either the King's government or his person: St. John had spoken out against the benevolence that James had tried to raise after the last parliament and was charged with seditious slander; Owen, a Catholic, was accused of having claimed it lawful to kill the King if he were excommunicated; and Peacham, whose case caused the greatest trouble because it was believed a more general plot against the government was involved and because it led to the confrontation with Coke over consulting with the judges, was a testy old Somersetshire parson who had penned some criticisms of the King, perhaps with the intention of using them as a sermon or pamphlet. Treason seemed to lie in the heart of all of the accused, and Bacon, with years of experience in dealing with this particular crime, gave a brilliant display of his expertise. He kept the King well briefed about his investigations by assiduously forwarding to him a succession of "private" accounts in which he sang his own praises while chiding the inadequacies of his fellows. "He [Peacham] never deceived me; for when others had hope of discovery, and thought time well spent that way, I told your Majesty *pereuntibus mille figurae,* and that he now did but turn himself into divers shapes to save or delay his punishment" (12.125-26). No man, he would have the King recognize as he carefully dates a letter, "This Friday late at night," goes so devotedly about affairs of state. And when it came to delivering the actual charges against Owen and St. John (Peacham was eventually tried in Somerset), Bacon showed that his old skills at composing a persuasive "narrative" of treason had not deserted him. On the evening of the day St. John's case was heard in Star Chamber, he wrote the King, "I set down as soon as I came home cursorily a frame of that I said; though I persuade myself I spake it with more life. I have sent it to Mr. Murray sealed; if your Majesty have so much idle time as to look upon it, it may give some light on the day's work"[85] Hardly a man in the kingdom understood so well the "nature and peril" of that nefarious crime, or how to make a profit from it.

Not long after these cases were out of the way, others, and more serious, took their place. Sir Thomas Overbury's murder, and subsequently the famous cases involving Chancery's jurisdiction, which culminated in Coke's dismissal from King's Bench, preoccupied the government through most of 1616. As Attorney-General and the most supple legal mind at the King's disposal, Bacon played at center stage. He argued the Crown's cause in the quarrel over the writ *De non procedendo Rege inconsulto,* advised the King in the *Praemunire* and *Commendans* disputes, and collaborated with James in the long and unsavory proceedings against the Somersets. He was particularly helpful in this last matter, where his task was to construct a plausible case against the accused couple and yet leave room for the King to grant them a pardon without tarnishing his own reputation; that is, without making it seem as if he were giving away to past affections. These cases are too well known to require retelling, but it should be stressed that they mark the high point of Bacon's public career. At no other time was the King to work so closely with him. And, more significantly, ample evidence exists to show that in each case James followed much of the advice given by his Attorney-General, who, no less than himself, was extremely sensitive to the political implications of these legal actions. "This great and public affront, not only to . . . your Chancellor . . . but to your high court of Chancery, which is the court of your absolute power, may not (in my opinion) pass lightly, nor end only in some formal atonement; but use is to be made thereof for the settling of your authority and strengthening of your prerogative according to the true rules of monarchy" (12.252). The King, though, probably cared far less for the "rules" than he did for the "strengthening."

Diligent though he was in managing these cases, Bacon still had time to send to the King reports and advices on various subjects. His confidence knows no bounds: "It [is] as easy," he tells the King when sending him a series of papers on the royal revenues which unfortunately have not survived, "for your Majesty to come out of want as to go forth of your gallery" (12.130). Nor his willingness, contrary to what Rawley will say, to be a "defamer of any man to his prince." In a matter touching recusants he tells the King that Secretary Winwood "bringeth *bonam voluntatem,* but he is not versed much in these things: and sometimes urgeth the conclusion without the premises, and by haste hindereth."[86] He also keeps the King regularly informed of the declining health of Lord Chancellor Egerton, and in February 1616, when it seems that the old man might finally die, Bacon sends the King a leter applying for the office which contains a revealing job description.

> I do presume also, in respect of my father's memory, and that I have been always gracious in the lower house, I have some interest in the gentlemen of England, and shall be able to do some effect in rectifying that body of parliament-men, which is *cardo rerum.* For let me tell your Majesty, that that part of the Chancellor's place, which is to judge in equity between party and party . . . concerneth your Majesty least. . . . But it is the other parts, of a moderator amongst your Council, of an overseer over your Judges, of a planter of fit justices and governors in the country, that importeth your affairs and these times most.
>
> I will add also, that I hope by my care the inventive part of your Council will be strengthened, who now commonly do exercise rather their judgments than their inventions. [12.243]

Whether as lawyer or judge, legal business was not his prime interest.

Having gained favor in this year "consecrate to justice" by means of the law, he hoped to turn that influence into other channels. Egerton, however, unexpectedly recovered and Bacon was left to seek a place on the privy council instead. At least then, he told the new favorite, George Villiers, his attempts to offer advice, "which may seem a kind of interloping . . . for one that is no councillor," would have greater legitimacy. He did not have long to wait. On June 9, 1616, the King appointed him to the council, a gesture without the significance Bacon would have preferred since James, particularly after Cecil's death, was not in the habit of listening to his council.[87]

Undoubtedly the new favorite had a hand in the appointment. He too had benefited from Somerset's disgrace and Coke's dismissal, and had received almost as many carefully drawn reports on the progress of these actions as had the King. Genuine admiration probably also inspired his support, for Bacon seems to have been able, once again, to charm a young man into believing in his powers. In his early letters to him Bacon is relaxed and witty, feeling as yet no threat from the youth. Favors are asked and returned with ease, and Villiers is trusted to pass on advice "I think myself bound to deliver to his Majesty." Gradually, as Villiers secures his position, the pedagogical instinct in Bacon is aroused; like Essex, Villiers is to be formed. In August, on the occasion of sending him his patent for becoming a viscount, Bacon begins his instruction with two lessons in fundamentals. The favorite should work to advance "able" and "meriting" men, something "never done since I was born," "for in the time of the Cecils, the father and the son, able men were by design and of purpose suppressed." This self-serving advice is followed by a warning that also recalls earlier frustrations. "Above all, depend wholly (next to God) upon the King; and be ruled (as hitherto you have been) by his instructions; for that is best for yourself " (13.6-7). Sending back a gracious reply to this avuncular message, Villiers moved Bacon to declare himself. Echoes of letters written over twenty years before roll like waves upon the reader.

> I took much contentment in that I perceive by your letter that you took in so good part the freedom of my advice, and that yourself in your own nature consented therewith. Certainly, no service is comparable to good counsel; and the reason is, because no man can do so much for another

as a man may do for himself. Now good counsel helpeth a man to help himself. But you have so happy a master as supplieth all. My service and good will shall not be wanting. [13.8]

If the role of advisor was the one he felt most comfortable playing, it is no less true that the people and situations of his early days continue to determine his outlook and his counsel.

Ample evidence for this can be found in two different copies of an advice that he drew up for Villiers at this time. Whether Villiers ever saw either is not known, nor does it really matter; they are important because they represent Bacon's mind as he passed through middle age. In each his primary concern is to teach the favorite how to perform his role, particularly in dealing with suitors. Five "rules to be observed" are set out showing how the purely mechanical part of the problem of dispatching petitions is to be handled. The "matter" of the suits themselves is divided into eight headings, and "some rules as land-marks to guide your judgment in the examination of every one of them" are offered. Having thus structured the problem to his satisfaction, Bacon offers detailed advice on each of the eight categories. Much of it can be traced back to earlier writings, but what is especially conspicuous is how he so openly identifies it with Elizabeth, "in whose times I had the happiness to be born and to live many years." For example, in discussing "the Council Board, and matters of State," he expresses the wish that the council be small so that its members "would be more venerable: and I know that Queen Elizabeth . . . was not so much observed to have a numerous as a wise council." Equally prudent was her policy of using a variety of councilors. "I conceive it will be most convenient to have some of every sort, as in the time of Queen Elizabeth was one Bishop at the least" (13.41). He is even more flattering when he devotes the entire section on foreign negotiations and embassies to recalling Elizabeth's practices, and urges straight imitation. "I shall tell you . . . what hath been and ever was the course in the happy days of Queen Elizabeth, whom it will be no dis-reputation to follow."[88]

In no other writing does Bacon so outspokenly recommend the Queen's practices. When speaking of parliament he has not feared to praise her example to James, but discreetly. Villiers, though, was a safe reader; he had, after all, been only a child when Elizabeth died.

Now that Bacon had a place at the council table and seemed destined to repeat his father's success by becoming Lord Chancellor, he was nerved to speak out on the discrepancies between the government of the Queen and that of her successor.

Things had come apart in twenty years. The Crown no longer enjoyed the majesty it once had, and subjects were no longer quite as obedient. What was needed was a return to the older methods of governing, those that had seemed to work so well. Only to Villiers, particularly in the early period of their association when he had so much faith in his pupil, could Bacon freely air his misgivings. Even in those parts of the advice that do not pay explicit respect to Elizabeth the writer is thinking of her. "If any question be moved concerning the doctrine of the Church of England expressed in the 39 Articles, give not the least ear to the movers thereof. That is so soundly and so orthodoxally settled as cannot be questioned without extreme danger to the honour and stability of our Religion" (13.17). Assuming, as Bacon did, that the "forms" and "rules" of government, properly applied, bring predictable results, his desire for a return to the Elizabethan model has at least the virtue of being logical. To his contemporaries, however, he may well have sounded at times like Justice Shallow.

In March 1617, as he was about to leave for Scotland, the King finally accepted Lord Chancellor Egerton's request for retirement and appointed Bacon to serve as Lord Keeper. How much his appointment owed to the influence of Villiers, recently created Marquis of Buckingham, is difficult to estimate, but he clearly felt himself obligated to "the truest and perfectest mirror and example of firm and generous friendship that ever was in court" (13.152). Times indeed had changed; Essex had had to struggle even to make a knight. Two months later, on the occasion of officially taking his seat in Chancery, Bacon spoke eloquently of the "rules" that would govern his tenure, and reminded his audience on several occasions that he had "a domestic example to follow." Sitting now at the top of the heap, he had at long last duplicated his father's achievement. Almost immediately, however, he was to compromise his position by conduct all too familiar.

Prior to his departure the King had given instructions that a proclamation was to be published ordering the nobility and gentry temporarily residing in London to remove themselves to their country seats. Order and stability required the natural leaders of society to "abide and continue in their severall dwellings in the Countrey, to performe the duties and charge of their places, and service."[89] In April the council, and particularly Bacon, who served in the King's absence as the principal official in the realm, drew James's anger after deciding not to publish the proclamation on the grounds that many of the gentry had already voluntarily left the city (13.161-63). A month later Bacon annoyed the King once more by the forward manner in which he recommended that Sir Lancelot Lowther, the Queen's Solicitor, be transferred to Ireland as a Baron of the Exchequer.[90] But the mistake that cost him heavily was his intervention in the proposed marriage between the daughter of Sir Edward Coke and the favorite's brother. Not realizing that both the King and Buckingham endorsed the match, he tried to stop it, justifying what seemed to benefit his "own particular" by arguing that "the King's service" would incur a "great weakening." Even after he was enlightened, Bacon defended the validity and sincerity of his judgment, and received in return sharp notes challenging his wisdom and faithfulness (13.217-53). Many months passed before the displeasure went out of Buckingham's letters, and it is very likely that neither he nor the King ever looked quite the same on a man who incessantly protested his "anxious and solicitous care" of their interests, but whose acts of supererogation, wrought and compounded by a singular obtuseness, made him undependable.

The years as Lord Chancellor—he was raised to the higher dignity in January of 1618—were not to be as Bacon imagined them. In what he had called the "least" part of his tasks, "to judge in equity between party and party," he was to gain his greatest success. He sat continuously during term time and always managed to clear the docket of cases, a feat that may explain why suitors were attracted to his court.[91] He also managed to compile a set of rules, *Ordinances in Chancery,* defining the proper procedures of that court, which summarized practices that had grown up during the last reign.[92] His pen also was kept busy. When, for example, the government needed a persuasive public declaration to justify its condemnation of Sir Walter

Ralegh—a man easily as popular as Essex had been—it was Bacon who undertook the task and performed it brilliantly.[93] But all this mattered little to him despite his incessant preening. "I have made even with the causes of Chancery, and comparing with the causes heard by my Lord that dead is, . . . I find them to be double so many and one more; besides that the causes that I dispatch do seldom turn upon me again, as his many times did" (13.283). Instead, he wanted to show "my care, and my strength too in council," and to have, as had been the case (he believed) with his father, his advice asked for and followed.

Logically enough, the advertising of talents is now confined to the particular advices themselves; he is no longer seeking office, but has the more difficult chore of persuading belief. The letters to the King and the favorite are filled with testimonies of his abilities and tirelessness. "No pains" are too much "for the servant that I am, or desire to be." Always he feels confident that even the most difficult of problems is soluble. "I see the straits and I see the way out" (14.40). There is, indeed, something tawdry yet pathetic about his declarations. "And as without flattery," he writes to the King in February 1620, "I think your Majesty the best of Kings, and my noble Lord of Buckingham the best of persons favoured, so I hope without presumption (for my honest and true intentions to state and justice, and my love to my master) I am not the worst of Chancellors" (14.78). Even in the days of pomp and power Bacon was obliged to speak as a suitor.

# CHAPTER 4

# *Historian,*
# *June 1621–March 1622*

n June of 1621 Bacon hoped that disgrace was behind him. Released from the Tower after a stay of only three or four days, his spirits "neither spent not pent," he looked to the future. "Now my body is out," he wrote Prince Charles, "my mind nevertheless will be still in prison, till I may be on my feet to do his Majesty and your Lordship faithful service" (14.281). The omens, however, were unclear. An immediate return to public life was out of the question: parliament, due to return in November, would not have tolerated so blatant a snub to its judgment. Also, the King had pointedly declined to remit that part of the penalty which forbade him coming within twelve miles of the court—evidence that James could do without his counsel. Still, with the King already requesting his opinion on the "reformation of your courts of justice, and relieving the grievances of your people," a return to service probably seemed only a matter of time. And so on June 23, "having (as shold seeme) no manner of feeling of his fall but continueng as vaine and ydle in all his humors as when he was at highest,"[1] Bacon left London by sentence of parliament. He went to Gorhambury and stayed there "out of use and out of sight," looking after his health, waiting for a summons to return to court, and working.

There was good reason not to be idle at Gorhambury. Repeated self-assurances that he had done no evil would never mend his broken reputation; besides, a skillful job of repair might hasten his return to royal favor. Already on June 16 he had written a letter to Gondomar announcing his hopes. "Myself, my age, my fortune, yea my Genius, to which I have hitherto done but scant justice, calls me now to retire from the stage of civil action and betake myself to letters, and to the instruction of the actors themselves, and the service of Posterity."[2] Both thought and metaphor chimed with the advice offered kings in the 1612 essay, "Of Counsel": "It is good to be conuersant in them [books], specially the books of such as themselves haue beene Actors vpon the Stage." That Bacon should have been contemplating a book was natural. Whenever in the past advancement had been slow he had turned to his pen, and now, with so much at stake—place, income, reputation—he needed to set about quickly to reclaim his position in the world. "In this it may be I shall find honour, and I shall pass my days as it were in the entrance halls of a better life." The only difficulty, since rapid composition had never been a problem, centered on what to write. Just any sort of book would not do. How, for example, could a Lord Chancellor impeached for bribery turn immediately about and publish on the law? On the other hand, to how large an audience would a weighty philosophical treatise appeal, assuming that this particular bow had not gone slack with the *Novum Organum?* There were, of course, the extremely popular *Essays,* but they had already seen a second edition. Something different was needed, something that could simultaneously display his "Genius" to the world and persuade the King that he was still a valuable counselor.

History was the natural, almost predictable, alternative. If, as he had told Gondomar, he wished to instruct the "actors" on "the stage of civil action," and at the same time gratify the reading tastes of both King and countrymen, he could not have made a better choice.[3] For popularity and respect no other genre challenged history, and Bacon himself shared that esteem. "Histories make men wise," he declared in 1597, and, as he noted about the same time, "the use which it [history] holdeth to man's life, if it be not the greatest, yet assuredly is the freest from any ill accident or quality." Men "conversant much in poets" were apt to be "conceited," while those learned in philosophy and "sciences" were prone to being "opinionate" or "perplexed and confused" (6.18). Along with these feelings went a thorough knowledge of the classical and modern historians, with Tacitus earning by far the greatest admiration.[4]

This was not the first time, however, that Bacon had thought of trying his hand at history. On a few other occasions he had volunteered his services to Clio—most recently in April, when he had promised "a good history of England, and a better digest of your laws" if James would intercede with parliament—and had twice even begun the labors. Sometime before 1603 he had composed five pages of *The History of the reign of K. Henry the Eighth, K. Edward, Q. Mary, and part of the reign of Q. Elizabeth,* and in 1610 had sketched out four pages of *The Beginning of the History of Great Britain.* The dates and titles of these two fragments suggest calculated self-interest as their inspiration; the same is undoubtedly true of the corrections at least twice offered to William Camden for inclusion in his *Annales.*[5] Insufficient time and interest probably best explains why none of his pre-1621 projects for writing history came to fruition. His impeachment, though, supplied him with an abundance of both.

As in most everything else he ever undertook, Bacon was confident he knew what a history ought to be. Brief discussions of its forms and uses, as well as comments on the historian's responsibilities, are scattered about his earlier writings, and while they hardly add up to a 'theory' of historical composition they do prepare the reader for Bacon's own effort.[6] The first obligation of the historian was to recognize that his task was not merely to record events, let alone to engage in the style of moralizing common to the traditional chroniclers. If a history was to teach men about politics it had to be stripped clean of irrelevant pageant and ethical dicta. What the historian should be doing instead was informing his readers of the reasons for events, the explanations in terms of power and character for why men had acted as they had, so that they (the readers) might use the information to conduct their own affairs more successfully. "In matter of Story," he had written in 1600, reporting "the things done, without the Councils and circumstances" was useless because the events themselves "cannot breed soundness of Judgement, which is the true use of all Learning."[7] Five years later, in the *Advancement of Learning,* he reiterated his contempt for histories composed "without the motives or designs, the counsels, the speeches, the pretexts, the occasions, and other passages of action" (3.333). A concern for art (and safety), however, muted Bacon's didacticism. "It is the true office of history to represent the events themselves together with the counsels, and to leave the observations and conclusions thereupon to the liberty and faculty of every man's judgment."[8] Lessons were to be taught, but never "magisterially"; ingenuity would enable a man to insinuate in a book what he might blanch to say in life. For Bacon, practiced as he was in dressing his thoughts in rare forms, and longing to speak his mind from an exile he felt unjust, history (as it has seemed to so many other discarded statesmen) provided an opportunity to explain the predicaments of political life.

The product of his labors was *The History of the Reign of King Henry VII*. Although composed in a matter of weeks, the book is undoubtedly Bacon's ultimate political testament, a virtuoso work encompassing the thoughts and talents of a lifetime of civil business. Like the *Novum Organum*, his supreme philosophical effort, the *History* will not be improved upon in the subsequent rash of writings.[9] The parallel between the two works extends, though, beyond their primary position in the Baconian corpus, for both have experienced a sharp reversal in reputation. Once praised as distinctive and original contributions to knowledge, neither is now deemed reliable. Science, it is argued, cannot be done by the method set out in the *Novum Organum;* the reign of Henry VII, though still dim to our eyes, cannot be rightly judged from the pages of the *History*. These are sound judgments, but they should not restrain study. At least in the case of the *History* we should look at how the work came to be what it is, if only because the qualities that render it untrustworthy as an assessment of Henry VII make it a valuable source for the career of its author.

If history was the logical genre, the reign of Henry VII may be said to have been an inevitable subject choice. Bacon's earlier attempts at writing history suggest that there was no likelihood of his going outside English history; besides, the lessons he desired to teach precluded, as we shall see, a foreign landscape. Of course, he might have undertaken the ambitious project he had publicly and privately often espoused: namely, a history of England beginning either with Henry VII, or as he usually noted, Henry VIII, and going up (at least) to the accession of James. The justification for examining this period indicates again what he believed to be history's special contribution to learning.

> For they be not the great wars and conquests (which many times are the works of fortune and fall out in barbarous times) the rehearsal whereof maketh the profitable and instructing history; but rather times refined in policies and industries, new and rare variety of accidents and alterations, equal and just encounters of state and state in forces and of

    prince and prince in sufficiency, that bring upon the stage the best parts
    for observation. [6.19]

But clearly in 1621 he had not the time for so vast a scheme if the work was to be his ticket back to power and reputation. The alternative, then, was to choose a portion of that "excellent period," and Bacon must quickly have realized that Henry VII, if only by a process of exclusion, was his man.[10] Henry VIII was beneath admiration,[11] Edward and Mary beneath respect, and Elizabeth already ably done by Camden.

    There were, though, more positive enticements to Henry's reign. Chief among them, perhaps, was the knowledge that King James greatly admired this earlier advocate of unions, the man who had both joined the houses of Lancaster and York and arranged the marriage that eventually brought the Stuarts to the English throne. Had not James's first son been named in honor of Henry?[12] Too, Bacon already had a clear view of Henry, which meant that it would be easier to tell his story. Included in the fragment *History* dating from Elizabeth's reign was a brief character sketch of the King that obviously foreshadows the later portrait. Its brevity and tone, however, suggest that the sketch was based on Bacon's general reading, rather than special research; it is the work of a writer outside of his subject. In 1621, once Bacon has had the chance to sift through more detail, the view of Henry will be enlarged, though, typically, not redesigned. What probably clinched the decision to write about Henry was that there was so little to be done. Bacon needed to prepare a work quickly and the materials for Henry's reign were scanty, a fact that had kept him, as he wrote at the time (6.19), from beginning the fragment *History* with the deeds of that King. A problem had now become a piece of luck. Thus, trusting his superior insight, and feeling no ugent requirement for what the records and papers in London might have told him, Bacon had, in effect, only to sit down and write.

    Not surprisingly the *History* fails to conform to any single category of civil history outlined in the *Advancement of Learning*. Definitions were easier to articulate than to execute. Later historians and students of biography have each disclaimed the work for not meeting all the standards of their particular genre, and even contemporaries—

Chamberlain referred to it as "the life or raign"—felt the confusion.[13] Yet it would be petty to charge Bacon with inconsistency. He mixed two kinds of "perfect" history ("history of times," and "history of lives") for very good reasons. To have restricted himself to a "history of times," which "representeth the magnitude of actions and the public faces and deportments of persons," would have meant losing the "smaller passages and motions of men and matters" that gave the reader a useful picture of events. For, as Bacon argued with a metaphor that he was to repeat in the *History,* "the workmanship of God" often suspends "the greatest weight upon the smallest wires," and only a fool would prefer "the pomp of business" to the "true and inward resorts thereof."[14] Also, those who expected history to teach knew the value of directing the reader's attention on another human being. "But lives, if they be well written [viz., not "barren eulogies"], propounding to themselves a person to represent in whom actions both greater and smaller, public and private, have a commixture, must of necessity contain a more true, native, and lively representation."[15] In other words, by focusing his (and our) attention on the King himself rather than on the outward face of events, as had the chroniclers, Bacon could fashion a more persuasive example.

A more complicated problem than form or purpose involves the sources used by Bacon. Spedding, though he never discussed the question in any detail, believed that Bacon relied on "the published histories then extant" (Vergil, Hall, Holinshed, Stow, Speed, Fabyan) and manuscripts (particularly the *Vita Henrici VII* of Bernard André and the city chronicle, *Vitellius Ms* A, XVI) drawn from the collection of Sir Robert Cotton (6,4). Several decades later Wilhelm Busch, after "a wearisome examination, sentence by sentence," of the *History,* concluded that the text was really founded on Edward Hall's *Chronicle* which in turn reproduced Polydore Vergil's *Anglica Historia* (assumed by Spedding to have been Bacon's principal guide). Further, Busch, while acknowledging the use of Cotton's manuscripts, discounted the histories of Speed, Holinshed, or Stow as sources for Bacon, presumed that the *History* revealed some knowledge of treaties and a "copious use" of the rolls of parliament, and supposed that the material on Cabot's voyage was obtained from Hakluyt.[16] Since his day Busch's conclusions have been accepted with little question.[17]

Neither list, however, is correct. Most importantly, Hall must share honors with John Speed as Bacon's narrative guide. Proof of the indebtedness dots almost every page, as Bacon freely copies from a man he undoubtedly trusted more than any of the other chroniclers.[18] This should come as no surprise. In the fragment *History* Bacon had said that what the aspiring (and impatient) historian required was a "tolerable chronicle" to give him "a simple narration of the actions themselves," to which were to be added the "acts, instruments, and negotiations of state themselves, together with the glances of foreign histories," so that he might find the "counsels and the speeches and notable particularities" (6.18-19). Of course, the latter "helps" were the best "originals and instructions out of which to write an history," but then the labor would be "much greater." When these remarks were made Bacon felt only contempt for the existing "public memories." But by 1621 Speed's *History of Great Britain* was available, and though it too did not measure up to Bacon's standard of political sophistication and literary style, it was a distinct improvement on Hall's *Chronicle*. Indeed, Bacon influenced the book, for Speed approvingly quotes from his early sketch of Henry. Whether Speed actually borrowed the sketch from Bacon, whom he spoke of as "a learned, eloquent Knight, and principal Lawyer of our time," or obtained it through another source, is not clear. And even if an answer were found, the not uncommon assumption that Bacon had been working on a history of Henry's times long before 1621 would still be in need of proof.[19]

What appealed to Bacon in the *History of Great Britain* was the author's capacity to see in Henry's actions qualities of calculation and dissimulation unbeknownst to earlier writers. There was, to be sure, still a loose thread of moralizing, but most of Speed's stitching showed political acuteness. Hall, on the other hand, had the advantage of relative completeness. His was the longest narrative available, and though its length was often merely a result of its verbosity, it did give additional information, especially on foreign affairs.[20] It should also be recognized that Bacon's judgment on certain events and persons was shaped by his recollection, if not by a rereading, of the histories of Commines and Guicciardini, the two modern historians he always praised.[21]

The question of Bacon's dependence on Bernard André is more complex. Busch believed that he had made direct and extensive use of André, basing his conclusion on a simple assumption: if Bacon says something that can be found in André he must therefore have taken it from André. But a check of Busch's examples shows that Bacon, except on two occasions, was using André as he was reproduced by Speed.[22] The two exceptions are noteworthy. Bacon took from the *Vita* the two prophecies about Henry that are to be found at the end of the *History,* and the story of the libel "dispersed . . . against the King" by the French ambassador, Gaguin. Both provide color, and that, as Speed had recognized, was André's chief virtue as an historian.[23] At some point Bacon looked at the *Vita* and jotted down the ornaments he thought usable, but that is the only way in which the blind poet's text can be thought of as a source for the politic historian.

There is also no good evidence that Bacon went to Hakluyt for what he had to say about Cabot's voyages. His remarks are based on Stow and his own fund of scientific opinions, opinions that were also to make his description of the sweating sickness of Henry's first year uniquely his own.[24] Nor, as Spedding originally pointed out, is there reason to believe that Bacon had use of the rolls of parliament. The mistakes he makes with Henry's sessions indicate ignorance not carelessness, a conclusion all the more reasonable when we remember that the rolls were locked away in London.[25]

Tracking down sources, however, will not ultimately tell us very much about the history that Bacon fashioned from them, for by disposition and training, as well as immediate purpose, he was committed to a basically interpretive method. His task was to discover, and then persuasively describe for the reader, the "real" explanations and meanings of past events so that the present might profit. What had before been wrongly understood, or not understood at all, would now be made clear. To do this he relied almost entirely on his extraordinary deductive powers. "Therefore we shall make our judgment," he announces when introducing the Lambert Simnel conspiracy, "upon the things themselves, as they give light one to another, and (as we can) dig truth out of the mine" (6.44). Any curiosity contained in that statement is directed to constructing explanations; thus the casual, sometimes irresponsible, manner of using sources, and the indifference to augmenting them.[26] So long as Bacon had the main lines of the story set out before him on his worktable, he could make do.

With utility as the goal, and deduction as the method, it followed that experience in politics was the essential qualification for an historian. No other training could prepare a man to comprehend the inwardness of politics. Bacon had made this clear in the opening pages of the *In felicem memoriam Reginae Elizabethae,* where he castigated those "monks or closet penmen" who "being keen in style, poor in judgment, and partial in feeling, are no faithful witnesses as to the real passages of business." If such men were allowed to continue could there be any mystery why, as he noted in the fragment *History,* there was "a greater difference between the good and the bad" in histories than between "the most excellent poet and the vainest rhymer," or "the deepest philosopher and the most frivolous schoolmen"? Instead, the men who ought to be writing histories were "ministers and great officers," those who had "handled the helm of government, and been acquainted with the difficulties and mysteries of state business." By his own definition, then, the former Lord Chancellor was eminently qualified to write a history.

Bacon dedicated the *History* "in part of my acknowledgment" to Prince Charles, who had (more or less) stood by him during the impeachment proceedings. Gratitude, though, was not the most demanding motive for thrusting this "ancestor to the King your father and yourself" before the Prince's gaze.

> For he was a wise man, and an excellent King; and yet the times were rough and full of mutations and rare accidents. And it is with times as it is with ways. Some are more up-hill and down-hill, and some are more flat and plain; and the one is better for the liver, and the other for the writer. I have not flattered him, but took him to life as well as I could, sitting so far off, and having no better light. It is true, your Highness hath a living pattern, incomparable, of the King your father. But it is not amiss for you also to see one of these ancient pieces.[27]

Charles—and perhaps his father—was clearly meant to learn from the portrait. If that had not been Bacon's intention he would have penned a dedication of mumbo jumbo flattery, something he was very capable of doing. The insistence that this was the true Henry, warts and all, underscored his purpose. Henry had made mistakes; to laud him as an almost perfect king, as had the chroniclers, was not only wrong, but useless. For an idealized portrait would not disclose that a considerable part of any king's wisdom lay in the recognition and avoidance of past error. Bacon probably had little hope that after all these years James would change his ways. By 1621 the King was noticeably old and unwell, "a living pattern" as tired as he was tarnished. But Charles, if only because he was young, was salvageable, particularly in the eyes of a man whose faith in the educability of other men was exceeded only by his belief in himself as the exemplary teacher.

The opening pages of the *History* display the qualities that characterize the work as a whole. Unconcerned with the machinations that brought the Earl of Richmond to the throne of England, Bacon begins his tale in the aftermath of Bosworth Field. Richard III is judged a false and seeming prince, "his virtues and merits" but "feigned and affected things," a "king in fact only, but tyrant both in title and regiment." Although seemingly out of place, this judgment of Richard, together with the assessment of his specific sins, prepares the reader to recognize a true king,[28] one who had the "nobleness" to order a proper burial for an enemy who would have shown him neither mercy nor respect. Henry's wish that Richard receive "honourable interment" gains additional merit when we are informed how the "common people" subsequently disposed of the corpse "after many indignities and reproaches."

But it is Henry the problem-solver who first draws our sustained attention.

> But King Henry, in the very entrance of his reign and the instant of time when the kingdom was cast into his arms, met with a point of great difficulty and knotty to solve, able to trouble and confound the wisest King in the newness of his estate; and so much the more, because it could not endure a deliberation, but must be at once deliberated and determined. There were fallen to his lot, and concurrent in his person, three several titles to the imperial crown. [6.29]

Almost two pages will be spent examining the advantages and disadvantages of the "several titles," with phrases like "he knew" or "it lay plain before his eyes" carefully presuming that the first Tudor was fully aware of (and concerned with) the fine points involved, or at least of all the points that Bacon himself was cognizant of.[29] In the discussion of the claim by conquest there is even the hint that Henry remembered how William the Conqueror "forbare to use that claim in the beginning, but mixed it with a titulary pretense."

In none of the earlier chroniclers shall we find a King "full of these thoughts before his departure from Leicester." Why then in Bacon? What was to be gained from exposing the King's thoughts as he determined to "rest upon the title of Lancaster"? The simplest solution would be to say that the lawyer in Bacon recognized a problem and was inspired to remark upon it; certainly there are other moments in the *History* where we sense that a discussion has been taken up or prolonged for that reason.[30] But the more important answer involves Bacon's feeling for what a history ought to be, and what that meant in this situation. That is, Bacon is here following his own dictum of providing the "counsels" and "motives" of business by lucidly separating the strands of a complex problem which had to have been crucial to a king who won a throne in civil war. Moreover, Bacon thought that Henry had made a disastrous mistake when he ignored Yorkist passions and took up the Lancastrian claim, "that title best which made him independent." This made an examination of the problem even more relevant. The discussion, then, is not a diversion into law, but a chance to see how a fundamentally political dilemma was presumably faced. And the reader has been given notice that the *History* will be considerably less concerned with narrative story than with informing disquisitions.

With the quandary over claims resolved, Henry "set forward by easy journeys to the City of London, receiving the acclamations and applauses of the people as he went." The joy was "true and un-feigned," Bacon declares, because the people thought Henry had been dispatched from heaven "to unite and put to an end the long dissensions of the two houses." The assigned motive, which assumes the people applauded for a conclusion probably beyond their knowing or caring, is Bacon's invention; his sources merely record the effusions, with Hall suggesting as a reason the people's relief at the death of the tyrant. Bacon pulls away completely from his sources, though, when he explains how the King had a shrewd hand in all this. "He on the other side with great wisdom (not ignorant of the affections and fears of the people), to disperse the conceit and terror of a conquest, had given order that there should be nothing in his journey like unto a warlike march or manner; but rather like unto the progress of a King in full peace and assurance" (6.32). Henry's solicitude is reminiscent of Bacon's own concern for James's entry into England in 1603, when he had urged that "some gracious declaration, for the cherishing, entertaining, and preparing of men's affections" be promulgated. Desiring always to give Henry a part, Bacon assumes a sensitivity in such matters equal to his own. It is a case of the historian imagining that his subject understood what he ought to have understood.

But this eagerness to find the "counsels" behind every situation, an eagerness that in the early paragraphs of the *History* sets in motion waves of deliberateness which will ripple through the entire book, necessarily causes discrepancies. Consider Bacon's description of Henry's entrance into London.

> The mayor and companies of the City received him at Shoreditch; whence with great and honourable attendance, and troops of noblemen and persons of quality, he entered the City; himself not being on horseback, or in any open chair or throne, but in a close chariot; as one that having been sometimes an enemy to the whole state, and a proscribed person, chose rather to keep state and strike a reverence into the people than to fawn upon them.
>
> He went first into St. Paul's Church, where, not meaning that the people should forget too soon that he came in by battle, he made offertory of his standards, and had orizons and *Te Deum* again sung. [6.32-33]

Why, if Henry was concerned with quieting the fears of his newly won subjects, and had marched from Bosworth "as if in a progress," did he enter London "in a close chariot"? The answer is that he did not. Bacon got the story from Speed, who had apparently read Bernard André's term *laetanter* (joyfully) as *latenter* (secretly). This error is commonly held up as proof of Bacon's slipshod scholarship, which it may be.[31] Far more importantly, though, it betrays the essential weakness of Bacon's method. For had he been able to correct the misreading, can there be much doubt that he would have supplied an equally shrewd motive for a joyful entrance? Our feeling of unease is increased if we then recall Bacon's description of Henry's thoughts after Bosworth. Can we believe in the reality of a King who so lucidly computes the contingencies of a dilemma and then promptly makes, as Bacon would have us think, a patently wrong decision?

Not very easily, if we have a skeptical turn of mind. Bacon's method of doing history guarantees a large measure of invention. According to tradition Henry had been a wise and successful monarch, and Bacon accepted that judgment wholeheartedly. But unlike the chroniclers, who (except for Speed) had little ability and perhaps less interest in such matters, he needed to ascertain the specific links between wisdom and success, for that was what it meant to compose a useful history. Thus the guesswork, since there was neither time nor inclination to search other sources. There is, however, a more intriguing result, one which will gradually become evident. Because Bacon knew that Henry was wise, and because he (Bacon) knew what policies were wise, the depiction of the King's statecraft becomes, in effect, an extension of his own policies and principles. Henry is generally made to act for the reasons his creator knew were right. Bacon did not imagine that he was creating a fiction, nor did he crudely intend to set out a mouthpiece for his own ideas. There is no disjunction in his mind between what he wants Henry to be and what he sees him to be. The reader, though, may always wonder whether Bacon is explaining events simply as they appear to him, or as he wants them to appear to his audience. This ambiguity is inherent in history when it is written to confirm and teach the Truth.

No one could deny, however, that Bacon consciously used his literary powers to convince his readers of what he said. The seeming artlessness of the *History* is a deception, inspired by the plainness of style. Every page reveals the effort to move men to truth by traditional rhetorical devices. This was to be expected, despite the hurry in which the work was written. Bacon's dream of reclaiming position and reputation required that men—kings and groundlings alike—enjoy and embrace what he wrote, otherwise the truth of Henry's reign was otiose. Proof of success lies in the general acceptance of his vision of Henry VII. Indeed, measured in terms of belief, the *History* may be the most successful piece of rhetoric Bacon ever undertook. No other work of his pen—with the possible exception of Book I of the *Advancement of Learning*—has had quite the power to persuade men of its truthfulness.

The touch of the master is to be seen in the opening sentence.

> After that Richard, the third of that name, king in fact only, but tyrant both in title and regiment, and so commonly termed and reputed in all times since, was by the Divine Revenge, favouring the design of an exiled man, overthrown and slain at Bosworth Field; there succeeded in the kingdom the Earl of Richmond, thenceforth styled Henry the Seventh. [6.27]

By deliberately recapturing and justifying the order of history with the order of his statement, Bacon has swept the stage clean; the sentence is less a notice of fact than it is a judgment, and the reader's mind is left both settled and attentive. We are then presented with the indictment of Richard, a brief made all the more weighty by the use of polysyndeton.

> And although he were a Prince in militar virtue approved, etc. And therefore it was noted by men of great understanding, etc. And that out of this deep root of ambition it sprang, etc. And as for the politic and wholesome laws, etc.

This device in turn sets up the use of the contrasting conjuction when we are reintroduced to Henry. "But King Henry, in the very entrance to his reign, etc." The subsequent analysis of the problem involving the "three several titles" exemplifies that concern for methodical presentation found in all of Bacon's works. The three titles are first briefly described in a single sentence, following which there is a long discussion of each in the same order as it was introduced. The resulting clarity draws us closer to Henry and gives us more trust in Bacon as our guide; orderly exposition bestows a more secure sense of where we are at in the narrative, and where we are headed.[32] Finally, there is a sample of how imagery will be employed in the *History*. At the end of the paragraph where Bacon has noted the King's decision to marry Elizabeth of York and described the journey from Bosworth to London is attached a summary image. "And as his victory gave him the knee, so his purpose of marriage with the Lady Elizabeth gave him the heart; so that both knee and heart did truly bow before him." The position and distilling character of the metaphor coaxes the reader to accept a point of view, and to read on with that view in mind. This explains why the images in the *History* usually appear at the beginning or end of a paragraph,[33] and why Bacon did not mind borrowing so many of them from Hall and Speed. It was a case of the professional knowing how to make better use of the amateur's lucky find.

Already it should be evident that the *History*–scissors and paste job though it is—has a special presence. The author has borrowed fact, format, and metaphor, and made of them an original creation. As such, the work should command a certain respect; it is far superior to the numerous other minimally researched and highly rationalistic histories of Bacon's day. They, after all, are for the most part no longer readable, and never contained the persuasive impact of the *History*. A closer look at its major parts will reveal how the *History* goes beyond the conventions of the period, and why Bacon's experiences and personality, not just his art and theories, must be taken into account if the book is to be understood.

Any political history of Henry's reign must largely be taken up with recounting the various conspiracies and rebellions that plagued the King. These dynastic challenges, colored always in dark tones by the chroniclers,[34] were Henry's main worry, at least until 1497. Having won his crown through guile and battle he would be obliged to spend much of his time defending it by the same means. Bacon, of course, was no stranger to "Tempests in State." For over twenty-five years he had been examining and prosecuting traitors, and felt himself enough of an expert on the subject to have already composed two essays on it.[35] Moreover, he had also trained his pen in these matters. The several tracts and briefs on conspiracies scattered through his career, with their superb command of narration and protraiture, promised that when he came to describe sedition in Henry's reign he would give a convincing performance.

The Lambert Simnel imposture, culminating in the battle of Stoke (1487), is a showpiece of Bacon's talents. A special confidence characterizes his account; he knows that his understanding of the *type* of event will enable him to clear away the confusions surrounding the case in hand. "Whereof the relations which we have are so naked, as they leave it scarce credible; not for *the nature of it,* (for it hath fallen out oft,) but for the manner and circumstance of it, especially in the beginnings" (6.44, emphasis added). The promise is made good when he solemnly announces who was pulling strings in the affair. "That which is most probable, out of the precedent and subsequent acts, is, that it was the Queen Dowager from whom this action had the principal source and motion" (6.46). His "conjecture" is based on the decision of a "close counsel, without any legal proceeding," to cloister the Queen Dowager and confiscate her lands on the "far-fetched pretences" that she willingly surrendered her daughter to Richard III. "Which proceeding being even at that time taxed for rigorous and undue, both in matter and manner, makes it very probable there was some greater matter against her, which the King upon reason of policy and to avoid envy would not publish."[36]

Whether Elizabeth Woodville actually had a role in the conspiracy—a point still unsettled[37]—does not need deciding to appreciate why it was Bacon who first made the charge. His sense of the "probable" in such cases, which made him reject the "subtile priest called Richard Simon" because he could not have known enough about Edward Plantagenet to have trained the imposter, and discount the published reasons for the Queen Dowager's disgrace, had been formed through years of presupposing Philip II of Spain to be the figure behind the conspiracies against Elizabeth. When he comes later to discuss Perkin Warbeck he will grossly exaggerate the part of Margaret of Burgundy for the same reason.[38] The logic of conspiracies demanded a chief architect, a man or woman behind the scenes who stood to profit from the overthrow of the legitimate sovereign, and the available evidence in both cases made deducing the answers relatively simple for so practiced an investigator.

In describing the rest of this conspiracy, Bacon sticks more closely to his sources, moving back and forth between Hall and Speed as it suits his purpose. Yet into his account he is ever weaving explanations and motives for events. So, for example, we are told why Simon took his "pupil" to Ireland, why the Irish entertained him with "incredible affection," why Henry did not imprison the Earl of Lincoln whom he suspected of traitorous designs, why the rebel army raised in Flanders went over to Ireland, and why, when the rebels finally came over to England, the people did not flock to their standards. These questions are not even raised by his predecessors; neither their backgrounds nor their sense of what a history ought to be would have prompted them to recognize their significance, and the undeniable result are narratives tedious to the modern ear. But because Bacon asked the right questions it does not follow that he gave the correct answers. Deduction has had to work with narratives plainly meagre in facts, and therefore the reader is often asked to swallow explanations that have only a sweet coating of style to recommend them.

Sometimes we can taste the political principle that has inspired analysis, as when he asserts, during the description of the "counsel" he imagines was held in Dublin to discuss whether Simnel and his army should descend on England, that it was basically the eagerness of the "men of war," "(as in such cases of popular tumult is usual)," rather than any rational considerations that decided the matter (6.54). At other times we see motives conforming to what the actor should, considering his position, have been thinking. Thus, Bacon portrays the Earl of Lincoln as figuring that the crown would wind up on his head, rather than Warwick's, once the conspiracy had succeeded and Simnel been disposed of.[39] This suggestion, not even alluded to in his sources, stems from Bacon's premise that because Lincoln was in the line of succession to the throne, he necessarily would have been operating only for himself. The twin to this cynical hypothesis is Bacon's assumption that Henry all along "secretly" kept an eye on the Earl, for that is what you do with those in the line of succession (6.52). Guesswork gets Bacon into trouble when he explains why the English did not welcome Simnel and his army. He mixes contradictory reasons, "partly by the good taste that the King had given his people of his government, joined with the reputation of his felicity" (Bacon had introduced the conspiracy by saying that Henry "was not without much hatred throughout the realm"), with a bit of wishful chauvinism, "and partly for that it was an odious thing to the people of England to have a King brought in to them upon the shoulders of Irish and Dutch."[40] Finally, Bacon assumes that Henry's charitable treatment of Simnel was a piece of shrewdness, "thinking that if he suffered death he would be forgotten too soon; but being kept alive he would be a continual spectacle, and a kind of remedy against the like inchantments of people in time to come."[41] Precisely *how* Simnel was to act as a "remedy" is never clarified. But we can readily appreciate why the former prosecutor and judge should have thought that Henry intended an object lesson. Believing the boy to have been "of the age of some fifteen years" when in fact he was only about ten—"a very chylde" in Hall's words—Bacon, himself childless, did not imagine that simple pity prompted Henry's pardon.

Skeptical though we should be of Bacon's explanations, we cannot deny that he tells a good story. Beginning with his introduction, which attempts to give the reasons for the "combustion," he enlists the reader's interest in the events themselves, whereas Hall, by luridly bemoaning the corruption of the times, and Speed, by discoursing on the commonness of "false pretenders," stall our concern. Bacon subsequently holds our interest by more carefully organizing his narrative. For example, although he generally follows his sources in shifting the reader's attention back and forth between conspirators and King, Ireland and England, his transitions are clearer, and he is willing to employ brief flashbacks to avoid the confusions consequent (particularly in Hall) upon following a strict chronology. This organic shaping of events, combined with the continual inspection of motives, impels the reader ever forward to the resolution of the story. Bacon at the same time sustains a sense of continuity by his exact use of metaphor. Almost all the images are drawn from his sources, but he is much more deliberate in his usage, carefully infusing in the reader, for example, a feeling of contempt for the "pageant" in general and Simnel, the "puppet," in particular. At the conclusion the recurring image of the conspiracy as a "play" is neatly tied up. "For which cause he [Simnel] was taken into service in his court to a base office in his kitchen; so that . . . he turned a broach that had worn a crown; whereas fortune commonly doth not bring in a comedy or farce after a tragedy."[42] The importance of all this is that Bacon, by forging a tale in which the reader has a more comfortable sense of structure—a beginning, a middle, and an end—is able to convince us of the correctness of his observations.

What is distinctive in Bacon's portrayal of the Lambert Simnel episode—the reliance on his own legal experience to elucidate events, the use of the typical, the ready-made "rule," to assess motives and situations, and a narrative style aimed at winning the reader—can be seen in his description of each of the other "tumults" that threatened Henry's crown.

In the Perkin Warbeck conspiracy, for example, we are shown a Margaret of Burgundy whose skill in instructing the imposter in how to make his story "hang together" is plausible only if we assume that she had had Bacon's experience as an examiner.

> She taught him only to tell a smooth and likely tale . . . warning him not to vary from it. . . . She taught him likewise how to avoid sundry captious and tempting questions, which were like to be asked of him.[43]

A similar fabrication occurs a little later when Bacon states that Henry had Sir James Tirrell and John Dighton, the two men still alive "that could speak upon knowledge" of the deaths of the princes in the Tower, examined in order to reveal Warbeck as a fraud. In reality, the two men were not examined until 1502, and Hall, whom Bacon follows in his report of what they confessed at the later date, makes this quite clear.[44] What has happened is that Bacon, knowing well the methods needed to "lay open" a conspiracy, has presupposed that Henry also knew what to do, a conclusion amusingly reinforced when we see Bacon then criticize the handling of the examination.[45] This is not the only occasion where Bacon's willingness to project his own legal experiences onto Henry forces him to reprimand the King. When Perkin is finally captured and brought to London, a confession is obtained and printed.

> Wherein the King did himself no right: for as there was a laboured tale of particulars of Perkin's father and mother and grandsire and grandmother and uncles and cousins, by names and surnames, and from what places he travelled up and down; so there was little or nothing to purpose of any thing concerning his designs, or any practices that had been held with him; nor the Duchess of Burgundy herself, that all the world did take knowledge of as the person that had put life and being into the whole business, so much as named or pointed at; so that men missing of that they looked for, looked about for they knew not what, and were in more doubt than before.[46]

It needed the man who had written the government's propaganda on Lopez, Walpole, Essex, and Ralegh to make that judgment.

In the account of the Cornish revolt, on the other hand, we see more of the rule-conscious philosopher. Miserably poor and unwilling to subsidize a war with the Scots, the people of the southwest refused in 1497 to pay the taxes levied by parliament. "And as in the tides of people once up there want not commonly stirring winds to make them more rough; so this people did light upon two ringleaders or captains of the rout" (6.176). Speed provided the image, but it is the author of the essay, "Of Seditions and Troubles," who pumps it up into a law of political conduct so that the reader might understand how this particular uprising instanced a perennial phenomenon. We are dealing not simply with a stylistic ploy, but a deep insistence on seeing people and events in a generic—thus useful—context. "The people upon these seditious instigations did arm, . . . and forthwith under the command of their leaders (which in such cases is ever at pleasure) marched out of Cornwall" (6.177). Still another rule is cited when we hear of how London received the rebels. "But the City of London, . . . was in great tumult; as it useth to be with wealthy and populous cities, especially those which being for greatness and fortune queens of their regions, do seldom see out of their windows or from their towers an army of enemies" (6.180). Bacon is not satisfied with describing the specific; the immediate fact is weighed to determine its prescriptive value.

No less evident in his version of the other rebellions are those small but crucial stylistic efforts to help the reader. His description of the Perkin Warbeck "personation" is a noteworthy example. That lengthy escapade, with its interruptions and wanderings, was difficult to follow in Hall and Speed, but Bacon is always at pains to organize each scene. Listen to him describe Henry's response to first learning about Perkin.

> His purposes were two: the one to lay open the abuse; the other to break the knot of the conspirators. To detect the abuse, there were but two ways; the first to make it manifest to the world that the Duke of York was indeed murdered; the other to prove that (were he dead or alive) yet Perkin was a counterfeit. For the first, thus it stood. [6.141]

This same concern leads him to relate the Cornish uprising in one piece, rather than let the narrative flow be interrupted, as had the chroniclers, with brief recitals of the other problems then burdening the King. Imagery, too, is effectively used, as can be seen in the introduction to the tax revolt in Yorkshire in 1489.

> But howsoever the laws made in that Parliament did bear good and wholesome fruit; yet the subsidy granted at the same time bore a fruit that proved harsh and bitter. All was inned at last into the King's barn; but it was after a storm. [6.88]

By indicating both the cause and outcome of the events to be described, the images—both old friends of the author—invite the reader forward; there is just the right mixture of suspense and certainty to stir the appetite. And when Bacon has finished with this affair and turns to sad matters in Scotland, he gives us a transition that has the same seductive qualities to it. "About the same time that the King lost so good a servant as the Earl of Northumberland, he lost likewise a faithful friend and ally of James the Third King of Scotland by a miserable disaster."[47]

What lessons were to be learned from watching Henry beat down the challenges to his throne? How did conspiracies founded on dynastic rivalries and popular rebellions sparked by heavy taxes relate to a sovereign who had come to his crown quietly, who had only recently been voted a subsidy for the first time in ten years, and whose son would unquestionably succeed him without a sword being raised? To Bacon the relation was obvious enough: rebellious and seditious subjects, whatever their faces or complaints, were a type. James may not have yet seen his people carry arms against himself, but there had been conspiracies on his life (though fewer than he imagined) and he had heard almost insulting discontent in his parliaments. Still, Bacon was much less conscious of pointing to exact correspondences than he was with portraying the specific qualities and strategies necessary to a king facing dangerous situations. Henry is intended to be a model of kingcraft, as well as a mentor to James and his son, and rare indeed was the king who had not faced the problem of sedition.

The picture of Henry confronting sedition is that of a King who learns of danger without trembling, and who then carefully analyzes the circumstances, acts swiftly to defeat his enemies, and, finally, metes out punishment with the wisdom of a Solomon. Fearless, prudent, and resolute, Henry is a worthy ancestor to the queen Bacon so admired. (Not once is there a hint that Henry felt any terror; he may be "moved" or "troubled," but he is never permitted to be "afflicted," in Hall's words, "with no small fear.") In the other chroniclers we do not see these characteristics very clearly; they are all there, either stated directly, or implied in the evidence, but there is no effort to focus them. It is Bacon, ever adjusting his lens for the sake of the reader, who makes them stand out sharply. Typical of the result is his account of the defeat of the Stafford-Lovell rising, where he manages to win all the credit for Henry, against the testimony of Hall and Speed.

> And as his manner was to send his pardons rather before the sword than after, he gave commission to the Duke [of Bedford] to proclaim pardon to all that would come in: which the Duke, upon his approach to the Lord Lovell's camp, did perform. And it fell out as the King expected; the heralds were the great ordnance.[48]

How important it was to imprint the proper image of the King upon the reader's mind is indicated by the trouble sometimes taken to explain the King's actions. For example, Henry's staying locked up in London during the Cornish revolt, contrary to his "former custom and practice" of going out to meet the enemy, obliges Bacon to spend almost a page justifying this seemingly unkingly backwardness. "And lastly, both reason of estate and war seemed to agree with this course. For that insurrections of base people are commonly more furious in their beginnings." And to scotch any lingering suspicions, Bacon then shows that Henry himself was aware of the potential embarrassment.

> The King, knowing well that it stood him upon, by how much the more he had hitherto protracted the time in not encountering them [viz., the rebels], by so much the sooner to dispatch with them; that it might appear to have been no coldness in fore-slowing but wisdom in choosing his time. [6.179]

This double dose of purposive thinking should not be regarded as an attempt by the author to deceive his readers. On the contrary, while persuading us Bacon is also persuading himself. Yet there comes a moment when even Bacon cannot quite comprehend the King, when the rationalizing capacity breaks down. At the conclusion of the Cornish rebellion Henry executed only three men, a fact that inspires some reflections.

> It was a strange thing to observe the variety and inequality of the King's executions and pardons: and a man would think it at the first a kind of lottery or chance. But looking into it more nearly, one shall find there was reason for it; much more perhaps, than after so long a distance of time we can now discern. In the Kentish commotion (which was but an handful of men) there were executed to the number of one hundred and fifty; and in this so mighty a rebellion but three. Whether it were that the King put to account the men that were slain in the field; or that he was not willing to be severe in a popular cause; or that the harmless behaviour of this people, that came from the west of England to the east without mischief (almost) or spoil of the country, did somewhat mollify him and move him to compassion; or lastly, that he made a great difference between people that did rebel upon wantonness, and them that did rebel upon want. [6.183]

The desire to make the King's actions result from a principle or rule is evident; "chance" is unacceptable as the determining factor. In part this search is a habit of Bacon's mind, but it is also based on his belief that a state has its fate largely determined by the way in which *praemium* and *poena* are dispensed. In the *Advancement of Learning* he had declared that "writers of histories" could teach men "how . . . to set affection against affection, and to master one by another . . . upon which foundation is erected that excellent use of *praemium* and *poena,* whereby civil states consist."[49] It was therefore necessary to make sense of Henry's apparently inconsistent actions if the King were to retain his reputation for wisdom. Indeed, in the fragment *History* it is even more clear that Bacon is groping for a principle just *because* of Henry's reputation for wisdom. "In the suppressing and punishing of the treasons which during the whole course of his reign were committed against him, he had a very strange kind of inter-changing of very large and unexpected pardons with severe executions; which (his wisdom considered) could not be imputed to any inconstancy or inequality."[50] There is no room for an explanation that says Henry acted upon spite, whim, or merely fatigue, for that would have smacked of failure, on both the King's part and the author's. Monarchs must act from consistent policy; historians must have the wit to name its parts.

"Stout without and apprehensive within," Henry withstood the bouts of sedition. Like all other kings, however, Henry had also "to hearken to foreign business," and there he showed a singular cunning and resilience. Or at least that is the way Bacon saw it. His descriptions of Henry's diplomacy, which for clarity are a striking improvement upon the often turgid pages of his predecessors, stress a capacity for managing events that would make any prince envious.

> Finding therefore the inconveniences and difficulties in the prosecution of a war, he cast with himself how to compass two things. The one, how by the declaraion and inchoation of a war to make his profit. The other, how to come off from the war with saving of his honour. For profit, it was to be made two ways; upon his subjects for the war, and upon his enemies for the peace; like a good merchant that maketh his gain both upon the commodities exported and imported back again. For the point of honour, wherein he might suffer for giving over the war, he considered well, that as he could not trust upon the aids of Ferdinando and Maximilian for supports of war, so the impuissance of the one, and the double proceeding of the other, lay fair for him for occasions to accept of peace.
>
> These things he did wisely foresee, and did as artificially conduct, whereby all things fell into his lap as he desired. [6.120]

Here especially we can see how the orderly presentation of Henry's scheming induces us to believe in the King's wisdom. But was there ever a king whose plans came to so perfect a conclusion?

Sublimely confident both of his own political insight and Henry's prudence, Bacon believed he could find the "true" interpretations for Henry's actions. His unsnarling of the tangled Brittany involvement, the major foreign business of the King's reign, vividly demonstrates what this entailed. Hall and Speed had given particularly unsatisfactory accounts: the former's was bloated almost beyond intelligibility, the latter's hurried and sketchy, especially where it dealt with events on the Continent. To be sure, there was no way to pretend that England had benefited from Brittany's being annexed by France; pride, pocket, and security had all been pinched. Instead, Bacon endeavors to make Henry look as good as the circumstances would allow, to persuade us that the King's reputation for wisdom was not bruised by the increase in French power. The result, while pleasing as narrative, mangles history.

To justify Henry's reputation Bacon emphasized that the King had seen through the designs of Charles VIII from the beginning. Accordingly, he greatly expands upon the interview at Leicester (1487) when ambassadors from the King of France first informed Henry of their master's "quarrel" with the Duke of Brittany, and requested either his "assistance" or his neutrality. From the brief reports of his sources Bacon had the gist of the ambassadors' message as well as the assumption that Henry could differentiate between the pretexts and the real motives for a French invasion of Brittany. With this he created two speeches in the third person, one belonging to the embassy and the other to Henry, which fill up three pages of his narrative. These inventions portray far more graphically than any short summary could the quality of dissimulation that Henry realized he was up against, and how, starting with artful eloquence, he hoped to deal with it. By being drawn within the meeting itself the reader more readily digests the necessary conclusion. "And so it was, that the King was neither so shallow nor so ill advertised as not to perceive the intention of the French for the investing himself of Brittaine" (6.67).

The problem here is not so much with the truth of the conclusion as with the means used to arrive at it. Bacon had been composing speeches to fit the lips of other men for decades, and given his large faith in the power of words to direct events, as well as the sanction of his favorite historians, it was inevitable that he should exercise his talent in the *History*. He was, though, careful to insert speeches only where his sources indicated they had occurred, or where it might reasonably be assumed they had, and he always cautioned that he was not reporting the actual words spoken. "[The] ambassadors . . . delivered their ambassage to this effect." As with the other rhetorical devices, Bacon did not feel that fabricated eloquence compromised the truth, only revealed it. But remarkable for their style and tone as the speeches are, serious distortions occur because the motive for composing them dictates their content, and because there is always the presumption (of both the artist and politician in Bacon) that they had a definite effect on the actors.

The distortions begin immediately, as Bacon invents an explanation for the opening remarks of the French so that the reader will acknowledge their slyness. "They first imparted unto the King the success that their master had had a little before against Maximilian in recovery of certain towns from him; which was done in a kind of privacy and inwardness towards the King; as if the French King did not esteem him for an outward or formal confederate, but as one that had part in his affections and fortunes, and with whom he took pleasure to communicate his business" (6.64). Hall simply cited the mention of the "success." Even more blatantly hypothetical, though necessary to Bacon's purposes as we shall see, is the statement that the ambassadors "entertained the King also with some wandering discourses of their King's purpose to recover by arms his right to the kingdom of Naples, by an expedition in person." This, Bacon says, was intended to "remove the King from all jealousy of any design in these hither parts upon Brittaine" (6.66). But since Charles did not march into Italy until seven years later it is improbable that he tried at this time to gull Henry with the prospect.[51] What apparently inspired the inference was Hall's later comment, made when discussing the Treaty of Etaples (1492), that Charles had "longe before thristed & sore wished" to "warre agaynst Ferdinand kynge of Napels."[52]

Similar tinkering is to be found in Henry's reported speech, although here too Bacon doubtless believed that he had not disturbed the truth. Did it matter, he might have argued, that he let Henry say what Hall described the King as instructing Christopher Urswick to report when he was sent to France shortly after the meeting at Leicester? This was only to allow Henry to speak his own thoughts. Besides, the switch was later obliquely confessed. "Urswick made declaration to the French King much to the purpose of the King's answer to the French ambassadors here" (6.69). Less easy to defend, however, was the inclusion in the King's reply (contrary to anything stated in the chroniclers) of a quiet warning to the French that he perceived their real aims. "And in this sort the French ambassadors were dismissed: the King avoiding to understand any thing touching the re-annexing of Brittaine, as the ambassadors had avoided to mention it; save that he gave a little touch of it in the word *envy*" (6.67, Bacon's emphasis).

What Bacon is doing in these speeches is asking the reader to share his faith in Henry's shrewdness on the basis of inventions he is able to control. The temptation is irresistible. We know the speeches are inventions yet we surrender to the larger vision of the King ("a wonder for wise men") that they hold out to us.

In the following pages Bacon continues to emphasize that Henry was not duped by the "art and dissimulation" of Charles VIII. "Neither was the King himself led all this while with credulity merely, as was generally supposed. But his error was not so much facility of belief, as an ill-measuring of the forces of the other party." This distinction is only vaguely felt in the pages of Hall and Speed, who never quite deny that Charles "abused the King of England's credulity"; Bacon significantly sharpens it by repeating, within the space of five pages, his analysis of how "the King had cast the business . . . with himself" (6.67-68,73). As with the earlier survey of Henry's "knotty" problem, Bacon convinces the reader of Henry's awareness and subtle strategies by portraying the King thinking about all the points that he (Bacon) knew were involved. That hindsight was crucial to his estimation of the King's mind is demonstrated by his comment on the Duke of Brittany's death: "an accident that the King might easily have foreseen, and ought to have reckoned upon and provided for" (6.83). Further disclosure of this approach comes in the verdict on Henry's strategy during the first stages of the Brittany business. "He promised himself money; honour, friends, and peace in the end. But those things were too fine to be fortunate and succeed in all parts; for that great affairs are commonly too rough and stubborn to be wrought upon by the finer edges or points of wit" (6.74). Quite unwittingly the author is actually criticizing his *own* elaborate reconstruction; Henry perhaps merited blame, but not for a strategy he did not plot. Bacon traps himself again in his portrayal of Charles VIII, whom he never tires of accusing of "dissimulation," when he explains why the French King protected the English ambassadors at his court from angry "young bloods" at the time of Lord Woodville's apparently unauthorized mission of aid to Brittany. "But the French King, both to preserve the privilege of ambassadors, and being conscious to himself that in the business of peace he himself was the greater dissembler of the two [viz., himself and Henry], forbad all injuries of fact or words against their persons or followers" (6.72). Charles VIII may have known himself to be a dissembler, but it is a queer sort of anachronistic deduction that assigns him a motive based on an integrity that would contradict what we have been previously led to believe about him.

The latter stages of the Brittany affair, culminating in the siege of Boulogne and the Treaty of Etaples (1492), saw Henry salvage his dignity and his purse. Bacon does what he can to lend the King a hand in his efforts, particularly (and predictably) by making it appear that success fell out according to a well-laid and intricate plan. The sequence of events is interpreted so as to substitute mind for accident and inertia. "Though he shewed great forwardness for a war, not only to his Parliament and court, but to his privy counsel likewise (except the two bishops and a few more), yet nevertheless in his secret intentions he had no purpose to go through with any war upon France" (6.119). To convince himself of this Bacon resorted to retrospective wisdom, "he knew well that France was now entire and at unity with itself, and never so mighty many years before," and assumptions contradicted by his sources, "he considered well . . . he could not trust upon the aids of Ferdinando and Maximilian for supports of war."[53] Forgotten in his enthusiastic rendition of Henry's masterful scheme is his earlier warning that "great affairs are commonly too rough and stubborn to be wrought upon by the finer edges or points of wit." The energy that before had been used to squeeze the best out of failure is now employed to enhance success.

The reader is also treated to another pair of speeches, wonderfully conveying Bacon's opinion of their speaker's position, when a second embassy is sent to Henry by Charles VIII, who hoped "to carry the marriage [of Anne of Brittany] as he had carried the wars, by entertaining the King of England in vain belief" (6.103). This time, though, the reader becomes a direct witness as Bacon switches from third person reports of what was said to first person deliveries. Since deception was basic to the aims of the French—Charles wanted Anne for himself (not merely the right to "dispose" of her marriage) and sought (according to Bacon) to gain peace with England in order to free himself to invade Italy—we are presented with a lengthy and "eloquent declaration" by the least important of the French ambassadors, Robert Gaguin, "(who though he were third in place, yet was held the best speaker of them)" (6.104). The aside nicely emphasizes that the French have only "sugared words" with which to defend their ambitions, and Bacon patiently strings out the flattery and empty arguments so that the reader is in no doubt of what to think. Properly hooked, we then relish Chancellor Morton's crisp reply, which punctures the French arguments with disdainful pleasure, leaving us satisfied that Henry was not fooled by the "wonted arts" of Charles

VIII. Further, Henry is carefully shown here to be practicing that discreet use of his counselors that Bacon had often, both privately and publicly, urged on James.

> Having therefore conferred divers times with his counsel, and keeping himself somewhat close, he gave a direction to the Chancellor for a formal answer to the ambassadors; and that he did in the presence of his counsel. And after, calling the Chancellor to him apart, bad him speak in such language as was fit for a treaty that was to end in a breach.[54]

Bacon has no evidence for such a tactic; history is being stretched to reach to his analysis.[55]

The use of the first person in these speeches befits the occasion, for the exchange is depicted as the turning point in the Brittany adventure as a whole. With an altogether incredible lucidity and swiftness, Henry revamps his strategy after being informed of the ambassador's message. "But weighing one thing with another, he gave Brittaine for lost; but resolved to make his profit of this business of Brittaine, as a quarrel for war; and of that of Naples, as a wrench and mean for peace; being well advertised how strongly the King was bent upon that action" (6.109-10). This is further evidence of why Bacon could insist that Henry plotted the denouement to "this business." Believing that Charles's designs on Naples had, from the start, played a spoken role in the negotiations —Gaguin speaks again of this ambition—he could imagine, especially as 1494 drew closer, that Henry would have had the wit to see how he could use that future event to escape from his present predicament. And so it is that Bacon is obliged to point out that Morton was given "a special caveat" by Henry not "to use any words to discourage the voyage of Italy," for that would have ruined the interpretation which gave the King highest honors.

Bacon's imagination had an easy run in most of the other diplomatic maneuvers of Henry's reign. At times, however, it goes wild, as in the description of how Henry subtly manipulated the Spanish ambassador, Pedro de Ayala, to initiate peace with Scotland, a description that ignores the fact, known to both Speed and Hall, that mediating a peace between England and Scotland was the prime purpose of Ayala's embassy.[56] As always, the key to each of Bacon's assessments is the desire to explain the King's prudence and show its rewards. "And yet this declaration of the King," Bacon says of Henry's response to Pope Alexander's call for a crusade, "(as superficial as it was) gave him that reputation abroad, as he was not long after elected by the Knights of the Rhodes protector of their order; all things multiplying to honour in a prince that had gotten such high estimation for his wisdom and sufficiency" (6.210-11). To make his point Bacon has had to compress events: Pope Alexander's call came in 1501, the honor in 1506. So long as they fell in the right order, past events served best those who had a meaning to give them.

Aside from the general helps for all kings, which rose close to the surface of the narrative, was there in Bacon's account of Henry's diplomacy a lesson for the Stuarts? Were these sections influenced by Bacon's reading of contemporary events? Undoubtedly yes. Henry was a sovereign who had preferred peace to war, and had succeeded by a deft combination of logic, threats, and occasional "succours" in getting his way, especially during the Brittany crisis. In 1621, James, who also was a lover of peace, was facing a situation not unlike Henry's: substitute Spain for France as ambitious trouble-maker, keeping in mind England's vested interests on the Continent, and the parallel sprung to life. But could James manage a similar success? Could he threaten and dissemble in such a way as to make the Habsburgs hesitate, or was his distaste for war so strong (more importantly, so well known) that he had no trumps to play in the complicated game of mediation? From the King's rejection of those parts of his pre-parliamentary proclamation that threatened war, and from the way matters had drifted since parliament had convened, Bacon must have felt that James needed urging on this matter. Thus the emphasis in the *History* on Henry's only playing with war, and, even more dramatically, the statement in the concluding portrait. "He knew the way to peace was not to seem to be desirous to avoid wars. Therefore would he make offers and fames of wars, till he had mended the conditions of peace" (6.238). Bacon is not, however, simply intoning a rebuke to James, the statement rises out of what he believed he saw.

When Bacon related the conspiracies that racked Henry's reign, "being almost a fever that took him every year," or recounted the twistings and turnings of the King's diplomacy, he depended on the chroniclers to provide him with the basic facts. But in his description of Henry's parliaments he was left almost entirely to his own knowledge and imagination, for Hall and Speed had given only occasional notice to the monies and laws that had come out of them. (In fact, Henry VII's parliaments are the least documented of any since the reign of Edward III.) This general silence did not discourage Bacon; if anything, it may have pleased him for once not to be burdened with unhusked reports. He knew, after all, what parliaments were like; he had sat in them for forty years. All he needed were copies of the statutes and the few details from his sources, and he could give a true picture of Henry's sessions. As a result, whereas the reports of Hall and Speed would together barely fill a page, more than fifteen per cent of Bacon's text is devoted to parliamentary activities.

Yet simply doing justice to an institution that he had long experience in was not the primary incentive to Bacon's effort, at least not in the summer of 1621. Instead, the almost transparent object was to show how a parliament should be conducted; and so it is that in these sections of the *History* the didactic pulse beats fastest. This was to be expected. On no other issue had Bacon spent more energy and ink advising James, and the session recently ended had (to his mind) proven once again that it was folly to disregard his opinion. Furthermore, the benefits to be derived were larger than they seemed at first glance. For if James could improve his relations with parliament, he would necessarily see the factious spirit of his subjects quieted, secure himself a better position to work his will abroad, and perhaps even see his way clear to finding a place for a deposed chancellor.

Henry's first parliament reveals the King as already the master of an institution hitherto unknown to him. He understands perfectly what can and cannot be obtained, and how the obtainable is best won. Moreover, he appreciates how parliament can serve, as Bacon for years had been telling James, "for the better knitting of the hears of your subjects unto your Majesty." The lesson is immediately drawn in the introductory discussion of motives. "Unto these three special motives of a Parliament was added, that he as a prudent and moderate prince made this judgment, that it was fit for him to haste to let his people see that he meant to govern by law, howsoever he came in by the sword." Following this statement Bacon describes how each of the three "ends" for summoning parliament was actually handled, easing the reader's path by keeping to the order in which they were originally announced. In the process Henry demonstrates a keen and sensitive legal mind.

> For that which concerned the entailing of the crown . . . he carried it . . . with great wisdom and measure. For he did not press to have the act penned by way of declaration or recognition of right; as on the other side he avoided to have it by new law or ordinance; but chose rather a kind of middle way, by way of establishment, and that under covert and indifferent words. [6.36]

Hall had quoted this "notable acte" but said nothing of its making or meaning. Bacon, pleased by its ambiguity, used the resolution—it is not actually an act of parliament[57]—as a proof of the King's wisdom. Hence the rhetorical device of making it seem as if Henry himself was the author, and the appearance of a favorite and always approving phrase ("middle way") to characterize it.

Henry also earns Bacon's approval, both as lawyer and politician, in his method of reversing the attainders against his followers. "But wisely not shewing himself at all moved therewith, he would not understand it but as a case in law, and wished the judges to be advised thereupon, who for that purpose were forthwith assembled in the Exchequer-chamber (which is the counsel-chamber of the judges), and upon deliberation they gave a grave and safe opinion and advice, mixed with law and convenience" (6.37). Here was formal justification for his opinion that the place of the judges was to serve as a support to the King, and a smug reminder to Coke as to who in 1615 had had more right on his side.[58] Finally, Henry's decision to forgo a subsidy is attributed to his appreciation of what was possible.

> As for money or treasure, the King thought it not seasonable or fit to demand any of his subjects at this parliament; both because he had received satisfaction from them in matters of so great importance, and because he could not remunerate them with any general pardon (being prevented therein by the coronation pardon passed immediately before); but chiefly, for that it was in every man's eye what great forfeitures and confiscations he had at that present to help himself. [6.39]

It was precisely this kind of sensitivity and restraint that Bacon had long urged on James, once even recommending that "subsidies should never be given nor spoken of in the next Parliament" so that the King might win a better "reputation" with the members and consequently strengthen his hand for "future" sessions (12.184). Once again Henry's motives are a witness to the historian's own thoughts, and a justification of them.

With Henry's first parliament Bacon was able to demonstrate the King's finesse in settling his claims and soothing his people. With the second he shows how the King worked a parliament to gain supply, and continues to celebrate the wisdom and skill to be found in the King's laws. The reader, meanwhile, feels his admiration growing.

Following his sources, whose interpretations might be scoffed at but whose facts and chronology he had neither the means nor the inclination to criticize, Bacon (mistakenly) believed that this parliament met at a critical moment in the "business of Brittaine."[59] But where Hall and Speed had seen Henry sincerely anxious to obtain money and sympathy "to support the warre of Brittaine," and reported his success, Bacon imagined that the King had no intention at this time of intervening but "thought to make his vantage upon his Parliament, knowing that they being affectionate unto the quarrel of Brittaine would give treasure largely" (6.73). Here, of course, was the strategy Bacon had often urged on James, and one (as is implicit in his rejected proclamation) that he felt suited the situation in 1621. The prospect, at least, of a foreign war might dispel tensions between the King and his subjects, and at the same time fill the royal coffers. Bacon remembered the willingness of Elizabeth's parliaments to vote subsidies at the rumor of war, and believed (though scarcely a man of martial feeling himself) that talking about the possibility of conflict was a legitimate method "to work upon to move a Parliament."[60] Especially if the prospective enemy was a popular villain. Henry, wise king that he was, had obviously understood this maneuver.

With this strategy in mind, Bacon created a speech for Lord Chancellor Morton to deliver at the opening of the session. Like the other speeches in the *History,* all of which owe some of their parts to statements made by Hall and Speed,[61] it is primarily a representation of what Bacon thought should have been said by the character in the particular situation. This speech, though, is a masterpiece, at once typical and worthy of its creator's own best performances. Indeed, given Bacon's constant hints and advices to James on how parliament was to be addressed, it is impossible to avoid regarding it as a deliberate lesson as well as an "ornament." Clearly organized and ingratiating in tone, the speech, particularly in the section dealing with Brittany, informs and flatters the members in equal measure. "Therefore by this narrative you now understand the state of the question, whereupon the King prayeth your advice; which is no other, but whether he shall enter into an auxiliary and defensive war for the Britons against France?" (6.77). Could even the most stubborn and suspicious backbencher deny a king who "hath made it a resolution to himself to communicate with so loving and well approved subjects in all affairs that are of public nature at home or abroad" (6.76)? This was the way to speak to men whose money was needed: they were to be caressed, not berated. Yet a diffident manner and a promise to "rely" on "your grave and mature advice" pledged Henry to nothing. The point is insisted upon. "This was the effect of the Lord Chancellor's speech touching the cause of Brittaine; for the King had commanded him to carry it so as to affect the Parliament toward the business; but without engaging the King in any express declaration" (6.79).

When Morton shifts to domestic matters the same blandishing tones are heard, but accompanied by a new note of concern.

> It is the King's desire that this peace wherein he hopeth to govern and maintain you, do not bear only unto you leaves, for you to sit under the shade of them in safety, but also should bear you fruit of riches, wealth, and plenty. [6.80]

Conventional though it might be, the image was the kind to stick in men's minds, the kind Bacon himself used in pressing a significant point. In this case it was that firm belief that a king ought to have "commonwealth" legislation ready to offer a parliament if he meant to ask for subsidies. Indeed, the very fact that he has Morton discuss those matters of internal peace and plenty subsequently dealt with by laws, thereby pre-empting for the King primary credit for their enactment, indicates Bacon's conviction. Whether Henry really understood this approach is a moot point, affecting in no way our recognition that Morton is made to speak about subjects like trade and usury in the way Bacon thought of them. Familiar phrasings are the clue to familiar arguments, as when the Chancellor finally asks for supply. "What comes from you is but as moisture drawn from the earth, which gathers into a cloud and falls back upon the earth again."[62] The request for money concludes the oration, the impact of which is immediately noticed. "It was no hard matter to dispose and affect the Parliament in this business; . . . Wherefore they did advise the King roundly to embrace the Briton's quarrel, and to send them speedy aids; and *with much alacrity and forwardness granted to the King a great rate of subsidy in contemplation of these aids*" (6.81-82, emphasis added). In the Latin translation of the *History,* prepared either by Bacon himself or under his direction, a sentence of praise is tied to the end of the speech that underlines the lesson and echoes the flattery he never minded bestowing on himself. *"Hanc orationem Cancellarius habuit, non comptam certe, sed solidam et perspicuam."*

Bacon confirmed his belief in Henry's dominance of parliament by the way he described the laws made in this session. "For according to the Lord Chancellor's admonition, there were that Parliament divers excellent laws ordained, concerning the points which the King recommended" (6.85). The emphasis on Henry's responsibility is then enforced by the device of beginning each of a sequence of paragraphs with phrases pointing directly at the King. "From the general peace of the country the King's care went on to the peace of the King's house, etc." "From the peace of the King's house the King's care extended to the peace of private houses and families, etc." With these transitions Bacon conveys the impression that all initiative flowed from the King, and that the two houses, by always following his lead, were little more than a rubber stamp. This sovereign-centered portrayal will be sustained throughout the *History;* rarely will we sense that "parliament" made a law.

Recognition of how Bacon, with simple strokes of his pen, could magnify Henry's role as a lawmaker prompts the question why so many pages of the *History* should be taken up with descriptions of the King's laws. Anticipating our curiosity, and eager to help us understand his purpose, he set out an explanation when surveying the statutes of 1489.

> And here I do desire those into whose hands this work shall fall, that they
> do take in good part my long insisting upon the laws that were made in
> this King's reign; whereof I have these reasons; both because it was the
> preeminent virtue and merit of this King, to whose memory I do honour;
> and because it hath some correspondence to my person; but chiefly
> because in my judgment it is some defect even in the best writers of
> history, that they do not often enough summarily deliver and set down
> the most memorable laws that passed in the times whereof they write,
> being indeed the principal acts of peace. For though they may be had in
> original books of law themselves; yet that informeth not the judgment of
> kings and counsellors and persons of estate so well as to see them
> described and entered in the table and portrait of the times. [6.97]

These reasons are all true, but in need of clarification.

The conclusion that Henry's laws were his chief "virtue and merit"
is a trifle strange, for at no time before the *History* has Henry been
praised outright as a lawmaker, let alone as "the best lawgiver to this
nation after King Edward the First."[63] Nor is the only comment on
Henry and his laws in the fragment *History* from Elizabeth's reign
flattering. "In his government he was led by none, scarcely by his
laws."[64] Indeed, the most frequent reference to the laws of
Henry—aside from citations of them in legal briefs—is the sorrow
expressed at how Empson and Dudley abused them.[65] As a result, it
would seem that Bacon defined his opinion of Henry as legislator only
in 1621, when he had occasion to peruse that wise King's statutes as a
*whole,* and was predisposed to seeing them as further testimony of the
royal wisdom.[66]

This brings us to the question of utility. What does Bacon mean
when he speaks of presenting Henry's laws so as to inform his reader's
"judgment"? The answer lies in noting whom he regarded as the
beneficiaries, "kings and counsellors and persons of estate." It is not
other lawyers he needs to instruct, nor is it simply respect for the King's
achievement he hopes to instill. Henry is a model for kings and counselors, and imitation is what Bacon has in mind. Accordingly, only laws
"touching public policy" that Bacon judges worthy are discussed; the
rest are passed over. "This year [1495] also the King called his Parliament, where many laws were made of a more private and vulgar nature
than ought to detain the reader of an history" (6.159). And we are

specifically instructed as to what laws developed wise policy, and how such laws were framed.

Already in Henry's first parliament we have seen how Bacon handled the latter concern. We are introduced to what the former entails in the second. "These were the laws that were made for repressing of force, which those times did chiefly require; and were so prudently framed as they are found fit for all succeeding times, and so continue to this day" (6.87). In other words, the wisdom of Henry's laws is determined by their continuing relevance. The point is made more rhapsodically a few pages later. "For his laws (whoso marks them well) are deep and not vulgar; not made upon the spur of a particular occasion for the present, but out of providence of the future; to make the estate of his people still more and more happy, after the manner of the legislators in ancient and heroical times."[67] Now insofar as this means that Henry made laws that still, in Bacon's day, worked their will it is unexceptionable. But the historian is up to something else when he points out the wisdom in Henry's laws. What he is more interested in doing is showing how the King's laws spoke to policies and principles that he (Bacon) knew were wise.

> There was also made a shoaring or underpropping act for the benevolence: to make the sums which any person had agreed to pay, and nevertheless were not brought in, to be leviable by course of law. Which act did not only bring in the arrears, but did indeed countenance the whole business, and was pretended to be made at the desire of those that had been forward to pay. [6.160]

No doubt his own frustrating experience with the benevolence of 1614, when he had tried in vain to persuade James to follow a course that had no odor of compulsion, made Bacon appreciative of Henry's method.[68]

The desire, however, to discover wisdom in Henry's laws sometimes lured Bacon into putting it into them. What the statutes can be interpreted to intend must be what that wise and secret King meant them to intend. To see this clearly let us look at what he has to say about two famous acts of 1489. The first (to which he devoted two pages) dealt ostensibly with depopulation, but had, as is claimed in one of those whispered asides meant to alert the reader, a deeper purpose: "[The] statute was made . . . (if it be thoroughly considered) for the soldiery and militar forces of the realm." Depopulation as a consequence of enclosures had led to a "decay of towns, churches, [and] tithes"; it had also caused a "diminution of subsidies and taxes," which, Bacon notes with heavy emphasis, "the King likewise knew full well, and in no wise forgot." The law subsequently passed (4 H. VII c. 19) was a masterpiece of indirection.

> In remedying of this inconvenience the King's wisdom was admirable; and the Parliament's at that time. Inclosures they would not forbid, for that had been to forbid the improvement of the patrimony of the kingdom; nor tillage they would not compel; for that was to strive with nature and utility: but they took a course to take away depopulating inclosures and depopulating pasturage, and yet not that by name, or by any imperious express prohibition, but by consequence. [6.94]

But admiration for Henry's cleverness does not stop there, for Bacon contends that the statute also "did wonderfully concern the might and mannerhood of the kingdom," because it "did advance the militar power." He knows this to be so "by the true principles of war and the examples of other kingdoms. For it hath been held by the general opinion of men of best judgment in the wars . . . that the principal strength of an army consisteth in the infantry or foot."

Henry, it is insinuated, understood these "principles" too, thus making him a precursor of Machiavelli and the other sixteenth- century writers who had needed the Italian wars to inform their judgments. "Whereas the King saw that contrariwise it would follow, that England, though much less in territory, yet should have infinitely more soldiers of their native forces than those other nations have. Thus did the King secretly sow Hydra's teeth; whereupon (according to the poet's fiction) should rise up armed men for the service of this kingdom" (6.95). Our sense that Bacon's ingenuity has deceived him, that he is seeing his own ideas in Henry's law, is supported by the striking verbal resemblance between the 1612 essay "Of the Greatness of Kingdoms," whose parent is the fragment *Of the True Greatness of Britain* (1603), and the passage where it is argued that infantry is the heart of an army. Once more language lets us see what is happening.

*History:*

> Therefore if a state run most to noblemen and gentlemen, and that the husbandmen and ploughmen be but as their workfolks or labourers, or else mere cottagers (which are but housed ɔeggars), you may have a good

cavalry, but never good stable bands of foot; like to coppice woods, that if you leave in them staddles too thick, they will run to bushes and briars, and have little clean underwood.

"Of the Greatness of Kingdoms":

Nobilitie & Gentlemen multiplying in too great a proportion, maketh the common subiect grow to bee a pesant and base swaine driuen out of heart, and but the Gentlemans laborer: like as it is in copices, where if you leaue your staddels too thick, you shall neuer haue cleane vnderwood, but shrubbes and bushes.

In the 1625 version of the essay Henry, naturally enough, will appear as the example for this principle.

The second gloss worth our notice follows directly in the text upon the first; position and phrasing suggest that it was to buttress the argument Bacon had made for its predecessor.

The King also (having care to make his realm potent as well by sea as by land), for the better maintenance of the navy, ordained, That wines and woads from the parts of Gascoign and Languedoc, should not be brought but in English bottoms; bowing the ancient policy of this estate from consideration of plenty to consideration of power: for that almost all the ancient statutes invite (by all means) merchants strangers to bring in all sorts of commodities; having for end cheapness, and not looking to the point of state concerning the naval power. [6.95-96]

As it happens, this statute, like the act of 1485 forbidding the import of Gascon wine in foreign bottoms (which Bacon neglects to mention), was the result of private rather than royal initiative.[69] Henry was probably concerned with keeping up a merchant marine, but the effective illusion—is there a sentence in the *History* more often quoted?—of a king preoccupied with a "policy" is a distortion.

It must be stressed, however, that Bacon was not consciously misrepresenting the statutes. Like any lawyer, he construed them to sustain an argument he was already convinced of. That others might contest his high estimate of Henry's laws was to be expected; thus, the defensive aside "whoso marks them well" when declaring their excellence. The aside also suggests how hard he himself had had to examine them.

Before leaving the parliament of 1489 we should glance at the explanation for why Henry summoned it.

> The former Parliament being ended somewhat suddenly (in regard of the preparation for Brittaine), the King thought he had not remunerated his people sufficiently with good laws, (which evermore was his retribution for treasure): and finding by the insurrection in the north, there was discontentment abroad in respect of the subsidy, he thought it good for to give his subjects yet further contentment and comfort in that kind. [6.92]

An error in chronology has again offered Bacon a chance to point a lesson. The "insurrection" actually occurred in the midst of this parliament, which began in January 1489 and was prorogued twice before concluding almost fourteen months later. Not realizing this, but certain that Henry understood as well as he did the need for a *quid pro quo* approach to parliament—the approach that he never could persuade James to adopt—Bacon has himself a motive. The point is intentionally emphasized by the parenthetical comment that makes it appear Henry was not merely responding to a situation but acknowledging a rule of political life.

The parliament of 1491, convened as Brittany was about to fall under French control, enabled Bacon to put the finishing touches on his portrait of Henry as a master parliamentarian. The outcome of this parliament was that the King raised great sums of money through a subsidy and a benevolence, although only a modest portion was spent during the abbreviated and highly profitable invasion of France. Bacon, as was discussed above, attributed the bountiful war to Henry's craft, an interpretation that the King of England in 1621 was to study. Also deserving of James's consideration was the speech that Henry is given to make at the beginning of the session, a speech suggested by Hall. "Wherfore he sommoned his courte of Parliament, and there declared first yᵉ cause why he was iustly prouoked to make warre agaist the Frenche kyng: And after desyred them of their beneuolent aide of men and money for the maintenaunce of the same."[70] It is Henry's only first person speech in the *History*, a sign of the importance Bacon attached to his accounts of the King's parliaments. The speech also shows that Henry was as good an orator as he was a lawyer.

Anyone familiar with James's scarcely pithy and often impenetrable rhetoric might surmise that Bacon was suggesting a change in the royal style of address. Henry's speech is brief, and marked by a confidence in tone that is given to no other speaker in the *History*. In short declarative sentences, wired with symmetries that lock our attention, the King states his intention to make war on France, discusses the possibility of alliances, and, at the end, seeks the "advice and aid" of his subjects.

> The French King troubles the Christian world. That which he hath is not his own, and yet he seeketh more. He hath invested himself of Brittaine. He maintaineth the rebels in Flanders: and he threateneth Italy. For ourselves, he hath proceeded from dissimulation to neglect, and from neglect to contumely. He hath assailed our confederates: he denieth our tribute: in a word, he seeks war. [6.118]

It is a stirring performance, designed to arouse the passions that take men into war, or (more to the point) make them open their purses. Which it did. "The Parliament . . . presently took fire." Yet as with Morton's speech, the reader is not meant simply to admire the historian's art: he is to learn how to move men to his advantage, even if it involves deception. Henry *speaks* differently because he is a king; the strategy of his remarks, and its lessons, are the same.

Although the last three parliaments of Henry's reign fill only a few pages in Bacon's narrative, they corroborate his point of view, even when, as in the introduction to the session of 1495, Henry's actions must be faulted. "And it may be justly suspected, by the proceedings following, that as the King did excell in good common-wealth laws, so nevertheless he had in secret a design to make use of them as well for collecting of treasure as for correcting of manners; and so meaning thereby to harrow his people, did accumulate them the rather" (6.159). Avarice was not a pretty sight, yet Bacon always had a liking for a well-executed double play. Most of what he has to say about this parliament, however, concerns its "principal law," the *De Facto Act*. Here he stumbled badly, wrongly imagining that the act was made to protect the King's "party" in the future, whereas its real purpose was to calm the former supporters of Richard III who might still have feared a purge. The reason for this error lies probably in Bacon's ill-founded belief that Henry was obsessed with "depressing" the Yorkists, and so was blind to the meaning of the act. His remarks also reveal the deeper misapprehension that pervades all his comments on the King's parliaments: namely, that there was no difference between the parliaments of his own day and Henry's. For his criticism of the "illusory" effectiveness of this law stems from a belief that the power of statute making (as understood in Henry's day) was "supreme and absolute," an attitude which was only beginning to gain acceptance in his own time.[71]

Two years later, in 1497, Henry repeats the strategy of 1491. "The King called again his Parliament; where he did much exaggerate both the malice and the cruel predatory war lately made by the King of Scotland." And again it worked. "The parliament understood him well, and gave him a subsidy."[72] No speech is offered this time, probably for fear of repetition, perhaps also for fear of offending the reigning Scottish King. The only law Bacon mentions was particularly appropriate. "There passed a law, at the suit of the Merchant Adventurers of England, against the Merchant Adventurers of London, for monopolising and exacting upon the trade; which it seemeth they did a little to save themselves, after the hard time they had sustained by want of trade. But those innovations were taken away by Parliament" (6.175). Here was the policy that in the fall of 1620 Bacon had continually backed. Henry, wise king that he was, had known how to let a parliament relieve abuses.

The parliament of 1504, Henry's last, is used as a kind of summing up.

> This year, being the nineteenth of his reign, the King called his Parliament, wherein a man may easily guess how absolute the King took himself to be with his Parliament; when Dudley, that was so hateful, was made Speaker of the House of Commons. In this Parliament there were not made many statutes memorable touching public government. But those that were had still the stamp of the King's wisdom and policy. [6.222]

Since the reputedly extortionary policies associated with Empson and himself only began about this time, it is not likely that Dudley was "so hateful" in January of 1504, or if he was, that Henry was particularly aware of it. And the chroniclers' silence on Dudley's appointment to the Speakership affirms the suspicion that Bacon is dramatizing an innocent event to make his point. The discussion of the laws passed in this session follows the familiar pattern.

Another statute was made, prohibiting the bringing in of manufactures of silk. . . . as ribbands, laces, cauls, points, and girdles, &c. which the people of England could then well skill to make. This law pointed at a true principle; That where foreign materials are but superfluities, foreign manufactures should be prohibited. For that will either banish the superfluity, or gain the manufacture. [6.223]

On more than one occasion Bacon had announced the same principle to both James and Buckingham (13.22-23, 74).

Like his granddaughter Elizabeth, Henry had known how to use a parliament. He had given his people good laws and received in return substantial subsidies. This reciprocity was at once the cause and the consequence of that understanding between king and parliament which Bacon had often spoken of to James, perhaps never more touchingly than in June of 1621. "It doth well in church-music when the greatest part of the hymn is sung by one voice, and then the quire at times falls in sweetly and solemnly, and . . . the same harmony sorteth well in monarchy between the King and his Parliament" (14.290). Bacon did not realize how warped his view of Henry's parliaments was, any more than he saw how inappropriate his lessons had become. Henry had probably not required the skills of Elizabeth; James needed something more.

In his dedication Bacon had told Prince Charles that he would not flatter the King. The promise is redeemed. Specific errors of judgment and character are cited and their impolitic consequences duly noted. Never, though, is Henry judged on moral grounds; besides being imprudent, that was irrelevant. The *History* assumes that effectiveness, not goodness, occupies the thoughts of men in politics, and that the choices they make, therefore, cannot be judged (or described) by a standard ignored in their deliberations.[73] The King's most notorious error, of course, was his avarice, a fault not invented by Bacon but certainly polished by his art and legal knowledge to a high tone. Thus, instead of confining his remarks to a summary and disapproving statement in the closing pages—the practice of the chroniclers, who saw the fault as a late development—Bacon will suggest it as an explanation for earlier exactions, thereby supporting his contention that the fault lay deep in the King's character. "But after many parleys," he writes of the loan given Henry after his first parliament, "he could obtain but two thousand pounds; which nevertheless the King took in good part, as men use to do that practise to borrow money when they have no need" (6.40). But what is perhaps most enlightening about Bacon's assessment of Henry's avarice is that it indicates the degree to which he was a prisoner of the sources he so despised. Relying on them for his basic information, he could not skim over the charge, especially as he had always himself believed that Henry had let his penal laws be used too rigorously. Had he dug about, Bacon might have discovered that the King had politic reasons for needing (and taking) the treasure he accumulated.

Yet avarice was not Henry's worst fault; at least it enabled him to stay afloat financially.[74] What to Bacon's understanding was the King's most serious flaw was his lack of foresight. "Being in his nature and constitution of mind not very apprehensive or forecasting of future events afar off, but an entertainer of fortune by the day" (6.31), Henry brought upon himself many troubles. Given Bacon's lifelong admiration for examples of "prudent and deep foresight" in politics as well as in law, and the extraordinary confidence he had in his own farsightedness, which was interminably advertised in his letters and advices to James and Buckingham,[75] it is quite understandable that Henry should be tested on this virtue. And Bacon's criticism seems simple enough: Henry just wasn't very good at envisioning the future. What complicates the matter, however, is Bacon's eagerness to exhibit instances of the King's foresight, such as in his discussion of Henry's legislation or his account of the last act of the Brittany affair. What then are we to make of the contradiction? Did Henry have foresight or did he not? Or should we content ourselves with the evasive answer that sometimes he did, sometimes he did not?

No answer need be given because the dilemma is essentially spurious. The charge that Henry lacked foresight—a deficiency unknown to the chroniclers (indeed, Hall opens his account by declaring that Henry had "the ingenious forcast of the subtyl serpent")—springs, like so much else in the *History,* from the deductive mode of interpretation. This becomes clear when we realize that Bacon largely confines the accusation to his disapproval of the King's treatment of the Yorkists. Despite continued success, Henry's reign posed (for Bacon) a disconcerting question: Why had so wise a king not been able to avert the succession of conspiracies and rebellions masterminded, or at least indulged in, by the party that lost out at Bosworth? We can see in the fragment *History* that the question was already bothering him.

> His times were rather prosperous than calm, for he was assailed with many troubles, which he overcame happily; a matter that did no less set forth his wisdom than his fortune; and yet such a wisdom as seemed rather a dexterity to deliver himself from dangers when they pressed him, than any deep foresight to prevent them afar off. [6.20]

In 1621 he was more sure of his position, there is no longer the tentative "seemed." His confidence was raised by his discovery that Henry had not adopted the conciliatory policy that he (Bacon)—a persistent advocate of soothing strategies—imagined would have saved the King considerable grief. Instead of appeasing the Yorkists Henry had neglected and spurned them. "The King . . . assumed the style of King in his own name, without mention of the Lady Elizabeth at all, or any relation thereunto. In which course he ever after persisted: which did spin him a thread of many seditions and troubles" (6.31). Unfortunately the evidence for this shortsighted policy is thin, consisting mainly (as Bacon tells it) of Henry's not mentioning Elizabeth, his delay in marrying her, and the subsequent delay in her coronation. Thus, lack of foresight is not really a concept describing an objective condition in the King, but a term hung on a weak peg to answer an embarrassing question. The evidence for shortsightedness, indeed, is no more convincing than the proofs Bacon advances for the King's farsightedness. Both depend on exaggerating Henry's immediate responsibility for the events of his reign.[76]

The intensity of Bacon's focus on the King was quite deliberate, however. The *History* is a book about kingship, not England, and the reader is obliged to spend his attention on the model for imitation. (Those who wanted to thrill in the national saga could read Hall.) Henry is placed at center stage in the very beginning, and despite the shifts to other scenes and actors he remains a palpable presence.[77] His immanence, in fact, has had much to do with the popularity of the work: the reader can forget facts and misplace dates but still never feel disoriented. Purpose, method, and art have combined to create a unique, unforgettable character.

Quite unintentional is our feeling that Bacon's portrait of Henry bears a remarkable likeness to himself. This, however, was inevitable. Proposing to uncover the working parts of the King's wisdom, to explain the motives for voiceless deeds, and not trusting the political sense of his sources, Bacon necessarily had to substitute his own thoughts and values for the historical Henry's. It was the unavoidable result of depicting a mind that would justify the King's reputation for political shrewdness. Yet the transference goes beyond the point of deducing policies and motives according to his own wisdom. Henry's balanced, highly rational manner of analyzing situations, together with his prevailing legal quickness, are a reflection of what Bacon saw in himself. "For as his Majesty hath good experience," he was fond of saying, "that when his business comes upon the stage I carry it with strength and resolution, so in the proceedings [viz., preliminaries] I love to be wary and considerate."[78] Nor can there be much doubt that Henry's more private side has been similarly invaded. When Bacon says that the King's "aversion toward the house of York was so predominant in him, as it found place not only in his wars and counsels, but in his chamber and bed," we sense that it is not just his wrong assumption about Henry's attitude toward the Yorkists that is operating, but his own familiar strictures on love and marriage.[79] The King's piety is also diminished. It was all right for Henry to be "religious," but Bacon was unwilling to let him cross the line from observance to true faith. "The King immediately after the victory [Bosworth], as one that had been bred under a devout mother, and was in his nature a great observer of religious forms, caused *Te deum laudamus* to be solemnly sung" (6.27). More striking, though, is the account of how Henry exploited Ferdinand of Spain's conquest of Granada in 1492. Bacon records that "King Ferdinando (whose manner was never to lose any virtue for the showing)" sent the King letters describing "all the particularities and religious punctos and ceremonies" observed in the entrance to the fallen city. Henry, "ever willing to put himself into the consort or quire of all religious actions, and naturally affecting much the King of Spain" (6.126), then ordered all the noblemen at court and the great men of the city to hear an oration from Chancellor (Cardinal) Morton. Bacon appears to have guessed at the existence of the letters; Hall, who is his source for this incident, and reports the oration as an inspired moment,[80] does not mention them. Yet while the surmise about the letters is credible, the estimate of Henry's motives all too clearly witnesses Bacon's own tepid beliefs.[81]

Thus Henry, both as man and king, comes close to being a mirror image of Bacon's talents, ideas, and personality. This projection, apparent throughout the *History*, derives from the purpose and method that created the work, not—it must be emphasized—from hubris. When Bacon interpreted Henry's actions, just as when he explicated the meaning of a law, he thought that he was finding the truth, albeit a truth fit for the present occasion. He wished to teach his contemporaries and imagined that the first Tudor had been as he portrayed him. However, a case can be made that Bacon at least half-consciously *did* identify himself with Bishop Foxe, "a wise man, and one that could see through the present to the future." Foxe plays a larger, more visible role in the *History* than he does in any of the other chroniclers, and is shown to have had that breadth of talent and responsibility which wise kings allowed to trusty counselors. "The chief man that took the care," Bacon writes of the pageants celebrating the entry of Katherine of Aragon to London and her subsequent marriage to Prince Arthur, "was Bishop Foxe, who was not only a grave counsellor for war or peace, but also a good surveyor of works, and a good master of ceremonies, and any thing else that was fit for the active part belonging to the service of court or state of a great King."[82] How often in a life spent seeking influence had the author of those words thought and said the same about himself!

At the end of the book, obeying the "law of an history" learned thirty years before, Bacon appended an eight-page "judgment" of Henry.[83] In orderly fashion he recapitulates the King's policies, often reducing his conclusions to terse comments. "If this King did no greater matters, it was long of himself; for what he minded he compassed."[84] For those without the time, intellect, or memory to appreciate the narrative, these maxims were a help. Later, Bacon would take special pains with the Latin translation of the 'character,' no doubt hoping, as he had with the *In felicem memoriam Reginae Elizabethae*, to see it used by foreign writers.[85] The two portraits also share an opening thought.

> This King (to speak of him in terms equal to his deserving) was one of the best sorts of wonders; a wonder for wise men.

> Elizabeth both in her nature and her fortune was a wonderful person among women, a memorable person among princes.

But the last sentences of Henry's memorial reach more obviously, and more gracefully, for future rewards.

> He was born at Pembroke Castle, and lieth buried at Westminster, in one of the stateliest and daintiest monuments of Europe, both for the chapel and for the sepulchre. So that he dwelleth more richly dead, in the monument of his tomb, than he did alive in Richmond or any of his palaces. I could wish he did the like in this monument to his fame.

For over three centuries men have turned that page, nodding.

On September 13, 1621, Bacon was given permission to return to London for a period of "one month or six weeks." To settle his debts and "be near help of physician" were the reasons stated in the royal warrant, a document he seems to have drafted himself. Undoubtedly there was also a strong desire to be nearer the court. "I am much fallen in love with a private life," he had written to Buckingham a few days before, "but yet I shall so spend my time, as shall not decay my abilities for use" (14.298). No reference is made in the warrant to needing any records from London.

Another warrant, dated September 20, greatly relaxed the penalties parliament had set. By its terms the fine of £40,000 had never to be paid, but instead would serve as protection against creditors.[86] The King was also willing to grant Bacon "a Coronation pardon," which freed him from all liabilities for past offenses. James made an "exception," however, to "the sentence given in our high Court of Parliament"; the former Lord Chancellor was still not worth a contest. Nonetheless, Bacon was gratified. On October 8 he wrote the King thanking him for the "remission," and informed him that he had turned his "poor talent upon those things which may be perpetual" now that he was not engaged in affairs of state. "I have therefore chosen to write the Reign of King Henry the 7th, who was in a sort your forerunner, and whose spirit, as well as his blood, is doubled upon your Majesty" (14.303). This letter is generally cited as marking the point at which the *History* was completed, but the sentences following Bacon's announcement offer another conclusion. "I durst not have presumed to intreat your Majesty to look over the book and correct it, or at least to signify what you would have amended. But since you are pleased to send for the book, I will hope for it." Apparently James had already heard from someone else how Bacon had spent the summer. Who the informant was can only be conjectured. Perhaps Gondomar? Less uncertain was Bacon's strategy. He was probably unsure how best to approach the King with this gift, and asked someone he trusted to mention the *History* to James. The King took the bait. The ploy suggests, moreover, that Bacon may have finished the work even before coming to London.

In any event, the King read the book and liked it. He had "very few" criticisms to make, as Thomas Meautys reported to Bacon on January 7, 1622, "and those rather words." The book was then passed on by the King to Fulke Greville for further editorial comment. He also approved, and hoped "that care should be taken by all means for good ink and paper to print it in; for that the book deserved it."[87] With these imprimaturs the *History* went to press sometime in February. Trouble arose in the middle of March, however, when the Bishop of London, Dr. George Montaigne, held up the sale of the volume. What prompted him to do so is a mystery. Perhaps he scrupled over Bacon's fitness to publish within the verge since he still was forbidden, except upon permission, to step within it.[88] Whatever the cause, the delay was short-lived—word of the King's prior approval probably stifled the bishop's "demur"—and by the end of the month the *History* was being sold in the bookstalls for six shillings.[89]

Praise for the work came quickly. Prince Charles, who along with the King and Buckingham received the first copies from the press, was very happy with it. No less a scholar than John Selden found it equal to Camden's *Annales*.[90] Even John Chamberlain, ever critical of Bacon but generous by nature, applauded: "Yt is pitie he shold have any other employment. I have not read much of yt, but yf the rest of our historie were aunswerable to it, I thincke we shold not need to envie any other nation in that kind."[91] Sales matched the words of praise. A second edition appeared the same year, two in 1628, and at least five more before 1700; foreign issues were a bit slower, but the book drew admiration.[92] Fittingly, the title page of one of the Latin editions referred to it as an *"opus vere politicum."*

Bacon was pleased by the reception; once more his pen had done him good service. When on April 20 he sent off a copy to Elizabeth, Queen of Bohemia, he was confident that he had begun to recover his reputation. "If King Henry the Seventh were alive again, I hope verily he could not be so angry with me for not flattering him as well-pleased in seeing himself so truly described in colours that will last and be believed."[93]

All these cheers ultimately joined in a nice irony: Bacon was in demand as an historian! Sometime in the summer or fall of 1622 he was asked by the Prince to continue his labors into the reign of Henry VIII. Help was forthcoming from the King, who ordered Sir Thomas Wilson, Keeper of the State Papers, to supply Bacon with any materials he might need. Word of the project must have gotten out, for there is an amusing confession by Chamberlain that while he had not time to look at two brief scientific works recently published by Bacon, he "shold find time and meanes enough to read" the rumored history.[94] But only a page, "one morning's work," Rawley claimed, was ever written, and its opening sentence clearly retraces the rhythm of the introductory sentence of the earlier *History*.

> After the decease of that wise and fortunate King, King Henry the Seventh, who died in the height of his prosperity, there followed (as useth to do when the sun setteth so exceeding clear) one of the fairest mornings of a kingdom that hath been known in this land or anywhere else. [6.269]

But why was it not finished? Bacon pleaded ill health and lack of sources—Cotton, he said, was "somewhat dainty of his materials in this." Later, Rawley intimated that had his master lived longer the book might have been completed. A more likely explanation for Bacon's holding back would be the ill opinion he had of Henry VIII, an opinion published in the *De Augmentis Scientiarum* (1623): "a king whose actions . . . [were] conducted more by impulse than policy" (4.306). What might such a negative lesson in kingship teach? What would be the use of recounting thirty-eight years of rash acts? Also worth noting in the same passage from the *De Augmentis* is a slight change from the *Advancement of Learning*. In the earlier work Henry

VII was judged "one of the most sufficient kings of all the number"; in the later he is declared "the most conspicuous for policy of all the kings who preceded him." Considering the author's own contribution, it was a just reformulation.

Nevertheless, the reception of the *History* cannot have been altogether satisfying to Bacon. For one thing, it seems not to have been appreciated for what it was, a book on kingship. Reaction of both King and Prince shows no evidence that either saw its purpose. Of course they would have realized that Bacon was giving them a portrait of a wise king who, in some vague manner, was worthy of imitation. But that is only to say that father and son read the book as all their contemporaries read history. Certainly it prompted no changes in policy or demeanor. Indeed, the only visible effect it may have had on the Stuarts was to inspire James with a momentary interest in England's antiquities.[95] Moreover, it did not return Bacon to office or favor. He spent his last five years in retirement preparing his reputation for posterity—if the world repudiated him as a counselor it must accept him as a philosopher. But he did not bear isolation gladly. Until his death he sought a return to influence, listening always for the call that never came. Letters of advice and offers of aid went out to the King, the favorite, and the Prince; in return he received disappointments and sometimes insults, as when Buckingham forced him to give up York House. There were no strings left on the suitor's lyre. He had become an embarrassment that only death could remove.

Still, the aging man persisted in seeing himself in the most flattering light. "For envy," he said to himself in 1622, "it is an almanack of the old year, and as a friend of mine said, the Parliament died penitent towards me." And shortly before he died he wrote, not unexpectedly, his own epitaph. To the essay, "Of Honour and Reputation," one of the original ten, and one that dealt with the subject closest to his heart, he attached in the 1625 edition a new concluding sentence. "There is an honour, likewise, which may be ranked amongst the greatest, which happeneth rarely; that is, of such as sacrifice themselves to death or danger for the good of their country; as was M. Regulus, and the two Decii."

Signs do exist, however, that the *History* was not without its perceptive readers. At Knole there lies a manuscript endorsed "collections out of the last edition of King Henry VII," which contains in tabular form with marginal epitomes a review of the courses taken by Henry "as well by parliament as by other means for raising treasure and supply of wants."[96] The presumed date of the paper is 1623, and the author may well have been Lionel Cranfield! More outspoken evidence is to be found in a tract dating from April 1657 entitled, *An English Traveler's First Curiosity: or the Knowledge of his own Country.* Written by Henry Bellasis, brother to Thomas, 2nd Lord Fauconberg, who was married to Cromwell's daughter Mary and served as an ambassador to Italy, the manuscript, as its title indicates, is no more than a chauvinistic survey. But under the heading "Good Scollers" there is a choice item.

> In prophane learning the most illustrious man that England hath bred this many years was Sir Francis Bacon, a man so famous abroad, that in the King of France's library in Paris there is no other picture but Bacon's, as if he alone were worthy of that honor, who had taught all Kings in his Henry the Seventh.[97]

# Conclusion

The story of Francis Bacon in 1621 ends as it began, in frustration. Once more his advice was disregarded. Indeed, his political career as a whole must be viewed as a failure if we measure it by the only standard that counted with the man himself: influence. Obviously clever and willing, he could never gain the love, trust, or even respect of those he yearned to serve. In April of 1626, as he lay slowly dying of pneumonia in another man's house, alone, he surely reflected on his father's more fortunate career.

Yet Bacon's writings on politics, both the private advices and the works intended for publication, have earned him acceptance and fame with posterity. Until very recently, in fact, they shaped the orthodox readings of two separate periods of English history. Besides being praised as the worthiest interpreter of Henry VII, Bacon was—and among some still is—regarded as the shrewdest commentator on the reign of James I. As a judge of people and events no man is more frequently cited to speak to us of his times.

By now, however, it ought to be evident that Bacon hardly deserves spontaneous trust as an observer of his own day, let alone of events a century before. What he sees is too obviously what he wants to see. The Henry VII of the *History* is a mixture of error, contrivance, and projection, although his creator was as much persuaded by him as generations of readers have been. And Bacon's hopeful memoranda to James, while not devoid of insight and sound tactics, are spun from a memory flawed by sentiment and propaganda. A mind that is in some ways uniquely brilliant and graceful is far less inquisitive and perceptive than its reputation suggests. It is not simply the anachronizing habit of his era that led Bacon to criticize James by the same standard—Elizabeth—as he created Henry.

Nonetheless, those cool, witty, seemingly wisdom-filled sentences, with their urge to settle a greater certainty on politics, still beguile

201

us. Bacon seems to know so well whatever subject he discusses. Frustrated though he was in his quest for influence during his life, the master of words has served as a trusted counselor ever after.

# Notes

## Chapter 1

1. D. H. Willson, *Privy Councillors in the House of Commons, 1604–29* (Minneapolis, 1940), pp. 40–41.
2. The full text of the proclamation is to be found in *Stuart Royal Proclamations*, ed. J.F. Larkin & P.L. Hughes (1973), 1. 493–94.
3. A disputed election at Oxford suggests that the King's words did not go unnoticed. The original winner, Sir Francis Blundell, used as an argument against his opponent, Thomas Wentworth, the fact "That the choyce of Lawyers was against the Proclamacion." *Commons Debates, 1621*, ed. Wallace Notestein, Frances Relf, and Hartley Simpson (New Haven, 1935), 4. 32. Cited hereafter as *C.D.*
4. John Chamberlain, writing to Dudley Carleton on October 28, conceded how tense things had become. "For mine owne part I cannot perceve any goode either way, for impositions and patents are growne so grievous that of necessitie they must be spoken of, and the prerogative on the other side is become so tender that (like a *noli me tangere*) yt cannot endure to be touched." *The Letters of John Chamberlain*, ed. N. E. McClure (Philadelphia, 1939), 2. 323. Cited hereafter as Chamberlain.
5. 14. 114. See also 135, 169.
6. Chamberlain, 2. 331.
7. Chamberlain, 2. 339.
8. Chamberlain, 2. 338.
9. *C.D.* 2. 2–13.
10. For a more appreciative view of this speech see Robert Zaller, *The Parliament of 1621* (Berkeley, 1971), pp. 31–36.
11. 14. 173. Bacon was originally to have spoken about "the true institution and use of a Parliament," but a letter from Buckingham on January 19 informed him that the King himself desired that topic, as well as the opportunity to discuss the reasons for calling parliament.
12. Chamerblin, 2.343–44.
13. See the debate on the subsidy in *C.D.* 2. 84–91, and the Venetian ambassador's letter to the Doge, *Calendar State Papers Venetian, 1619–21*, pp. 589–90.
14. *C.D.* 2. 92–93.
15. On the Commons' growing sense of identity, see Elizabeth Read Foster, "The Procedure of the House of Commons against Patents and Monopolies, 1621–1624," *Conflict in Stuart England. Essays in Honor of Wallace Notestein*, ed. W.A. Aiken and B.D. Henning (New York, 1960), pp. 60–63.
16. *C.D.* 4. 20.
17. *C.D.* 4. 108.
18. John Hacket, *Scrinia Reserata, A Memorial of John Williams* (London, 1693), 1. 49-50. Unfortunately it is impossible to date the advice. Gardiner believed it to have been given on March 11, and assumed that it caused an abrupt change in James's policy. S. R. Gardiner, *History of England from the Accession*

*of James I to the Outbreak of the Civil War* (London, 1883–1884), 4. 52 note 2. Zaller implies it was given on March 12. Zaller, p. 74. But the King's speech of March 10 and Buckingham's surprise speech on March 3, when he disowned Mompesson, suggest an earlier date.

19. *C.D.* 2. 147. Even while he was preparing for parliament, Bacon was certifying another patent for Kit Villiers. 14. 140–41; Zaller, p. 23. See also W. J. Jones, *Politics and the Bench* (London, 1971), p. 57.

20. Danila Cole Spielman, "Impeachments and the Parliamentary Opposition in England, 1621–1641" (unpublished Ph.D. dissertation, University of Wisconsin, 1959), chap. 1.

21. *C.D.* 2. 127–32; Edward Nicholas, *Proceedings and Debates in the House of Commons in 1620 and 1621* (Oxford, 1766), 1. 83–85. Cited hereafter as *P.D.* The debate on February 23 makes it clear that the members became carried away with themselves.

22. For a good discussion of the medieval heritage to which the lawyers went, see Colin G. C. Tite, *Impeachment and Parliamentary Judicature in Early Stuart England* (London, 1974), chap. 1.

23. *C.D.* 2. 148.

24. *C.D.* 4. 116. Less principled concerns may also have motivated Rich on this occasion. Tite, p. 97 note 43.

25. *C.D.* 2. 114. The writer of the anonymous journal then added, "A good motion."

26. On the difficulties between the two houses in James's first parliament see *Privy Councillors,* pp. 226–28, 298; Wallace Notestein, *The House of Commons, 1604–1610* (New Haven, 1971), *passim.* Cited hereafter as Notestein. Even the comparatively productive session following the Gunpowder Plot was wracked by disagreements.

27. *C.D.* 7. 648. This is taken from an anonymous parliamentary diary for 1614. See T. L. Moir, *The Addled Parliament of 1614* (Oxford, 1958), chaps. 9 and 10.

28. Tite argues, however, that in James's earlier parliaments the Commons had "compelled" the Lords to get used to collaborating on matters of judicature. Tite, chap. 3, especially pp. 80–82.

29. *C.D.* 2. 36.

30. The house agreed with Alford's objection. *C.D.* 4. 80; 5. 460–61.

31. *C.D.* 2. 88.

32. For a careful examination of the make-up and changing disposition of the Lords see Jessie Lucinda Stoddart, "Constitutional Crisis and the House of Lords, 1621–1629" (unpublished Ph.D. dissertation, University of California, Berkeley, 1966), chap. 2.

33. Chamberlain, 2. 348. This is from a letter to Carleton dated February 27. For more details see *Acts of the Privy Council, 1619–21,* pp. 352–53.

34. *The Hastings Journal of the Parliament of 1621,* ed. Lady De Villiers, *Camden Miscellany,* 20 (London, 1953), p. 7. See also Stoddart, pp. 25, 35–37, 48–49.

35. Even physically Mompesson fitted his role. "He is a little man of a black swart complection with a little black beard and of the age of about fortie yeares." *C.D.* 2. 160, note 16.

36. See Bacon's letter to the King, carefully dated "at xi of our forenoon" (March 1), in which he describes the tactics employed, particularly the use of the Archbishop. 14. 190. Willson suggests that this was not Bacon's only effort at obstruction. *Privy Councillors.* p. 151 note 41.

37. *C.D.* 2. 158–59.

38. *Notes of the Debates in the House of Lords, 1621, 1625, 1628,* ed. Frances Relf, Camden Society, third series, 42 (London, 1929), p. 12. Cited hereafter as Relf. Southampton's own connections with members of the lower house were very close. See the notes of his examination in July, after he was arrested. *P.D.* Appendix; *C.D.* 7. 615–17.

39. *Journals of the House of Commons* (1803), 1. 536. Cited hereafter as *C.J.*
40. *Journals of the House of Lords* (1846), 3. 34. Cited hereafter as *L.J.*
41. The Proclamation appeared the same day. *Stuart Royal Proclamations*, 1.499–500.
42. The best accounts of this conference are in *C.D.* 2. 160–61; 6. 302–4. *L.J.* 3. 34 should also be consulted. Mompesson's brother-in-law, Alexander Choke, gave his maiden (and only recorded) speech in the Commons that morning, and took the opportunity to disown him. *C.J.* 1. 535.
43. For Coke's entire speech see *C.D.* 2. 193–98. His precedents scarcely justified his conclusions. Relf, p. xv. Cf. Tite, p. 101 note 59.
44. *C.D.* 2. 205.
45. Relf, p. 13; *Hastings Journal*, p. 25.
46. *Hastings Journal*, pp. 25-29. The avian reference alludes to a precedent—4 H. 4.c.4: Brangwyn, or "white crow"—that Coke had cited at the conference on March 8. The former Chief Justice was accused of having "devised [it]... of his owne head." *C.D.* 5. 36 and note 1.
47. *Hastings Journal*, pp. 29–31. It was after his speech that the King dispatched Coventry. While leaving the Lords, he learned that Coke had come up requesting a conference for that afternoon. James immediately returned to the house and asked the Lords to deny the request, but since they had already accepted it, and were unwilling to reverse themselves, they recommended that he himself send someone to the Commons.
48. Relf, p. 20.
49. Relf, p. 20.
50. *C.D.* 2. 212. This is Coke's summary of the speech. The conjectural emendation is the editors'.
51. *C.D.* 5. 43. Sir Dudley Digges took it upon himself to repeat the Prince's remarks to the Commons when the committee returned. Coke was given special thanks for his speech.
52. These are the words of John Finch speaking on February 14 in behalf of Bacon to the committee. *C.D.* 4. 51–52. This willingness was later reported to the whole house. *C.J.* 1. 525.
53. Coke gave a succinct explanation of their name. "A man oweinge money to many pretended his inabilitie to paie all, and one by reason of his misfortunes beinge content with part of their debts, Hee exhibited his bill to have the rest conformable." *C.D.* 5. 39.
54. For a discussion of the cases see Gardiner, 4. 58–64. See also Joel Hurstfield's "Political Corruption: the Historian's Problem," in his *Freedom, Corruption and Government in Elizabethan England* (London, 1973), pp. 145–47.
55. 14. 212; *P.D.* 1. 161–62; *C.D.* 2. 238–39; 5. 44–45; 6. 67.
56. Even Mrs. Prestwich, who comes upon conspiracies at every turn, cannot connect Aubrey and Egerton with either Coke or Cranfield. Menna Prestwich, *Cranfield: Politics and Profits under the Early Stuarts* (Oxford, 1966), p. 300. But see Zaller, p. 204, note 130.
57. *C.D.* 2. 233.
58. *C.D.* 6. 70.
59. *C.D.* 2. 234. Sandys is obviously alluding to Phelips's assertion.
60. The precedent Phelips presumably referred to, the case of Michael de la Pole, Lord Chancellor in the reign of Richard II, had been noted by Coke in his speech to the Lords on March 8.
61. *P.D.* 1. 187. There was precedent for this suggestion. Zaller, p. 205, note 147.
62. Aubrey had sent his gift through his counsel, Sir George Hastings; Egerton had used Sir Richard Yonge. Both Hastings and Yonge were part of Bacon's household. Indeed, what Phelips reports of Hastings's conscience is reminiscent of Bacon's own protestations twenty years before in the case of Essex. "Sir George Hastings... hath been struggling with himself

betwixt ingratitude and honesty. But public and private goods meeting together, he preferred the public." *C.D.* 2. 237.

63. *C.D.* 2. 244–45; 5. 51. It is tempting to think that Gondomar, who had "a very long audience" with James on the night of March 17, had something to do with this proposal to help a man he admired and respected. For the audience see Thomas Birch, *The Court and Times of James the First*, ed. R. F. Williams (London, 1848), 2. 240; for the friendship 14. 228, 285, 318–19; Chamberlain, 2. 356; A. J. Loomie, "Bacon and Gondomar: An Unknown Link in 1618," *Renaissance Quarterly* 21 (1968). 1–10. At some period Bacon was on Gondomar's pension list. Garrett Mattingly, *Renaissance Diplomacy* (Boston, 1955), pp. 259–60.

64. A contemporary broadside on Mompesson reflects this feeling. It compares the monopolist to Empson and Dudley, and tells how King and parliament found him out and punished him. The last lines strike a note of thanksgiving:

> our gracious Kinge is bent
> To give his faithfull subiects all content;
> Where love is dwe, hee lovingly doth show't,
> Where mercies meete by pardon many know't,
> By rendring Iustice vnto great and small,
> The smale one trippe & great ones downeright fall,
> Oh what more needs a Loyall Subiect crave
> Then mercy, love and iustice choice to have.

*Catalogue of Prints and Drawings in the British Museum: Political and Personal Satires*, ed. F. G. Stephens (London, 1870), 1. 55–56.

65. *Politics and the Bench*, p. 68.
66. *C.D.* 5. 51. See also *P.D.* 1. 194. Cf. Zaller, pp. 82–83.
67. Chamberlain, 2. 355.
68. *L.J.* 3. 55; Relf, pp. 27–28.
69. See Gardiner's discussion of the complex and damaging case of Lady Wharton. Gardiner, 4. 72–81.
70. *C.D.* 4. 184.
71. Chamberlain, 2. 356.
72. Chamberlain, 2. 356. The punning potential of his name always made Bacon an easy target. See a letter written by Samuel Albyn on March 28, 1621, where he is said to be "in his sty, at york House." *C.D.* 7. 591. See also L. B. Osborn, *The Life, Letters and Writings of John Hoskyns* (New Haven, 1937), p. 210.
73. But did he ever see it? Bacon left to Buckingham's discretion the decision "to deliver it." (14.225).
74. This proclamation was issued on March 30. *Stuart Royal Proclamations*, 1. 503–5.
75. L.J. 3. 69-70.
76. See, for example, Chamberlain, 2. 358; *Calendar State Papers Venetian, 1619–21*, p. 15; *Hastings Journal*, p. x; *The Court and Times of James the First*, 2. 243. Even Lord Say was impressed. Relf, p. 46. The speech was subsequently published.
77. *C.J.* 1. 574.
78. The added penalty was officially announced in a proclamation issued on March 30. *Stuart Royal Proclamations*, 1. 502–3.
79. *C.D.* 4. 207–9; 5. 327–28.
80. *C.D.* 5. 326.
81. 14. 229–31. Chamberlain was also unimpressed with its tone: "I send you here a psalme or kind of pharisaicall prayer of his [Bacon] made since his

trouble, which me thincks savors litle or nothing of true humiliation."
Chamberlain, 2. 365.
82. *C.D.* 2. 306.
83. *L.J.* 3. 81. When James issued the proclamation finally dissolving parliament
[January 6, 1622], he cited as evidence of his concern for the "weale of
Our people" the fact that "Our Justice . . . extended not only to persons of
ordinary rank and qualitie, but even to the prime Officer of Our
Kingdome." *Stuart Royal Proclamations,* 1. 528.
84. *Notes of the Debates in the House of Lords, 1621,* ed. S. R. Gardiner, Camden Society,
103 (London, 1870), p. 13. Cited hereafter as *Notes.*
85. *Notes,* p. 13.
86. *Notes,* p. 17.
87. Nor, perhaps, did Ley's close connection to Buckingham enhance his reputation. Chamberlain, 2. 338.
88. The report of Ley's summary is brief. "To postill all the matters of charge in the
margent therof in wryghting. To have Satterday come sennight [10 days],
for that the same tyme was gyven to another [Yelverton]," Ley was
granted permission to answer Bacon "by him selfe as a pryvate man, yf he
wyll." *Notes,* p. 18.
89. *Notes,* p. 22.
90. *Notes,* p. 23. This is a report of Bacon's written message, which has itself not
survived.
91. *L.J.* 3. 102.
92. *Notes,* p. 54.
93. *Notes,* pp. 62–64, for the whole debate, most of which took place in committee.

# Chapter 2

1. Most of the evidence dates from Bacon's three-year stay in France in the
embassy of Sir Amias Paulet. Paulet's few references to Bacon in his letters
show a concern for the boy's health. *Copybook of Sir Amias Paulet's Letters,*
ed. Octavius Ogle (London, 1866), pp. 78, 130; *Calendar State Papers
Foreign, 1578–79,* p. 462. Regrettably, no letters from Bacon's own hand
during this period have been found, but two of the three direct references
to it in his later works—the presentiment of his father's death and the
cure obtained from Paulet's wife for a case of warts—point to a high-
strung temperament. 2. 666–67, 670.
2. 1.4 *The Life of the Right Honourable Francis Bacon* was first published in 1657 as an
introduction to the volume entitled, *Resuscitatio; or bringing into public light
several pieces of the works, civil, historical, philosophical, and theological, hitherto
sleeping, of the Right Honourable Francis Bacon.*
3. Edward Levi, *An Introduction to Legal Reasoning* (Chicago, 1948), pp. 1–8;
Huntington Cairns, *Legal Philosophy from Plato to Hegel* (Baltimore, 1949),
pp. 220–36. Cf. W. S. Holdsworth, *A History of English Law* (London,
1922–52), 5. 239–40.
4. 7. 513. See A. G. Guest, "Logic in the Law," *Oxford Essays in Jurisprudence,* ed. A.
G. Guest (Oxford, 1961), pp. 177–78, 182–83.
5. The particular statute explicated was Westminster 2, c. 5. A copy of the reading
is in B.M. *Stowe* MS. 424, fols. 145–50.
6. *Acts of the Privy Council, 1588,* p. 417.
7. The fact is clearly seen if we look at the admission dates to the inns of court of
the other men and assume, as with Bacon himself, that fifteen or sixteen
was the standard age at entrance. In a couple instances there are birth and

death dates available: *Grays Inn,* John Brograve 1555, William Daniell 1556, John Spurlinge 1562; *Inner Temple,* Edward Drue 1542–1598, Francis Beaumonde, utter barrister 1568, John Cooper, utter barrister 1571, John Eyre, no information; *Lincolns Inn,* William Lambarde 1536–1601, Edward Heron 1564, John Tindall 1562, Thomas Owen 1562; *Middle Temple,* Myles Sandes 1551, Thomas Fermor 1553, James Morrys 1558, Thomas Harrys 1566.

8. For Nicholas Bacon's interest in legal reform, Robert Tittler, "Sir Nicholas Bacon and the Reform of the Tudor Chancery," *University of Toronto Law Journal* 23 (1973), 384. Cf. 7. 319.

9. 8. 14. See also Paul Kocher, "Bacon and His Father," *Huntington Library Quarterly* 21 (1957), 133–58. Kocher is somewhat rigid in his belief that Bacon was always looking for someone or something to replace his father. He does not, for example, consider that Bacon's repeated references to his father may have often been for consciously calculated reasons. Indeed, it is likely that his mother, Lady Ann Bacon, with her overbearing puritanism, had a more direct effect on him.

10. Bacon was permitted to move up to the Reader's Table before his time. *Pension Book of Grays Inn,* ed. R. J. Fletcher (London, 1901–10), 1. 42, 43, 72.

11. Conyers Read, *Lord Burghley and Queen Elizabeth* (New York, 1960), p. 258.

12. Speeding believed that the tract "possibly and not improbably" belonged to Bacon, a view shared by Conyers Read. 8. 46; *Burghley,* p. 565, note 49. A good case, though, has been made for Burghley's authorship. Christopher Devlin, *The Life of Robert Southwell, Poet and Martyr* (London, 1956). pp. 330–32. To see Bacon composing it at the behest of Burghley, however, dissolves the dilemma. For stylistically the work, as Read lamented, is beyond Burghley's capacities, although there are passages where a cruder pen than Bacon's is at work. Also, despite Bacon's audacity, it is unlikely that at twenty-four he would have presumed to send the Queen advice, a conclusion sustained by his failure ever to mention this work later. Finally, all his other political writings during this decade were government inspired.

13. Napoleone Orsini, *Bacone e Machiavelli* (Genoa, 1935), pp. 72–76. For the connection between the two men see also Felix Raab, *The English Face of Machiavelli* (London, 1965), pp. 73–76.

14. On Elizabethan propaganda see Gladys Jenkins, "Ways and Means in Elizabethan Propaganda," *History* 26 (1941), 105–14; Conyers Read, "William Cecil and Elizabethan Public Relations," in *Elizabethan Government and Society,* ed. S. T. Bindoff, J. Hurstfield, C. H. Williams (London, 1961), pp. 21–55.

15. The passion for orderly exposition is also very noticeable in his 1588 reading. B. M. *Stowe,* 424, Fols. 145–45b, 148b.

16. Spedding offered no reasons for his belief that Bacon wrote the tract solely to circulate it among friends. While possible, this assumption does not take into account certain other—admittedly slight—evidence. 1) Why did Bacon bother to translate into English the dozens of Latin citations to be found in the work? Surely his friends would not have required that favor. 2) The first Marprelate tract appeared in October 1588, the last in September 1589, one month after the press on which they were printed had been seized by the government. The *Advertisement* was obviously written toward the end of this period, probably (as Spedding suggested) in the summer of 1589. In October, Burghley, who was angered by Martin Marprelate but scarcely a loud backer of the bishops *(Burghley,* pp.

444, 470), gave to Bacon, over "great and vehement opposition" (9.52), the remainder right to the office of Clerk of Star Chamber. Is there any connection?

A plausible explanation would be that Burghley, unhappy with both the radical tracts and the responses of the bishops, asked his nephew in the summer of 1589 to draw up a more temperate response, but decided to let the matter drop *after* the press had been discovered. The gift, then, would have been an appropriate gesture for service rendered, both present and past.

17. An interesting comparison could be drawn between Bacon and Sir Thomas More in their supposed reluctance to engage in public life. For More, see G. R. Elton, "Thomas More, Councillor," *St. Thomas More: Action and Contemplation*, ed. Richard Sylvester (New Haven, 1972), pp. 87–122.

18. It comes from a collection, Rawley's *Supplement*, that is made up of copies of letters—or, perhaps, simply drafts of letters. Hence we cannot assume that they were sent to the addressee, or that if sent they went in the form we have them. All that we can be certain of is that they "represent something which was in Bacon's mind to say" (8.344).

19. 8. 123. For the fragments of the other two speeches, see *A Conference of Pleasure*, ed. James Spedding (London, 1870).

20. There is still some doubt whether Bacon did compose the speeches for the Grays Inn festivities in 1594. *Gesta Grayorum*, ed. Desmond Bland (Liverpool, 1968), p. 100. Also, it should be mentioned that Bacon had a hand in working on the dumb show part of a masque, *The Misfortunes of Arthur*, which was produced at Grays Inn in 1588. A. Wigfall Green, *The Inns of Court and Early English Drama* (New Haven, 1931), p. 151.

21. Brian Vickers, "Bacon's Use of Theatrical Imagery," *Studies in the Literary Imagination* 4 (1971), 190–91. Cf. Paul Kocher, "Francis Bacon on the Drama," *Essays on Shakespeare and Elizabethan Drama in Honor of Hardin Craig*, ed. Richard Hosley (Columbia, Missouri, 1962), pp, 297–307.

22. The masque for Elizabeth and Frederick was written by Francis Beaumont and produced jointly by Grays Inn and the Inner Temple. Both it and the Somerset's 'gift' are to be found in *A Book of Masques; in honour of Allardyce Nicoll* (London, 1967), pp. 127–77. See also 11. 343–44, 392–95.

23. Spedding dated its composition to January or February of 1593. 8. 146. Read called the section describing Burghley "the greatest tribute ever paid to Burghley," but added that "it would be rash to assume that Bacon meant all that he said." *Burghley*, pp. 478–79. It is also possible that the work was not published *because* of Bacon's offense.

24. "An edition of Bacon with marginal references and parallel passages would show a more persistent recurrence of characteristic illustrations and sentences than perhaps any other writer." R. W. Church, *Bacon* (London, 1884), p. 221. On the same point see the discussion of the recurrent image patterns in Bacon's work in Brian Vickers, *Francis Bacon and Renaissance Prose* (Cambridge, 1968), pp. 174–98.

25. J. E. Neale, "The Elizabethan Political Scene," in *Essays in Elizabethan History* (London, 1958), p. 82.

26. J. E. Neale, *Elizabeth I and her Parliaments 1584–1601* (New York, 1958), pp. 241–325. See the same author's *The Elizabethan House of Commons* (rev. ed., London, 1963), pp. 179, 192.

27. 8. 254. And Burghley may have had honest doubts as to Bacon's fitness for the office. *Burghley*, pp. 494–96, 586 note 26.

28. A brief and worshipful description of Bacon's performance that day was written

by Henry Gosnold, a young lawyer at Grays Inn, and a personal friend. 8. 268. For their friendship, unnoticed by Spedding, see *Memoirs of the Reign of Queen Elizabeth*, ed. Thomas Birch (London, 1754), 1. 79.

29. 9. 34. This comment is contained in a letter written to Lord Keeper Egerton in May 1596. Essex defined the idle life as one "not spent in public business."

30. 7. 618. Spedding's footnote to this passage is deceptively understated. "The professional rivalry with him [Coke] seems to break out here and below, though they were on the same side."

31. 7. 625. See also 628.

32. 8. 297. Essex's own reaction to hearing the case is recorded in a letter written to Robert Cecil. *Historical Manuscripts Commissions, Salisbury*, 4. 525.

33. 8. 292. See also 291, 313, 320, 352, 358.

34. 8. 354. See also 345.

35. 9. 34. See also 35.

36. As early as 1587 Bacon was assisting the Attorney-General, but the scanty evidence indicates the occasional nature of his service. *Calendar State Papers, Domestic, 1581–90*, p. 427. In April 1594 Bacon also received a minor post in the administration of the Duchy of Lancaster. Robert Somerville, *History of the Duchy of Lancaster, 1265–1603* (London, 1953), p. 433.

37. The Lopez case remains a mystery, but it is clear that Bacon's tract was not written at the behest of Burghley, who originally set William Waad to the task of explaining the government's case but then finally did it himself. "Elizabethan Public Relations," pp. 52–55. In addition, both Burghley's effort and the anonymous account printed in *Burghley Papers*, ed. Samuel Haynes and William Murdin (London, 1740–59), 2. 669–75, lack the particular stress that is to be found in Bacon's. His tract was aimed at convincing the reader that a heinous plot against the Queen had existed. The others simply assume that it did and concern themselves with the part Philip II of Spain had in it. Considering the Queen's reluctance to believe the whole sorry story, and the pressure upon Essex, even after the trial, to prove his case, the emphasis in Bacon's account is quite logical. Bacon attended Lopez's trial.

38. Spedding's guess that this tract was written by Bacon has been definitely proven. Corinne Rickert, "An Addition to the Canon of Bacon's Writings," *Modern Language Review* 51 (1956), 71–72. Bacon was involved in the examination of Squire, which may account for why he was chosen to write the government's case. *Calendar State Papers Domestic, 1598–1601*, pp. 107–10.

39. 10. 111. This Walpole, Richard, was a younger brother of the more well-known Jesuit, Henry, who had been executed by the government in 1594. Bacon had participated in the several examinations of Henry and drawn up a brief, typically felicitous "Remembrance" of them. For the examinations and the "Remembrance" see the *Publications of the Catholic Record Society* 5 (1908), 244–69. Henry Walpole also was the English translator of Parson's *Responsio*. For the Walpole brothers see Augustus Jessopp, *One Generation of a Norfolk House* (London, 1879), *passim*.

40. Chamberlain, 1. 70.

41. As with the famous 1592 complaint to Burghley, this letter is from the *Supplement*. Also, there is no reference to it in the *Apology*, where we would naturally expect to see it mentioned.

42. There is simply no evidence—even from Bacon himself—that he did. And it is worth noting that he did not mention the gift in 1616, when he sent to James *A Proposition Touching the Compiling and Amendment of the Laws of*

*England*. It is also possible that he may have sent Elizabeth only a sampling. James Spedding, *Evenings with a Reviewer* (Boston, 1882), 1. 101. On the dating and relationship of the existing texts, prefaces, and dedications see 7. 309–11.

43. This report is in a letter from Anthony to his mother, dated December 31, 1596. *Memoirs of the Reign of Queen Elizabeth*, 1. 241.

44. 7. 320. In each of the paragraphs discussing his procedure, there is a direct or oblique claim that he has eschewed self-display. "So that, to conclude, you have here a work without any glory of affected novelty, or of method, or of language, or of quotations and authorities, dedicated only to use, and submitted only to the censure of the learned, and chiefly of time" (7.323).

45. It seems that Bacon had been jotting down these rules for some time. 7. 310–11, 323.

46. See also on this point Paul Kocher, "Francis Bacon on the Science of Jurisprudence," *Journal of the History of Ideas* 18 (1957), 7–9.

47. See Jerome Frank, *Law and the Modern Mind* (New York, 1930), pp. 90, 337; Cairns, pp. 217–20; Henry van Leeuwen, *The Problem of Certainty in English Thought 1630–1690* (The Hague, 1963), chap. 1. Van Leeuwen argues that Bacon's concept of certainty is the one part of his thinking that his later followers in science found unacceptable.

48. 1. 5. The "great masters of the law" is a transparent reference to Coke. In the 1616 *Proposition* for amending the laws, Bacon, after noting the value of his maxims for such a project, went out of his way to set the record clear. "And I do assure your Majesty, I am in good hope, that when Sir Edward Coke's Reports and my Rules and Decisions shall come to posterity, there will be (whatsoever is now thought) question who was the greater lawyer?" (13.70). See also 7. 523.

49. For the circumstances of the attempted piracy see W. W. Greg, *Some Aspects and Problems of London Publishing* (Oxford, 1956), pp. 56–58, 76.

50. Spedding found a rough draft of a letter written by Anthony to Essex and dated February 8, 1597. In it he gives the Earl "the first sight and taste of such fruit as my brother was constrained to gather," and transfers "my interest" in the "property" to him. 6. 521. Was this a private way of apologizing for what would appear publicly as an oversight? It is difficult to imagine why Anthony would compose such a letter on his own.

51. See also Jacob Zeitlin, "The Development of Bacon's Essays and Montaigne," *Journal of English and Germanic Philology* 27 (1928), 508, 512.

52. The sentence appears in the dedication to Buckingham. Whenever he speaks to friends of this latest edition he emphasizes its newness. 14. 429, 536.

53. The cuts amount to less than a hundred words. *Renaissance Prose*, pp. 218, 298 note 1.

54. 8. 290–91, 344–45, 348–49, 364–66.

55. Cf. Stanley Fish, *Self-Consuming Artifacts* (Berkeley, 1972), chap. 2. Fish's argument—that Bacon's essays are to be seen as strategies to induce further critical thinking, not merely as nuggets of wisdom—has considerable merit, but seems too convenient an explanation for *all* of the inconsistencies that appear as a result of the additions to the essays.

56. Even Rawley claims no more for him. 1. 14. And Tobie Matthew, who admired his "noble and true friend" to a fault, was astonished at Bacon's naiveté in matters of theology. "He was in very truth (with being a kind of monster both of wit and knowledge also in other things) such a poor kind of creature in all those which were questionable about religion, that my wonder takes away all my words." *A True Historical Relation of the Conversion of Sir Tobie Matthew to the Holy Catholic Faith; with the Antecedents*

*and Consequences thereof*, ed. A. H. Mathew (London, 1904), p. 112.

57. 7. 219–26. This work dates from before the summer of 1603. The prayers ascribed to Bacon show the same fine rationality. 7. 259–60.

58. 7. 70. The phrase comes from a draft letter to Lord Mountjoy. By the "best book" Bacon means the *Rhetoric*. See Karl Wallace, *Francis Bacon on Communication and Rhetoric* (Chapel Hill, 1943), pp. 67–68; James Stephens, "Bacon's New English Rhetoric and the Debt to Aristotle," *Speech Monographs* 39 (1972), 248–59.

59. Bacon was given to using the term in law to indicate a false principle. 7. 625, 632–33.

60. He was also elected for Ipswich, at the nomination of Essex. Considering the Earl's aggressive attempts to seat his followers in this parliament, it is possible that Bacon took a seat that would not obviously identify him with his friend—a decision that would square with his not dedicating his first book to him. What Bacon's connection was with Southampton is not clear. *Elizabethan House of Commons*, pp. 174, 229–31.

61. *Acts of the Privy Council, 1596–7*, pp. 373–74, 412–13; E. P. Cheyney, *History of England From the Defeat of the Armada to the Death of Elizabeth* (London, 1914–26), 2. 30–35. Bacon had also recently argued a case in Star Chamber against a band of ingrossers and forestallers. John Hawarde, *Les Reportes del Cases in Camera Stellata 1593–1609*, ed. W. P. Baildon (London, 1894), pp. 78–79. And is it possible that he knew of a census of the poor taken in Ipswich presumably in October 1597, just prior to parliament? *Poor Relief in Elizabethan Ipswich*, ed. John Webb, *Suffolk Records Society* 9 (1966), 119–20.

62. To see Bacon as the "official" or "unofficial" leader of the house in this parliament is both to read his words in a mechanical fashion and to assume that the Queen was a bit dim. Is it likely she would have allowed a man she distrusted to hold so important a position? For the standard interpretation see "Hayward Townshend's Journals," ed. A. F. Pollard and M. Blatcher, *Bulletin of the Institute of Historical Research* 12 (1934), 11; Joel J. Epstein, "The Parliamentary Career of Francis Bacon" (unpublished Ph.D. dissertation, Rutgers University, 1966), p. 64. Neale is more modest in his estimate of Bacon's position. *Elizabeth I and her Parliaments, 1584–1601*, pp. 326, 338.

63. Unfortunately there is no good work on Bacon as a speaker, although (typically) there are many discussions of his ideas on rhetoric. The following are of limited use. Robert Hannah, *Francis Bacon: The Political Orator* (New York, 1926); Egon Jungmann, *Die politische Rhetorik in der Englischen Renaissance*, in *Brittanica et Americana* 5 (1960), 91–129; *Renaissance Prose*, pp. 47–49; Karl Wallace, "Discussion in Parliament in Francis Bacon," *Journal of Speech* 42 (1957), 12–21; "Chief Guides for the Study of Bacon's Speeches," *Studies in the Literary Imagination* 4 (1971), 173–88; *Francis Bacon on Communication and Rhetoric, passim*.

64. 9. 85. The words further suggest that Bacon was not an official leader. The custom alluded to was not very old. *Elizabeth I and her Parliaments, 1584–1601*, p. 359.

65. This preoccupation with his audience's needs is defined in his essay, "Of Discourse," and in the *Short Notes for Civil Conversation*, 7. 109–10. See also *Francis Bacon on Communication and Rhetoric, p. 183*.

66. *Proceedings in Parliament, 1610*, ed. Elizabeth Read Foster (New Haven, 1966), 2. 29. See also 10. 197, 309.

67. 8. 223. Perhaps the best testimony is to be found in the brief summaries of his

speeches contained in the *Commons Journal*. Almost always they are built around a figure of speech the reporter remembered. For example, *C.J.* 1. 192, 209, 994.

68. 1. 12–13. See also Notestein, p. 3.
69. Jonson's well-known and hyperbolic appraisal is to be found in *Timber*. For a more critical view see Notestein, pp. 28, 105.
70. "I am little acquainted with the country," he would remark in 1610. *Proceedings in Parliament, 1610*, 2. 344. See also his admission in 1604 of knowing only at "second hand" the specific abuses arising from purveyance. 10. 185–86. Cheyney's comment too is apt. "There is frequent reason to observe in Bacon's writing that he was not very familiar with the local institutions of his time." Cheyney, 2. 390.
71. The inspiration for this comment came from the musings of a gardener in modern day East Anglia. Ronald Blythe, *Akenfield* (London, 1969), pp. 106–7.
72. *Aubrey's Brief Lives*, ed. Oliver L. Dick (Ann Arbor, 1957), p. 12.
73. For Bacon's own susceptibility to this 'Idol of the Tribe,' see Virgil Whitaker, "Bacon's Doctrine of Forms: A Study of Seventeenth Century Eclecticism," *Huntington Library Quarterly* 32 (1969), 209.
74. 7. 423. For Bacon's hope that this reading might gain him a greater legal reputation than Coke's, see J. E. G. de Montmorency, "Bacon," *Great Jurists of the World*, ed. J. MacDonell, E. Manson (Boston, 1914), pp. 152–53.
75. On the analogy see Holdsworth, 4. 410 note 1.
76. The apt phrase is from James Whitelocke, *Liber Familicus*, ed. John Bruce, Camden Society, 70 (London, 1858), p. 8. Bacon seems to have been a witness to the assault on the city. *Calendar State Papers Domestic, 1598–1601*, p. 573.
77. So worthy that those later writers who condemn him for appearing at the trial seem really to be protesting his *skills*. W. B. Devereux, *Lives and Letters of the Devereux, Earls of Essex* (London, 1853), 2. 159; Robert Lacey, *Robert, Earl of Essex* (New York, 1971), pp. 305–6.
78. 9. 225. The particular historical figure Bacon relies on as an example is Pisistratus.
79. He had earlier been commissioned to write up a narrative of the proceedings against Essex at York house on June 5, 1600. 9. 175–88. For Bacon's "very eloquent speech" at this hearing see Fynes Moryson, *An Itinerary* (Glasgow, 1907–8), 2. 315–17.
80. 10. 159. The Queen herself, according to Bacon, made changes in the tract.
81. See the references to him in *The Diary of John Manningham*, ed. John Bruce, Camden Society, 94 (London, 1868), pp. 62–63, 81–82.
82. In 1601, though, he was appointed to High Commission. R. G. Usher, *The Rise and Fall of the High Commission* (Oxford, 1913), p. 346.
83. Chamberlain, 1. 123. When his mother died in 1610 Bacon himself provided evidence of lack of feeling in a letter written to Sir Michael Hicks. 10. 217–18.
84. Spedding argued that the work was written in the summer of 1603. The possibility of an earlier date, however, has been suggested by J. G. Crowther, *Francis Bacon: The First Statesman of Science* (London, 1960), p. 213. An exact date would be helpful for what it might tell us about the progress of Bacon's frustration. Internally the work has only teasing clues, the sum of which could place it almost anywhere between his thirty-fifth and fiftieth year. Whatever the date, the view of himself is the familiar one.

# Chapter 3

1. Helen G. Stafford, *James VI of Scotland and the Throne of England* (New York, 1940), pp. 117, 203–4. For evidence of Bacon's peripheral connection, see *Memoirs of the Reign of Queen Elizabeth*, 1. 122, 147.
2. 10. 67. A few days before Elizabeth's death Bacon had written to Northumberland promising him the "use" of his "head, tongue, pen, means, or friends." It was not "any straits of my occasions," he assured Northumberland, that induced him to offer his services, but the Earl's "love towards studies and contemplations of an higher and worthier nature than popular" (10.58).
3. A good example comes from the summer of 1604 when Bacon drew up a proclamation proposing a change in the King's style. Whether James ever saw this unsolicited effort is not known, but there is no evidence to support Spedding's contention that it served as the basis for the proclamation finally issued in October, when James, despite his promise to wait upon the work of the Commission of Union, had himself declared King of Great Britain. For a careful comparison with the King's opening speech to parliament the previous March plainly shows the source for the proclamation. Bacon's composition is half again as long, and seeks to *defend* the King's initiative in adopting the new style. The strident concern for persuading the "multitude" finds Bacon writing long-winded though well-organized briefs. The King's manner, on the other hand, is more desultory yet very assertive; a proclamation was clearly conceived as an act of his will. For Bacon's effort, 10. 235-39; for the proclamation eventually published, *Stuart Royal Proclamations*, 1. 94–98.
4. From James's opening speech to parliament, March 19, 1604. *The Political Works of James I,* ed. C. H. McIlwain (Cambridge, Massachusetts, 1918), p. 278.
5. Spedding placed the fragment in 1608 on the basis of an entry in the *Commentarius Solutus* (1608): "Finishing my treat. of $y^e$ Great. of Br. $w^{th}$ aspect ad pol." He assumed that the work, if it had been finished, was intended to persuade James to undertake a foreign policy that would keep mens' minds off of domestic difficulties. Virtually all later commentators have accepted this date, although a few years before Spedding's edition appeared, 1605 had been offered as an alternative date. Charles de Rémusat, *Bacon* (Paris, 1857), p. 69. Rémusat supposed that Bacon had included the tract (presumably complete) as a kind of preliminary show of seriousness with a letter he had sent to Lord Chancellor Egerton in 1605 suggesting the need for a history of Great Britain. The letter, however, contains no hint of an accompanying gift, an omission very unlike Bacon. More recently Farrington suggested that it was "written about the time James mounted the throne." Benjamin Farrington, *Francis Bacon: Philosopher of Industrial Science* (New York, 1949), p. 151. Despite his failure to provide either evidence or argument for his guess, Farrington seems to be right. The question is a serious one since it directly involves the purpose and interpretation of the work. If we date it back to 1603 Spedding's judgment of its purpose must be wrong. Evidence for doing this is available. In several letters dating from the time of James's accession, Bacon promises to send his contacts at the Scottish court "some means . . . to verify" their "commendation" of him. 10. 59, 64, 66. This "means" was presumably something he was *then* in the process of writing, which would exclude the several pieces that came from his pen in the early months of the reign since they all were manifestly responses to specific situations. Moreover, a sentence on the first page of the treatise

sounds very much as if it were written soon after James came to the throne. "Therefore, that it may the better appear what greatness your majesty hath obtained of God, and what greatness this island hath obtained by you, . . . I have thought good, as far as I can comprehend, to make a true survey and representation of the greatness of this your kingdom of Britain; . . . being out of doubt that none of the great monarchies which in the memory of times have risen in the habitable world, had so fair seeds and beginnings as hath this your estate and kingdom (7.47)." What probably happened is that Bacon began the treatise shortly before Elizabeth's death but then put it aside when he realized that a particular problem—James's desire to effect a union of the two kingdoms—offered him an opportunity for more relevant advice. This explanation would also square with the entry in the *Commentarius Solutus.* As it was, the treatise never did get finished and part of it was put into the 1612 essay "Of the Greatness of Kingdoms."

6. Orsini, pp. 49–51.
7. Herbert Butterfield, *The Statecraft of Machiavelli* (London, 1940), pp. 78, 126.
8. Within a few days of Elizabeth's death there appeared in the bookstalls of London the first public edition of the *Basilikon Doron.* The book was a great success and Bacon, it is fair to assume, was probably one of its early readers. He may have also already perused the King's *Trew Law of Free Monarchies* (1598) as well as the *Daemonologie* (1597). Certainly by the time he was writing the *Advancement of Learning* he knew them, since all received flattering and knowledgeable mentions.
9. See the section on the *Philosophia Prima* in the *Advancement of Learning,* 3. 346–49, and the discussion in Robert McRae, *The Problem of the Unity of the Sciences* (Toronto, 1961), chap. 2.
10. Hardin Craig, *The Enchanted Glass* (New York, 1936), *passim*; Donald Davie, *The Language of Science and the Language of Literature, 1700–1740* (London, 1963), p. 65; Philip C. Ritterbush, *Overture to Biology* (New Haven, 1964), chap. 3.
11. A reference to the *Brief Discourse* in the introductory pages dates it beyond June. No allusion, however, to the Hampton Court Conference, originally scheduled for November but postponed to January 1604, suggests that it was completed before the late fall. Also, the reference to the "extremities" of both the Puritans and bishops points to the summer, when each side was trying to outdo the other in petitioning and speaking out. See Patrick Collinson, *The Elizabethan Puritan Movement* (London, 1967), pp. 449–55. The tract was published anonymously in 1604.
12. Another good example of this can be found in the 1608 paper, *Answers to Questions Touching the Office of Constable,* where he discusses the "obscure" origin of the office. 7. 749–54.
13. For a good general discussion of what construing statutes involves, see Felix Frankfurter, "The Reading of Statutes," *Of Law and Men* (New York, 1956), pp. 44–71.
14. In July Bacon had told Cecil that his civil ambition was "quenched," and that henceforth his time would be spent improving his estate and using his pen "to maintain memory and merit of the times succeeding" (10.80). It is the familiar rationalization, inspired not only by disappointment but also probably by Coke's unwillingness to employ him in the legal counsel. The two men had had a bitter quarrel two years before and neither felt comfortable working with the other (10. 1–5, 78). Also, soon after James came to the throne, Coke seems to have been trying to undercut his rival.

On April 6, 1603, he wrote to Cecil explaining the progress of his efforts in the prosecution of Valentine Thomas, a hapless pseudo-conspirator, and carefully included a suggestion that Bacon had botched an earlier examination. *Historical Manuscripts Commission, Salisbury,* 15. 34–35.

15. 10. 181–87. Bacon kept a full report of this speech also.

16. *Privy Councillors,* pp. 114–15; J. P. Kenyon, *The Stuart Constitution* (Cambridge, 1966), p. 28; Theodore K. Rabb, "Sir Edwin Sandys and the Parliament of 1604," *American Historical Review* 69 (1964), 647. Willson realizes, however, that Bacon was continually "striving to make his activities in the Commons a stepping stone to advancement." *Privy Councillors,* p. 106. See also Notestein, p. 119.

17. Two letters dating from the session of 1605-6 are the first evidence of collaboration. Both are addressed to Cecil and contain brief messages of business, but they are also characterized by an air of uncertainty and zealousness, the mark of a man new to a position and watchful of the impression he is making. "I purpose, upon promise rather than business, to make a step to my house in the country this afternoon: Which because your Lordship may hear otherwise, and thereupon conceive any doubt of my return, to the prejudice of the King's business, I thought it concerned me to give your Lordship an account, that I purpose (if I live) to be here to-morrow evening" (10.275). See also 277. This quality is perhaps all the more striking since Bacon had been writing to his cousin for many years. More significant evidence is to be found in a letter written to the King sometime during the summer of 1606 in which Bacon speaks of the Solicitor-Generalship (vacant once again) as being practically owed to him. "For both in the commission of Union, . . . and this last Parliament, in the bill of the Subsidy . . . ; in the matter of Purveyance; in the Ecclesiastical Petitions; in the Grievances, and the like; as I was ever careful (and not without good success) sometimes to put forward that which was good, sometimes to keep back that which was not so good; so your Majesty was pleased to accept kindly of my services. . . . In all which nevertheless I can challenge to myself no sufficiency, but that I was diligent and reasonable happy to execute those directions, which I received either immediately from your royal mouth, or from my Lord of Salisbury" (10.294). That Bacon, especially considering the letter's object, goes no further back than the Commission of Union while listing his "former services strongly suggests that his efforts in the 1604 session had not been officially inspired, however much they may have been appreciated. Never backward in blowing his own horn, Bacon, had he been formally working with Cecil in 1604, would have mentioned the fact.

18. This was essentially the view of Spedding and Gardiner. Recently it has been refurbished by Joel J. Epstein, "Francis Bacon: Mediator in the Parliament of 1604," *The Historian* 30 (1968), 219–37.

19. It is also possible that Bacon's efforts in investigating the Gunpowder Plot gained him some notice. Spedding found little to connect him with the investigation, but printed evidence showing greater participation is available. 10. 255–58; *Historical Manuscripts Commission, First Report,* p. 58; *Third Report,* p. 281.

20. 10. 312. See Notestein, pp. 222–24.

21. This sentence comes from a speech delivered May 22, 1610, when Bacon used precedents from Elizabeth's reign to prove that the Commons had permitted debate to be stayed upon royal command. *Proceedings in Parliament, 1610,* 2. 110–11; Notestein, p. 328. The scriptural text is

Jeremiah 6:16. Bacon quotes more frequently from the Bible than from any other source. Harold Fisch, *Jerusalem and Albion* (London, 1964), pp. 90–91.

22. *The Parliamentary Diary of Robert Bowyer*, ed. D. H. Willson (Minneapolis, 1931), p. 120. For the diarist's own compliments on Bacon's speeches, pp. 65, 165. See also *Journal of Sir Roger Wilbraham*, ed. H. S. Scott, *Camden Miscellany*, 10 (London, 1902), p. 81. For doubts about Bacon's persuasiveness, *Proceedings in Parliament, 1610*, 2. 92; Notestein, pp. 28, 105, 551 note 5.

23. See the letter of advice to his niece touching the offer of marriage made to her by Sir Thomas Edmondes. 13. 174.

24. *The Political Works of James I*, p. 10. The phrase is from the *Basilikon Doron*.

25. A small incident is suggestive. On November 16, 1610, thirty members of the Commons were summoned to Whitehall and directly asked by the King if they "thought he was in want." Bacon was among the group and immediately began "to answer in a more extravagant style than his Majesty did delight to hear," who then "picked out Sir Henry Neville, commanding him to answer." Ralph Winwood, *Memorials of Affairs of State*, ed. Edmund Sawyer (London, 1725), 3.235; Notestein, p. 567 note 4. It is perhaps no accident that among the dozens of compliments (including Elizabeth's and Cecil's) on Bacon's oratory that have survived, there is not a word from James. See also David Mathew, *James I* (London, 1967), p. 9; James Rowley, "Francis Bacon: His Public Career and Personal Character," *Wordsworth and other Essays* (Bristol, 1927), pp. 125–68.

26. For evidence that at least some Scotsmen saw Bacon as the betrayer of Essex, see the letter Archibald Douglas, a former ambassador to London, wrote to his cousin Richard in 1601. *Calendar of Scottish Papers, 1597–1603*, Part II, pp. 918–19.

27. Certainly other men thought so. Writing to Carleton on April 12, 1603, Chamberlain observed, "your old friend Tobie Mathew was sent with a letter [to the King] from Master Bacon but I doubt neither the message nor messenger were greatly welcome." Chamberlain, 1. 192. See also the letter Bacon sent to the Earl of Southampton, who had been involved in the Essex fiasco, shortly before the Earl was released from the Tower. 10. 75–76.

28. E. A. Abbott first questioned the reliability of the *Apology* in his *Bacon and Essex* (London, 1877), pp. 112–15, 183. Abbott, however, was only concerned with demonstrating where Bacon went astray factually and did not look at the *Apology* as a purposeful creation. It is interesting to note that Spedding had some doubts about the work when he discussed it in *Evenings with a Reviewer*, written in 1846 but not published until 1882. "What he tells us is of course to be taken with caution, being his own story told in his own defense when nobody could contradict him." Expressed differently in the *Works*, this caution loses its impact. *Evenings with a Reviewer*, 1. 141; 10. 161–62.

29. See, for example, the words Elizabeth is credited with having spoken in the summer of 1600. 10. 156.

30. R. W. Gibson, *Francis Bacon, A Bibliography of his Works and of Baconiana to the Year 1750* (Oxford, 1950), p. xiv.

31. *Historical Manuscripts Commission, Hastings*, 4. 2. The statement comes from a letter written (c. 1604) by Egremont Thynne, a lawyer, to Sir John Davies, the lawyer and poet who was then serving as Solicitor-General for Ireland. "Kinge" is a mystery (perhaps Humphrey King, the comic verse-writer?), nor do any dictionaries help with "philosoter." If the word is not a

mistake, Thynne would seem to be punning with the idea of a fondness for preserving. In any event, the tone of the comment is clearly mocking. It is also worth noting that none of Bacon's biographers has cited this letter. Indeed, his latest biographers, Fulton H. Anderson, *Francis Bacon: His Career and his Thought* (Los Angeles, 1967), Catherine Drinker Bowen, *Francis Bacon: The Temper of a Man* (Boston, 1963), and Crowther, avoid serious discussion of the *Apology* altogether.

32. D. G. James, *The Dream of Learning* (Oxford, 1951), p. 21; Geoffrey Bullough, "Bacon and the Defense of Learning," *Seventeenth Century Studies Presented to Sir Herbert Grierson* (Oxford, 1938), p. 1.

33. 11. 146, 281; 14. 230. Although he almost always used the phrase to portray himself as a man "fitter to hold a book," on one occasion at least he reversed its message and used it to ask the King for employment. See *The Essays of Francis Bacon*, ed. S. H. Reynolds (Oxford, 1890), p. 275.

34. It has been argued that the first book is patterned on the model of a classical oration. Maurice McNamee, "Literary Decorum in Francis Bacon," *St. Louis University Studies*, ser. A. Humanities, 1 (1950), 47–48.

35. 3. 270. Was not Cecil, to Bacon's mind, the archetype of the "empiric" statesman? See above his comments to Cecil on sending him advice about Ireland. 10. 45.

36. 3. 272. Compare this to what he had to say in the *Apology* about his efforts on Essex's behalf. 10. 143.

37. See his comments in the *Apology* on serving self. 10. 157.

38. *The Political Works of James I*, pp. 4, 40, 48.

39. Emil Wolff, *Francis Bacon und seine Quellen* (Berlin, 1910–13), 2. 27.

40. 10. 291. This description is quoted from a letter of Dudley Carleton to John Chamberlain. For other examples of Bacon's love for pomp and splendor see Chamberlain's description of his formal entry into Chancery. Chamberlain, 2. 72–73, also 61–62. In addition see Aubrey's comments. *Brief Lives*, pp. 9–10. Bacon was wont, however, not to acknowledge his liking for the trappings of position. "This matter of pomp," he tells Buckingham when reporting on his entry into Chancery, "which is heaven to some men, is hell to me, or purgatory at least" (13.194). The fact and the attitude are both sincere, paralleling so many other discontinuities in his life.

41. 1.8; *Catalogue of the Exhibition Organized by the St. Albans City Council . . . to Commemorate the 400th Anniversary of the Birth of Francis Bacon* (St. Albans, 1961), p. 6.

42. 10. 371. Bacon also drew up a proposal for a proclamation on the issue, but it was not used.

43. Bacon also appears to have arranged Constable's marriage to his wife's sister, much to the displeasure of the mother, Lady Packington, a "litle violent Lady" as Chamberlain calls her. 11.14. See also *Historical Manuscripts Commission, Salisbury*, 19. 346.

44. 11. 119. This is taken from a discourse, *Certain Considerations Touching the Plantation in Ireland*, that Bacon subsequently sent the King.

45. In reaction to Fulton Anderson's non-historical approach to Bacon's philosophy, *The Philosophy of Francis Bacon* (Chicago, 1948), Paolo Rossi, *Francis Bacon: From Magic to Science*, trans. Sacha Rabinovitch (Chicago, 1968), and Benjamin Farrington, *The Philosophy of Francis Bacon* (Liverpool, 1964), have, it seems, gone to the other extreme and emphasized intellectual development where considerations of stylistic presentation are probably more important. Both men see Bacon gaining greater historical insight with the passing years and applying it to his critique of ancient learning. Neither

man, however, can provide very much evidence for his position, and at one point Rossi inaccurately summarizes a passage from the *Advancement of Learning* to make his case. Rossi, p. 45. Cf. 3. 329–30.

46. Farrington, *Philosophy*, p. 72. I have used Farrington's translations of these three works. They follow his essay on Bacon's intellectual development.

47. 3. 223. For an interesting discussion showing how Christian teachings buttressed Bacons's criticisms of traditional philosophy (and philosophers) and justified his own ideas for the reform of knowledge, see Paolo Rossi, "Bacone e la Bibbia," *Archiwum historii Filozofii i mysli spolecznej* 12 (1966), 105–25.

48. Farrington, *Philosphy,* p. 62.

49. Moody E. Prior, "Bacon's Man of Science," *Journal of the History of Ideas* 15 (1954), 348–70, connects the lecturer of the *Redargutio* with the father of the *New Atlantis* while arguing that Bacon was forming a new ideal for the scientist. He does not, however, mention the speaker in the *Temporis Partus Masculus* or consider how the ideal might connect with Bacon's own life.

50. The image is still persuasive. See Loren Eiseley, *The Man Who Saw Through Time* (New York, 1973).

51. Hellmut Bock, *Staat und Gesellschaft bei Francis Bacon* (Berlin, 1937), pp. 69–70.

52. 11. 50–52. The "Att." was Attorney-General Hobart.

53. The last observation belongs to Menna Prestwich, *Cranfield*, p. 270.

54. He sent a copy to Sir George Carew, the English ambassador at Paris and a man he had lost touch with over the years ("I thought to provide your remembrance of me by my letter"), requesting him to pass it on to the great French scholar. 11. 109.

55. In July 1609, for example, Bacon played a key role in the three-day debate at Whitehall on the question of prohibitions and their effect on the ecclesiastical courts. For his performance and the King's response, see R. G. Usher, *The Reconstruction of the English Church* (New York, 1910), 2. 231–35.

56. Lines composed by John Davies of Hereford at about this time for his *Scourge of Folly* accurately reflect Bacon's own feelings.

> Thy bounty and the Beauty of thy Witt
> Comprised in Lists of Law and learned Arts,
> Each making thee for great Imployment fitt
> Which now thou hast, (though short of thy deserts)
> Compells my pen to let fall shining Inke
> And to bedew the Baies that deck thy Front; . . .

57. 6. 696. Four of the fables had been written up as early as 1604 to be included in a work entitled *Cogitationes de Scientia Humana.*

58. Some contemporaries realized (and applauded) the considerable invention that went into these pieces. Vittorio Gabrieli, "Bacone, La Riforma e Roma nella versione hobbesiana di un carteggio di Fulgenzio Micanzio," *English Miscellany* 8 (1957), 205.

59. Spedding set the work among Bacon's literary productions. Anderson thinks differently: "The work is unquestionably one of the most significant contributions to philosophy in the history of English thought." *Philosophy*, p. 57. Rossi and Farrington have followed the same line. Douglas Bush originally saw them as "virtually another series of civil and moral essays." *Mythology and the Renaissance Tradition of English Poetry* (Minneapolis, 1932), p. 241. More recently he has shifted a little to Anderson's position. *English Literature in the Earlier Seventeenth Century 1600–1660*, 2nd edition (Oxford, 1962), p. 197. See also Charles W. Lemmi, *The Classic Deities in Bacon*

(Baltimore, 1933); Barbara C. Garner, "Francis Bacon, Natalis Comes and the Mythological Tradition," *Journal of the Warburg and Courtauld Institutes* 23 (1970), 264–91.

60. 11. 282. It is likely that this letter—which Spedding assumed was written in 1612—was actually composed several years before, perhaps as early as 1604. The introductory character of the references to his father and himself, as well as other comments, do not sound as if they come from a man who had been Solicitor-General for five years. And the phrase Spedding thought described Cecil *(quo vivente virtutibus certissimum exitium)* could apply to other servants of the King.

61. 9. 282. In both matters he also had a private interest. He had hoped to capture the Mastership of the Wards and in June 1612 had been mentioned as the likeliest candidate. In the case of Sutton's will it appears that Bacon was acting in collusion with Simon Baxter, the cousin who brought the legal action to set aside the will. W. K. Jordan, *The Charities of London, 1480–1660* (London, 1960), p. 152; *Philanthrophy in England, 1480–1660* (London, 1959), p. 285.

62. "Of Seditions and Troubles" appears in the Harleian manuscript set of essays which dates from the period 1607–12. Both essays were printed in 1625.

63. *Essays*, Reynolds, p. xii.

64. Chamberlain, 1. 397.

65. 11. 59. Bacon seems to have been successful in winning the Prince—another example of his talent for dealing with the young. At some point after 1608 he was made the Prince's Solicitor-General, and in 1611 Henry appointed him Steward of King's Langley in the Duchy of Lancaster. Somerville, p. 433.

66. On Bacon's failure to appreciate the growing self-consciousness—hence power—of parliament, see Notestein, p. 558 note 7.

67. *Proceedings in Parliament, 1610*, 2. 92.

68. James Whitelocke had provided Sir Robert Mansell, Treasurer of the Navy, with arguments challenging the legality of the King's method of investigating abuses in the navy. Bacon played a major role in the charges subsequently brought against the lawyer. Also, when Whitelocke, after a twenty-six day confinement in the Fleet, finally penned a submission to the King, Bacon helped him to write it out in a form pleasing to James! *Liber Familicus*, pp. viii, 40.

69. Moir, pp. 82–83. The memorial will be found in 12. 24–30.

70. For the Cambridge election see Millicent Rex, *University Representation in England, 1604–90* (London, 1954), pp. 64–65. For the debates in parliament on seating the Attorney-General, see *C.J.* 1. 456, 459–60; Moir, pp. 85–87.

71. See also *Politics and the Bench*, p. 45.

72. Parry, the Chancellor of the Duchy of Lancaster, was accused of unlawfully intervening in the election at Stockbridge. Thought to be one of the infamous "undertakers," he was expelled from the house. James completely avoided involving himself in the case except to offer to punish Parry. Moir, pp. 45, 102–103.

73. Gardiner, 2. 193; *Privy Councillors*, p. 132; Epstein, "The Parliamentary Career of Francis Bacon," p. 236; Clayton Roberts, *The Growth of Responsible Government in Stuart England* (Cambridge, 1966), p. 18; J. W. Allen, *English Political Thought, 1603–1660* (London, 1938), p. 62.

74. Certainly other men of his day were inclined to regard Elizabeth's reign as a touchstone. See, for example, W. J. Jones, "Ellesmere and Politics, 1603–1617," *Early Stuart Studies*, ed. Howard S. Reinmuth (Minneapolis, 1970), pp. 12, 62–63; Ronald A. Rebholz, *The Life of Fulke Greville* (Oxford, 1971), *passim*.

75. 12. 184. For more general comments on Bacon's conservatism see Theodore K. Rabb, "Francis Bacon and the Reform of Society," *Action and Conviction in Early Modern Europe: Essays in Memory of E. H. Harbison,* ed. Theodore K. Rabb, Jerrold E. Seigel (Princeton, 1969), pp. 169–93.

76. As late as 1620 Bacon was still damning the policy "begun first by the Earl of Salisbury," of openly "divulging and noising of your wants" (14.87). Modern historians are more willing to give Cecil credit for ingenuity, but tend to come up with some strange arguments for assuring themselves that the policy could not (or ought not to) have worked. See, for example, Joel Hurstfield, *The Queen's Wards* (Cambridge, Massachusetts, 1958), pp. 322–23.

77. W. H. Greenleaf notes the discrepancy but does not attempt an explanation. *Order, Empiricism and Politics: Two Traditions of English Political Thought, 1500–1700* (London, 1964), pp. 206, 231. On Bacon's own instinctive impatience with empiricism, see also Fisch, 82–83.

78. 3. 715–26; F. R. Johnson, *Astronomical Thought in Renaissance England* (Baltimore, 1937), pp. 245–47.

79. See his comments in the *Advancement.* 3. 359–60. It has recently been suggested that Bacon neglected mathematics also because he associated it with magic. Frances A. Yates, "The Hermetic Tradition in Renaissance Science," *Art, Science, and History in the Renaissance,* ed. Charles S. Singleton (Baltimore, 1967), pp. 268–69.

80. The frequent political metaphors and analogies in Book II of the *Advancement of Learning* reveal the same quality. Sometimes they are obtrusive, e.g., 3. 325.

81. The work is generally ascribed to sometime before 1616 because it contains no reference to Galileo's theory of tides, which was announced that year. For a good discussion of the connection between the thinking of Bacon and Galileo on the tides, see Paolo Rossi, "Galileo e Bacone," *Saggi su Galileo Galilei. Pubblicazioni del Comitato Nazionale per le Manifestazioni Celebrative* (Rome, 1972), vol. 3 pt. 2, 256–68. This essay also compares the method and thinking of the two men on science in general. Cf. W. Mays, "Scientific Method in Galileo and Bacon," *Atti dei Convegni. Pubblicazioni . . . Celebrative* (Rome, 1967), Vol. 2 pt. 5, 309–16.

82. Ernst Cassirer, *The Platonic Renaissance in England,* trans. James P. Pettegrove (Austin, 1953), pp. 48–49; Joseph Needham, *The Skeptical Biologist* (London, 1929), pp. 81–82; Barbara J. Shapiro, "Law and Science in Seventeenth Century England," *Stanford Law Review* 21 (1969), 732, 736, 743.

83. 11. 391. This Biblical tag (Luke 10:41), a favorite of Bacon's, appears first in his writings in the 1596 advice to Essex, when he urged the Earl to "win the Queen" (9.40).

84. The statement comes from a letter written to Bacon in April 1616. Earlier Matthew had apologized for interrupting Bacon with some excerpts of a letter of Galileo's. *Le opere di Galileo Galilei,* ed. G. Barbéra (Florence, 1929–39), 12. 255.

85. "Mr. Murray" was Sir John Murray, Groom of the Bedchamber, and a conduit for much of James's correspondence.

86. 12. 101–2. For Rawley's view of Bacon's treatment of other men, see 1. 14–15. Wit alone distinguishes Bacon from his contemporaries when it came to political infighting.

87. *Privy Councillors,* pp. 17–20.

88. 13. 42. See also 20.

89. *Stuart Royal Proclamations,* 1. 370.

90. 13. 207–8, 244. For evidence that Bacon may have had his own personal reason for desiring this switch see *Letters from George Lord Carew to Sir Thomas Roe,*

ambassador to the court of the Great Mogul, 1615–1617, ed. John MacLean, Camden Society, 76 (London, 1860), 106.

91. *Report of Cases Decided by Francis Bacon in the High Court of Chancery*, ed. John Ritchie (London, 1932), pp. v–xviii. There were, however, complaints. See the case of John Wraynham. 13. 311; Chamberlain, 2. 159, 161; *A Complete Collection of State Trials*, ed. W. Cobbett, T.B. Howell *et al.* (London, 1816–98), 2. 1059–86.

92. 7. 759–74; Holdsworth, 5. 254; W. J. Jones, *The Elizabethan Court of Chancery* (Oxford, 1967), pp. 286, 313.

93. For the *Declaration* 13. 384–413. See also Chamberlain, 2. 188; V. T. Harlow, *Ralegh's Last Voyage* (London, 1932), p. 94.


# Chapter 4

1. Chamberlain, 2. 385.
2. 14. 285. This is Spedding's translation of the original Latin.
3. For James's fondness for history see his comments in the *Basilikon Doron. The Political Works of James I*, pp. 40, 44.
4. "Off all Stories I think Tacitus simply the best." Vernon F. Snow, "Francis Bacon's Advice to Fulke Greville," *Huntington Library Quarterly* 23 (1960), 373. See also Edwin Benjamin, "Bacon and Tacitus," *Classical Philology* 60 (1965), 102–10; Mary F. Tenney, "Tacitus in the Politics of Early Stuart England," *The Classical Journal* 37 (1941), 154–56, as well as the same author's unpublished dissertation, "Tacitus in the Middle Ages and the Early Renaissance and England to about the year 1650" (Cornell University, 1931), pp. 180, 356–69; Robert Adolph, *The Rise of Modern Prose Style* (Cambridge, Mass., 1968), chap. 2 *passim*; Else-Lilly Etter, *Tacitus in der Geistesgeschichte des 16. und 17. Jahrhunderts* (Basel, 1966), pp. 191–93. On July 16, 1621, Bacon, clearly hoping for restitution himself, quoted in a letter to James the speech Tacitus assumed Seneca spoke to Nero. "*Utar*, saith Seneca to his Master, *magnis exemplis; nec meae fortunae, sed tuae* . . . . Seneca banished for divers corruptions; yet was afterward restored, and an instrument of that memorable *Quinquennium Neronis*" (14.297). See Tacitus, *Annals* 14. 53. The similitude appears again in the "epistle dedicatory" to the *Advertisement Touching a Holy War*. 14. 372; 7. 12. Cicero and Demosthenes were also comfortable parallels.
5. In 1610 the corrections had to do with his father's career. 11. 212–14. Sometime after 1615 further suggestions were offered dealing with matters dating from the last years of Elizabeth. Bacon, as lawyer and propagandist, had either been directly involved or familiar with all of them. 6. 353–64.
6. There are several discussions of Bacon's ideas on the writing and significance of history. Most rely on Leonard F. Dean's "Francis Bacon's Theory of Civil History Writing," *English Literary History* 8 (1941), 161–83. See also F. Smith Fussner, *The Historical Revolution* (New York, 1962), chap. 10; F. J. Levy, *Tudor Historical Thought* (San Marino, 1967), pp. 252–58; Enrico De Mas, *Francesco Bacone da Verulamio: La filosofia dell 'uomo* (Turin, 1964), pp. 151–56; George H. Nadel, "History as Psychology in Francis Bacon's Theory of History," *History and Theory* 5 (1966), 275–87; B. Wylie Sypher, "Similarities between the Scientific and the Historical Revolutions at the End of the Renaissance," *Journal of the History of Ideas* 26 (1965), 353–68; D.S.T. Clark, "Francis Bacon: The Study of History and the Science of Man" (unpublished Ph.D. dissertation, Cambridge University, 1970), chaps. 1, 4–6. Clark's thesis now stands as the most ambitious effort to

connect Bacon's thinking on history to his general philosophical outlook and program.

7. Snow, p. 371.

8. 3. 339. Bacon knew well the dangers that lurked for the unwary historian. He had himself in 1615 "charged" William Martin (the Recorder of Exeter) before the council with having inserted many questionable "passages" into his "lately written" *The Historie, and Lives, of Twentie Kings of England. Acts of the Privy Council, 1615–16*, p. 100. More familiar is his connection with Sir John Hayward's *First Part of the Life and Raigne of King Henrie the IIII* (1599). Bacon played no part in the government's examination of the author, but he did introduce the matter of Essex's patronage of the book at the York House hearing in June 1600. *Calendar State Papers Domestic, 1598–1601*, pp. 404–5, 449–53, 539–40; Moryson, 2. 316–17. The famous bons mots about Hayward's "felony" and "stile" (10.150), which Bacon claims in the *Apology* to have delivered to the Queen, should be treated—like all the remembered conversations in that book—with skepticism.

9. Only in the law would Bacon fail to write a major work. There is no question, however, that he was thinking about it. In a memorandum from March 1622 there is listed as a possible "contemplative" work "for my Pen" a "General Treatise *de Legibus et Justitia*" (14. 351–52).

10. It has been suggested that Bacon might have been self-consciously following up Sir Thomas More's *The History of King Richard III. History of the Reign of King Henry VII*, ed. Vittorio Gabrieli (Bari, 1964), p. xiv.

11. For Bacon's attitude toward Henry, 3. 336; 4. 306; 6. 306; 14. 362.

12. D. H. Willson, *King James VI & I* (London, 1956), pp. 249–50. See the same author's "King James and Anglo-Scottish Unity," *Conflict in Stuart England*, pp. 43–54; *The Political Works of James I*, p. 328. James had already decided to use Henry's chapel as the final resting place for Stuart royalty, and he eventually had himself buried in the tomb of Henry and Elizabeth.

13. Chamberlain. 2. 430. John Selden seems to have experienced the same problem. Marc Friedlaender, "Growth in the Resources for Studies in Early English History 1534–1625" (unpublished Ph.D. dissertation, University of Chicago, 1938), p. 188. Recent confusion over genre is witnessed in printed references to it as *The Life of Henry VII*. See G. R. Elton, *The Practice of History* (Sydney, 1967), p. 2; R. L. Storey, *The Reign of Henry VII* (London, 1968), p. 4.

14. 3. 334. See 6. 198–99.

15. 3. 334. In the *De Augmentis* a revealing clause is tacked on to the sentence: " . . . and one which you may more safely and happily take for example in another case" (4.305).

16. Wilhelm Busch, *England Under the Tudors: King Henry VII*, trans. Alice M. Todd (London, 1895), pp. 416–23.

17. See, for example, *The History of the Reign of King Henry VII*, ed. F. J. Levy (Indianapolis, 1972), p. 51; Edward I. Berry, "History and Rhetoric: Bacon's *History of Henry VII* and its Relation to the Humanist and 'Politic' Traditions" (unpublished Ph.D. dissertation, University of California, Berkeley, 1969), pp. 12, 212.

18. Spedding noted several occasions where Bacon followed Speed, but drew no conclusions. More recently, Robert Adolph noted the dependence in his fine discussion of Bacon's style, though he includes no real analysis of the source question. Adolph, p. 69. Some examples of where the language alone shows Bacon copying Speed are as follows: the introductory paragraph to the Brittany affair (6. 63–64; John Speed, *History of Great Britain* [London, 1611], p. 734); the death of James III (6.90–91; Speed, p. 735); the proxy marriage between Maximilian and Anne of Brittany (6. 101;

Speed, p. 736); the introductory paragraphs to the Perkin Warbeck conspiracy (6. 132–34; Speed, p. 737): Cliffords's confession in the Tower (6. 149; Speed, p. 739); Perkin at the court of James IV (6. 166; Speed, p. 741); Henry's treatment of Perkin's wife (6. 193; Speed, p. 744); the arrival of Archduke Philip in England (6. 230; Speed, p. 749).

19. Busch, and more recently Roger Lockyer, believed in Bacon's earlier research, presumably on the basis of Speed's borrowing. Busch, p. 416; *The History of the Reign of King Henry VII*, ed. Roger Lockyer (London, 1971), p. 12. But since Speed always carefully mentions who his sources are, and there is nothing from Bacon that is not contained in the fragment portrait, we are left wondering just what "materials" were collected. The assumption is advanced also in a study of Sir Robert Cotton. Hope Mirrlees, *A Fly in Amber* (London, 1962), p. 349. There the suggestion is based on a letter written by Walter Hawkesworth (d. 1606) to Cotton asking for books dealing "either in the life of Henry VII, or in the story of his times." Hawkesworth, secretary to Sir Charles Cornwallis, mentions that he himself is not the "principal in the study," but is only doing the collecting. Considering that the "principal" is not identified, that there seems to be no other evidence for a connection between Bacon and Hawkesworth, and that the date of the letter is illegible, it is difficult to accept such a guess. The Hawkesworth letter is to be found in *Cotton Ms. Julius* C, III. f. 24. Levy suggests that the very rapidity with which Bacon produced the work indicates earlier "notes," an argument that fails to appreciate Bacon's extraordinary facility at composition. *History,* ed. Levy, p. 16.

20. The few manuscripts obtained from Cotton were also helpful here. The famous antiquarian was the only source Bacon chose to mention in his text: "A worthy preserver and treasurer of rare antiquities: from whose manuscripts I have had much light for the furnishing of this work" (6.167).

21. Bacon's interpretation of how Henry used Archduke Philip as a prisoner in 1506 comes originally from the *Istoria Italia,* 7. 2., but he had referred to it once before in a legal brief prepared in 1612 against the Duchess of Shrewsbury. 11. 298–99. Bacon also relied on Guicciardini for his view of the characters of Ferdinand and Maximilian. Vincent Luciani, "Bacon and Guicciardini," *PMLA* 62 (1947), 96–113, and Edward Fueter, *Geschichte der neuren Historiographie,* 3rd edition, (Munich, 1936), pp. 168–70. For more discussion on the relationship between the two historians see Berry, "History and Rhetoric," chap. 3. Bacon uses Commines for his account of Charles VIII's invasion of Italy. *Memoires,* 7. 14, 17. Here, too, though, we may be dealing with a remembrance. Evidence of how that ill-fated venture had stuck permanently in Bacon's mind can be seen in his frequent use of the mocking metaphor (taken from Commines) with which Alexander VI characterized it. 3. 363; 4.53; Farrington, *Philosophy,* p. 104.

22. Busch, p. 417. The title of "Juno" for Margaret of Burgundy appears twice in Speed, and on the first occasion Speed cites André as his source. Speed, pp. 734, 740. The "distorted" story of Perkin Warbeck comes from Speed not André: the fact that Bacon alluded to "one that wrote in the same time" only proves that he was picking up Speed's own citation (p. 737), not that he was actually quoting André. The same mistaken assumption occurs in the question of Stanley's supposedly promising aid to Perkin (6. 151; Speed, p. 739), and on the matter of Perkin's confession being printed (6. 195· Speed, p. 744). As for the negotiations between Chancellor Morton and the French ambassadors, Bacon was quite able to make up the speeches delivered on the basis of what Hall and Speed told him.

If Bacon had been using André at first hand it is hard to believe that he would have made the famous mistake about "laetanter" (see below), that he would have confused the story of Perkin's heritage, and that he would not have given (as André does but Speed and Hall do not) the correct date of Prince Arthur's birth.

The modern editor of André, James Gairdner, thought that Bacon made use of the notes Speed had taken of André. *Memorials of King Henry the Seventh* (London, 1858), p. xxvi note 2. This seems unlikely, or academic, since Bacon follows the text of Speed so closely. Gairdner (p. xvi) also thought Bacon "must have been composing" the *History* "about the time" Speed was doing his.

23. "This Andreas . . . meant to haue historified and poetized the Acts of this king, but (for want of competent and attended instructions in many places of chiefe importance) left his labour full of wilde breaches, and vnfinished; yet in such points as he hath professed to know, not vnworthy to bee vouched; for there is in him a great deale of cleare elocution, and defaecated conceit aboue the ordinary of that age." Speed, p. 728.

24. On Cabot's voyages, John Stow, *Annales* (London, 1592), p. 802. Bacon is far more interested than Stow or Hall—his sources on this matter—in analyzing the disease as a medical phenomenon. 6. 33–34. Cf. Stow, p. 784; Edward Hall, *Chronicle,* ed. Henry Ellis (London, 1809), pp. 425–26.

25. Presumably in the Rolls House or Rolls Chapel. R. B. Wernham, "The Public Records in the Sixteenth and Seventeenth Centuries," *English Historical Scholarship in the Sixteenth and Seventeenth Centuries,* ed. Levi Fox (Oxford, 1956), p. 18. See also *C.D.* 6. 231.

26. Interestingly enough, there is no evidence of a connection between Bacon and the Society of Antiquaries.

27. 6. 25. The historian as painter is a favorite conceit with Bacon. 3. 336; 10. 249–52.

28. On the opening pages see also Edward I. Berry, "History and Rhetoric in Bacon's Henry VII," *Seventeenth Century Prose,* ed. Stanley E. Fish (New York, 1971), pp. 282–84. Cited hereafter as Berry. Berry's article, although it exaggerates the calculated "scientific" approach of the *History,* is a very perceptive discussion.

29. On the lack of contemporary discussion of Henry's claims to the throne, see S. B. Chrimes, *Henry VII* (London, 1972), p. 50.

30. See, for example, the glowing description of Star Chamber, the discussion of Stanley's "hard case," and the summary of how Empson and Dudley "turned law and justice into wormwood and rapine." 6. 85, 151, 217–19.

31. Speed, of course, may have been using a bad copy of André, a conclusion all the more possible when the reader senses the uneasiness with which he (Speed) reports the fact: "But Henry staied not in ceremonious greetings and popular acclamations [when he entered London], which (it seemes) hee did purposely eschue, for that (Andreas saith) hee entred couertly, meaning belike, in a Horse-litter or close Chariot." Speed, p. 729. And if Bacon, when he looked at André, saw the same copy, he would at least in this instance be cleared of the charge of doing shoddy work, for he would have had no reason to doubt what Speed gave him.

32. For other examples of careful division in the *History,* 6. 35–39, 59–62, 141–44, 225–26.

33. On the positioning of images in Bacon's works, *Renaissance Prose,* p. 158. For some other particularly effective examples in the *History,* 6. 42, 43, 60, 88, 95, 120, 139, 141, 192, 202, 211, 219.

34. Vergil's *Anglica Historia,* the source, directly or indirectly, for all subsequent narratives, had been written in part to serve as a defense of Henry's

rightful claim. Denys Hay, *Polydore Vergil* (Oxford, 1952), p. 9.

35. "Typhon," *De Sapientia Veterum*, 1609. "Of Seditions and Troubles," 1607–12.

36. 6. 47. It is possible that Speed inspired Bacon's deduction. "Shee being so iust an obiect of his [Henry] commiseration, . . . it cannot bee reasonably thought, but that there were other most important motiues, perswading such a sharpe course." Speed, p. 731.

37. Chrimes, p. 76.

38. See Agnes Conway, *Henry VII's Relations with Scotland and Ireland, 1485–1498* (Cambridge, 1932), p. 48; James Gairdner, *Henry the Seventh* (London, 1889). pp. 106-7; Chrimes, p. 81.

39. 6. 52, 54. See also his later assessment of what gave the Earl of Suffolk "confidence" to rebel. 6. 220–21.

40. 6. 56–57. Speed used this patriotic motive only to account for those who came in to fight on Henry's side. Speed, p. 732.

41. 6. 59. For Bacon's concern for "example and public justice" see his comments in 1616 about John Bertram, a disappointed litigant in Chancery who had first murdered a Master and then later hanged himself. 13. 100. The situation was a potentially embarrassing one for the government, and Bacon oversaw the preparation of "a little pamphlet" explaining what had happened. 13. 106, 115. See also Chamberlain, 2. 36, 39; *Elizabethan Court of Chancery*, p. 109 note 2.

42. 6. 59. See also Berry, pp. 286–87.

43. 6. 135. In Chudleigh's Case twenty-five years before Bacon had made the same point. "In cases as in testimonies, if one is found faulty in one point it deserves no credit in others" (7.619–20). Gairdner noticed Bacon's exaggerated description of Perkin's "tuition" but offered no explanation for it. *Memorials of King Henry the Seventh*, pp. xxx-xxxiii.

44. Hall, pp. 377–78. It is even possible that Tyrell never confessed. Chrimes, p. 93 note 1.

45. "Thus much was then delivered abroad, to be the effect of those examinations; but the King nevertheless made no use of them in any of his declarations. Whereby, as it seems, those examinations left the business somewhat perplexed" (6.143).

46. 6. 195–96. Bacon's lofty dismissal of the "tale of particulers" overlooks the fact that Henry (and his subjects) could not be certain that Perkin was an imposter. See Mortimer Levine, *Tudor Dynastic Problems, 1460–1571* (London, 1973), p. 38.

47. 6. 90. The germ of this transition is in Speed. "The vnworthy death of the Earle of Northumberland was seconded by a more vnworthy, of Iames the third King of Scotland, so as King Henrie lost at home a most honourable stay of his Northerne affaires, and a sure Ally abroad." Speed, p. 735. The thought is the same and the words similar, but the rhythm of Bacon's sentence shows how the artist can make gold out of a commonplace. See *Renaissance Prose*, chap. 4, for a general discussion of syntactical symmetry in Bacon's writings.

48. 6. 43. Hall states that it was Bedford's idea to try a pardon, and he subsequently praises the Duke for his "pollitique Wisdome." Hall, p. 427. Speed is briefer and more vague on the matter, simply saying that Henry sent Bedford "with conmission to pardon, or to fight." Speed, p. 730.

49. 3. 438. See 10. 50; 11. 260–61 for instances of Bacon's concern for this matter in his official life. See also Thomas Wheeler, "The Purpose of Bacon's *History of Henry the Seventh*," *Studies in Philology* 54 (1957), 1–13. Wheeler limits the purpose of the *History* to giving instruction to Charles only in this one matter.

50. 6. 21. The same phrasing will reappear in the character at the end of the *History*. 6. 239.
51. Spedding tried to justify the mention of Italy (and, unfortunately, several other statements in the *History*) by proposing that Bacon had used materials destroyed in the fire that ravaged the Cotton library in 1731. For other instances where he cites possible "independent" sources, see the footnotes on 6. 41, 75, 104, 109, 117, 142, 205.
52. Hall, p. 457.
53. 6. 119–20. For Henry's surprise and disappointment at hearing of Maximilian's unreadiness, Speed, p. 736; Hall, p. 456.
54. 6. 110–11. In the 1612 version of the essay, "Of Counsel," Bacon noted that, "for secrecy, Princes are not bound to communicate all matters with all Councellors, but may extract and select." In the 1625 edition Henry was inserted as an example of this wise policy. Also, Bacon's advice to James before the parliament of 1621 had stressed the same point. 14. 114.

     When he comes to his final comment on Henry's use of his council, Bacon gives a judgment that fits neatly with his own ideas. "To his counsel he did refer much, and sat oft in person; knowing it to be the way to assist his power and inform his judgment" (6.242). See the essay "Of Counsel"; "Metis" (*De Sapientia Veterum*); 13. 19. It is probable that his opinion was founded on what he knew of the workings of Elizabeth's council. 13. 40–41.
55. There is no hint of this tactic in André, presumably the source for Bacon's knowing that it was Morton who replied to Gaguin. *Memorials of King Henry the Seventh*, pp. 55–56.
56. 6. 185; Hall, p. 482; Speed, p. 743.
57. G. R. Elton, *The Tudor Constitution* (Cambridge, 1960), p. 1.
58. See the letter to the King written in 1615 where Bacon, in telling a story on Coke, makes clear his opinion of the place of the judges. 12. 108. See also "Of Judicature."
59. Henry's second parliament met in November 1487, many months before events the chroniclers assumed had preceded it.
60. 12. 183–84. The sentence introducing this second parliament of Henry's, with its awkward repetition, also points to this strategy. "He presently summoned his Parliament, and in open Parliament propounded the cause of Brittaine to both houses by his chancellor" (6.74–75).
61. In this case, Speed suggested some of the basic headings for the speech. Speed, p. 734. Hall gave only a two-sentence summary of the parliament. Hall, p. 440.
62. 6. 81. Bacon had first employed the image in the parliament of 1597. 9. 86.
63. 6. 92. Bacon often praised Edward as a lawgiver. 7. 314, 647; 8. 155; *Diary of Robert Bowyer*, p. 269.
64. 6. 21. This abrupt judgment will be toned down in the character at the end of the *History*. 6. 239. The lack of comment further indicates that the view of Henry in the fragment was not based on any 'research.'
65. 11. 98; 12. 144.
66. For more on Bacon's exaggeration of Henry's merits as a lawgiver see Chrimes, pp. 136, 183.
67. 6. 92. In 1625 neither Henry nor Edward will be placed in the second category (lawgivers) of the "degrees of sovereign honour," in "Of Honour and Reputation." Henry, though, will make it into the third, "*liberatores*, or *salvatores*, such as compound the long miseries of civil wars, or deliver their countries from servitude of strangers or tyrants." Cf. Bacon's praise for the "makers" of the Statute of Uses. 7. 432.

68. See his advice to James. 12. 81–83.
69. Storey, p. 175; Chrimes, p. 220.
70. Hall, p. 451. There is no record of the speech in the *Rotuli Parliamentorum*.
71. Kenneth Pickthorn, *Early Tudor Government: Henry VII* (Cambridge, 1934), pp. 152–55. See also G. R. Elton, *England Under the Tudors* (London, 1958), pp. 35–36; Chrimes, pp. 178–79; and particularly, A. F. Pollard, "The De Facto act of Henry VII" *Bulletin of the Institute of Historical Research* 7 (1929), 1–12.
72. Spedding, 6. 173–75. Speed is the source here for his cynicism. Speed, p. 741.
73. Cf. Berry, pp. 284, 294–95.
74. Levy has suggested that Bacon exaggerated Henry's "penny-pinching" to effect an object lesson for the spendthrift James. *Tudor Historical Thought*, p. 257. This observation gains support by what Bacon has to say about the "reasons" for it in the final character sketch. 6. 240. Cf. Berry, p. 308 note 38.
75. 11. 312; 12. 119, 172; 13. 117, 171, 224; 14.70.
76. For his insistence ("certain it is") that "some great defects" accounted for Henry's "perpetual troubles," see his comments in the final portrait. There he adds two other possible candidates, "the strength of his will," and "the dazzling of his suspicions" (6.244). The same false premise is involved however.
77. Events completely beyond the King's direction are often run through quickly and without much spirit. See, for example, the reports of the French-Flemish contests. 6. 98-100, 123–25.
78. 14. 47. The permanent justification for Bacon's methods of doing business is contained in the essay, "Of Dispatch."
79. Bacon certainly had no evidence for his assumption that Henry was largely indifferent to Elizabeth. Hall said Henry showed "perfyght loue and syncere affeccion" toward her. Modern commentators have now begun to reject the legend of Henry's coldness. Storey, pp. 62–63; Chrimes, p. 302.
80. Hall, pp. 453–55.
81. For modern judgments on Henry's faith see David Knowles, *The Religious Orders in England* (Cambridge, 1948–59), 3.3; Chrimes, p. 304.
82. 6. 212. It is not clear, however, that Foxe actually played the role given to him in these ceremonies by Bacon. Sydney Anglo, "The London pageants for the reception of Katherine of Aragon: November 1501," *Journal of the Warburg and Courtauld Institutes* 26 (1963), 55.
83. The "law" had come from Guicciardini. See 8. 186; 11. 219. Cf. Benjamin Boyce, *Theophrastian Character in England to 1642* (Cambridge, Massachusetts, 1947), p. 174.
84. For sharp criticism of this famous quotation, see Chrimes, p. 319.
85. Spedding suggested Bacon's immediate involvement to account for the "unusually numerous" differences in this section between the translation and the original, but he offered no reason for this concern. 6. 237 note 6.
86. In cases involving fines the Crown had first claim on a man's property, thereby serving as a kind of protection. In the warrant James agreed to assign Bacon's fine "unto such persons as he himself shall nominate." In effect, then, the fine would never have to be paid.
87. Both James's and Greville's opinions are contained in Meautys's letter. 14. 325–26.
88. This was Spedding's suggestion. 14. 353, 355. A more personal motive might have been involved. The careers of the two men crossed at many places—beginning with Essex. Montaigne had been his chaplain on the voyage to Cadiz. *Dictionary of National Biography*, "Montaigne."

89. Later there would be complaints about the price and it would be reduced to four shillings. *Records of the Court of the Stationers Company 1602–1640*, ed. W. A. Jackson (London, 1957), p. 149.
90. Friedlaender, pp. 188–89.
91. Chamberlain, 2. 430. The letter is dated March 30. For Chamberlain's feelings about Bacon see Wallace Notestein, *Four Worthies* (New Haven, 1957), pp. 77–82.
92. Gibson, *Bibliography*, p. xiv; *Supplement* (1959), p. 2. For the reception in France, G. Ascoli, *La Grande-Bretagne devant l'opinion française* au XVII$^e$ siecle (Paris, 1930), 2. 61. See also "Bacone, la Riforma e Roma," 214, 217; *The Letters of Peter Paul Rubens*, ed. Ruth S. Magurn (Cambridge, Massachusetts, 1955), p. 212.
93. 14. 365. Elizabeth liked it, but also seems to have not been altogether sure of its genre. "I thank you very much for your letter and your book, which is the best I ever read of the kind; . . . I consider that worthy Prince fortunate in having found so faithful a biographer as you are" (14.366).
94. Chamberlain, 2. 476.
95. In 1622 James assigned Patrick Young, Keeper of the Libraries, to conduct a search in all cathedrals for old manuscripts and ancient records, and to bring an inventory of them to him personally. Young was granted £100 "and more if needful" for his task. *Calendar State Papers Domestic, 1619–23*, p. 40. See also Friedlaender, chap. 3.
96. *Historical Manuscripts Commission, 4th Report*, p. 298.
97. *Historical Manuscripts Commission, Various Collections*, 2. 195. According to Professor René Pintard of the Sorbonne, who was very kind to respond at length to an inquiry on this point, the assertion about the portrait may be true. Whether this is the portrait mentioned by Rawley, which an admirer "carried . . . over with him into France, as a thing which he foresaw would be much desired there," is unknown. 1.15.

# Index

Jonathan Marwil is assistant professor of history, Department of Humanities, University of Michigan.

The book was designed by Richard Kinney. The text is set in Mergenthaler's Baskerville designed for Mergenthaler's Variable Input Phototypesetter (VIP) and based on designs originally cut by John Baskerville in the 18th century. The display face is Mergenthaler's Caslon Old Face based on designs originally cut by William Caslon about 1725.

The Initial Letters used on the chapter openings are 16th century woodcuts from *The Handbook of Medieval Alphabets and Devices* by Henry Shaw, reprinted in *Decorative Alphabets and Devices* edited by Alexander Nesbitt. The Old Style headpieces are from the Caslon Letter Foundry of Stephenson, Blake & Co. Ltd. England.

The book is printed on offset paper and bound in Columbia Mills' Financial Deluxe cloth over boards. Manufactured in the United States of America.